ALSO BY TARA-LEIGH COBBLE

*The Bible Recap: A One-Year Guide to Reading
and Understanding the Entire Bible*

*The Bible Recap Study Guide: Daily Questions to Deepen
Your Understanding of the Entire Bible*

The Bible Recap Journal: Your Daily Companion to the Entire Bible

*The Bible Recap Discussion Guide: Weekly Questions
for Group Conversation on the Entire Bible*

The God Shot: 100 Snapshots of God's Character in Scripture

Israel: Beauty, Light, and Luxury

*The Bible Recap Kids' Devotional: 365 Reflections
and Activities for Children and Families*

THE BIBLE RECAP KNOWING JESUS SERIES*

Knowing Jesus as King: A 10-Session Study on the Gospel of Matthew

Knowing Jesus as Servant: A 10-Session Study on the Gospel of Mark

Knowing Jesus as Savior: A 10-Session Study on the Gospel of Luke

*General editor

THE
BIBLE
RECAP
FOR KIDS

A 365-DAY GUIDE
THROUGH THE BIBLE
FOR YOUNG READERS

TARA-LEIGH COBBLE

BETHANYHOUSE
a division of Baker Publishing Group
Minneapolis, Minnesota

© 2024 by Tara-Leigh Cobble

Published by Bethany House Publishers
Minneapolis, Minnesota
BethanyHouse.com

Bethany House Publishers is a division of
Baker Publishing Group, Grand Rapids, Michigan

Printed in the United States of America

Library of Congress Cataloging-in-Publication Data
Names: Cobble, Tara-Leigh, author.
Title: The Bible recap for kids : a one-year guide through the Bible for young readers ages 8-12 / Tara-Leigh Cobble.
Description: Minneapolis, Minnesota : Bethany House, a division of Baker Publishing Group, [2024] | Includes index. | Audience: Ages 8-12
Identifiers: LCCN 2024002311 | ISBN 9780764240355 (paper) | ISBN 9780764243905 (casebound) | ISBN 9781493443888 (ebook)
Subjects: LCSH: Bible—Juvenile literature. | Devotional literature—Juvenile literature. | Bible—Paraphrases.
Classification: LCC BS551.3 .C665 2024 | DDC 220.5/20817—dc23/eng/20240220
LC record available at https://lccn.loc.gov/2024002311

Cover design by Dan Pitts and Heath McPherson
Illustrations by Heath McPherson
Interior design by Brian Brunsting

The author is represented by Alive Literary Agency, AliveLiterary.com.

Baker Publishing Group publications use paper produced from sustainable forestry practices and postconsumer waste whenever possible.

24 25 26 27 28 29 30   7 6 5 4 3 2 1

To my parents, who raised me in a home where Christ is King and gave me every opportunity to watch them love Him first. Because of you, He is part of even my earliest memories.

To all the teachers who helped me read, understand, and love Scripture as a child, specifically Norma Chapman, Nell Reynolds, Clara King, Mary Evans Turner, and Karen Rodriguez. And special thanks to Dorothy Reynolds who helped me navigate my way through the aisles and pages of the Christian Book & Gift Shop from the time I could barely walk.

To every parent or caregiver who prays that the child they love will come to know Jesus. And to every child who picks up this book. May you feel the gentle tug of the Holy Spirit, the kindness of Jesus, and the deep love of the Father.

CONTENTS

A NOTE TO GROWN-UPS

Dear Grown-Ups,

The Bible is the most amazing book ever written, and we want kids to be excited to dig into it for themselves! *The Bible Recap for Kids* is designed to help young readers love God's Word and understand its value in their lives.

This book follows the same 365-day chronological reading plan as the original book and podcast. As wonderful as daily Bible reading is, please know your child can read this book at the pace best for them. Each day starts with a suggested Bible reading that averages three chapters. Your child may want to read the passage on their own, or they can listen to an audio version of those Bible chapters. If you are also going through *The Bible Recap*, that's even better. You and your child (and other family members too!) can read or listen to the Bible chapters together, and then you can read that day's two-page recap in the original edition of *The Bible Recap* while your child reads the more streamlined one-page recap in this book. Another option is to read the shorter recaps and Seven-Day Roundups from this book together.

We recommend using a standard Bible because most chronological Bibles are laid out differently from the plan we are doing. This book quotes Scripture most from the New Living Translation, but other translations are also quoted, so your child should feel free to use your family's preferred version of the Bible.

One important note: The Bible covers a lot of challenging topics. You may feel that some passages are too mature for your child. This may include well-known passages in Song of Solomon and in Revelation, and also lesser-known passages such as Ezekiel 23. The Bible Recap team and I believe God's Word has benefits for all those who engage with it, and we encourage people of all ages to dig into Scripture! As the parent of your child, though, we believe you are best equipped to guide your child's Bible reading and determine how to handle the conversations that may arise as your child approaches new or challenging topics.

A NOTE TO KIDS

Hey, kids! I am so excited you're going to read the Bible with me. The Bible is made up of many stories, but the Bible is also *one* story. It's the story about who God is, what He's doing, and how much He loves His kids.

Every day you'll read (or maybe listen to!) a few chapters in the Bible. Then you'll read the recap page. At the end of every day, you'll read a God Shot, which shows a snapshot—a picture—of who God is.

After seven days, there's an extra page called a "roundup." It's a review of what you've been reading, and it'll include a few things:

- **Zoom Out**—Here, you'll read a few sentences summarizing what you've just finished reading in the Bible.
- **Big Picture**—When you finish reading a book of the Bible, you'll get a short summary reminding you what the whole book is about.
- **Words to Remember**—Here's where you'll find definitions for important words that will help you understand the Bible. While you're reading, if you get to a word you don't know, turn to the back of the book on page 437 to see if that word has already been defined for you. If it has, that page will tell you what page number to turn back to. Let's get started with a few now!
  - » Bible—God's Word, made up of 66 books, recorded by around 40 different authors, written over 1,500 years. Every word of the Bible is true and given to us by God.
  - » Scripture—another word for the writings in the Bible.
  - » Old Testament—the first 39 books of the Bible. It was originally written in the Hebrew language.
  - » New Testament—the last 27 books of the Bible. It was originally written in the Greek language.
- **Application**—An application is a way you can *apply* what you're learning about God to your own life. It helps answer the question "Now what do I do?"

As you read the Bible and *The Bible Recap for Kids*, you may want to spend more than one day on each "day" of our reading. That's great!

Take all the time you want to soak up God's Word. Every day that you're in God's Word is a good day.

One more thing—in this book you'll come across a phrase we use a lot: "He's where the joy is!" That phrase appears so much because we believe it's true. I'm praying for you as you read, that God will teach you about Himself and show you that He's where the joy is!

THE
RECAPS
AND
CHRONOLOGICAL
READING PLAN

DAY 1

GENESIS 1–3

ZOOM IN

God said, "Let us make human beings in our image, to be like us. . . ."

Genesis 1:26

Today we start at the beginning: creation. The heavens and the earth and everything in them were created on purpose by God. In 1:26, God talks about Himself in the plural form: "Let us make human beings in our image." The **Trinity** is one God in three persons: God the Father, God the Son, and God the Spirit. They're all there at creation, working together!

God tells us His personal name in 2:4. When you see the word LORD written in all capital letters, it represents an ancient Hebrew—the language the Old Testament was written in—spelling of YHWH (you'll hear this pronounced "Yahweh" or "Jehovah"). This is God's personal name, and He tells it to us in His Word because He wants you to know Him!

When Adam and Eve **sin**, they believe the lie that they know better than God—their Creator and their LORD. This is a lie that we're often still tempted to believe today.

TODAY'S GOD SHOT

God is our Creator and our LORD, and He knows everything. He knew that Adam and Eve would sin, and that we all would sin. He's had a plan all along to make everything right again, and one day, He will! And until then, God is still with us, and He seeks us out with His perfect love. When Adam and Eve hide from God, they know they've disobeyed and sinned against Him. But God calls out to them because He loves them. There are consequences when you sin, but even in your sin, there is always God's great kindness toward you. He's where the joy is!

ZOOM IN

Noah found favor with the LORD.

Genesis 6:8

When God created the world, He said it was very good. It was *good*, but it wasn't—and isn't—*perfect*. We saw this when Eve ate the fruit. We saw this when Adam hid from God. We see this when Cain kills Abel. And we see this as more and more people are born. Sin damages the world God made good and the people in it.

As the number of people on earth grows, so does their wickedness. In Genesis 6, the "sons of God" (probably fallen angels) take any woman they want and tell her she has to be their wife. This isn't God's way, but they follow their selfish hearts anyway. The children born as a result of this sin are completely wrapped up in evil.

This makes God sad. He says He'll shorten life-spans in the future, and He'll bring a great flood to wipe out everyone who has been consumed by evil now. This is almost all people, except for one family. Noah lives the way God wants him to, so God tells Noah to build an ark to keep him, his family, and the animals safe during the coming flood. Noah obeys, and the rains come.

TODAY'S GOD SHOT

God is **sovereign**. That means that He has the ultimate power over everyone and everything He created. He created the rain, and He tells it when to start and stop. He's had a plan all along to fix the things we've broken, including our relationship with Him. And evil can't ruin God's plan. You can be joyful knowing that His plan works through all things, even the things you don't understand. He's where the joy is!

GENESIS 8–11

ZOOM IN

God said to Noah, "Yes, this rainbow is the sign of the covenant I am confirming with all the creatures on earth."

Genesis 9:17

When the rains stop, Noah and his family have a lot to get used to. They live in a new place. The land is muddy and soggy. Everyone else on earth has died. And they know they'll live shorter lives than people before them did. Everything seems to have changed for Noah and his family, and change can feel scary sometimes.

But God—who never changes—makes them a promise: He'll never again destroy the earth with a flood. God tells Noah that His promise is a **covenant** between Him and Noah and all people who will ever live on the earth. This is the first covenant in the Bible, and it's unconditional. God knows that people will continue to sin, and He makes the promise anyway. God gives them a rainbow as a sign of His covenant, and He invites them to join Him in the covenant relationship by filling the earth with people again.

Noah's family gets part of the invitation right, and many more people are born. But they miss the second part. They don't fill the earth; they stay put in one place, ignoring God's instructions. So God spreads them out by changing their languages and dividing them into groups.

～TODAY'S GOD SHOT～

God's covenant with Noah and all people on earth includes you! Even though our sin continues today, God will never again destroy the earth with a flood. God sent Noah and his family a sign of this promise: a rainbow. Can you imagine the joy they must've felt every time they saw a rainbow for the rest of their lives? You can share their joy today, because He's where the joy is!

About four hundred years after the flood, we meet a man named Job, who might remind you a little bit of Noah. Job lives his life the way God wants him to. The Bible calls him "blameless."

The "sons of God"—fallen angels—are back, and they present themselves to God. God starts a conversation with one of them (Satan) about Job. Satan tells God that Job only lives God's way because God has blessed Job with land and riches and family. Satan tells God that if those blessings were taken away, Job would curse God.

Satan attacks Job, and all of those blessings are taken away. Even Job's health is attacked—his whole body is covered in sores. Satan creates the plan to test Job, but God allows it. However, God tells Satan that he's not allowed to take Job's life. Through all of this—and even through the bad advice of the friends who show up—Job does not sin or blame God.

TODAY'S GOD SHOT

God is in charge, even over His enemies. (Remember the word *sovereign*?) He puts limits on what the enemy can do. In fact, in 1:12 and 2:6, Satan had to wait for God's permission to test Job. Job's story is hard to read at times, and can be hard to find joy in. But keep reading and keep looking for God in the hard places. When you see God, you'll see joy, because He's where the joy is!

JOB 6–9

ZOOM IN

What are people, that you should make so much of us, that you should think of us so often?

Job 7:17

Job has lost everything, and now his friends give him some terrible advice. His first friend, Eliphaz, insists that the attacks of Satan are Job's fault. And his second friend, Bildad, tells Job to say he's sorry for his sin so that all his troubles will go away.

We all sin, and sometimes really bad things happen as a result of that sin, but Job knew that his sin had not caused all the tragedy that just happened in his life. Because we have the Bible, we know that the tragedy happened not because he was sinful, but because he was blameless.

Job is heartbroken, but in his grief he doesn't say anything untrue or unkind about God. Job tells his friends that they're wrong and reminds them of who God is.

TODAY'S GOD SHOT

God is infinitely powerful, and He's also personally close. Job reminds his friends that God "spread out the heavens" (9:8) and "moves the mountains" (9:5) and "does great things too marvelous to understand" (9:10). And Job also marvels in 7:17 that the same all-powerful God comes close to us. God is big enough to create the entire universe and caring enough to want to be close to you. He's where the joy is!

ZOOM IN

God might kill me, but I have no other hope.

Job 13:15

After Eliphaz and Bildad take turns with their terrible advice, Job's third friend, Zophar, speaks up. Like the two before him, he also urges Job to turn away from his sin. All three friends believe God is punishing Job because of some deeply hidden sin, and all three friends tell him this over and over again. These friends are the perfect example of what *not* to do when people in our lives experience tragedies that we don't understand.

While the advice Job's friends give is terrible for his situation, some of what they say is still true. In 11:6, Zophar says, "God is doubtless punishing you for far less than you deserve!" And he's right about that. Because of our sin, we deserve death. But God doesn't give us what we deserve—this is called **mercy**. And God goes beyond mercy, giving us so many good gifts that we don't deserve—this is called **grace**.

Job trusts so strongly in God that he declares that even if God kills him, he will still trust God.

~ TODAY'S GOD SHOT ~

God is the only place where hope can be found. Job knows this, and holds on to that hope so strongly, even when everything around him falls apart. While it's true that sometimes the consequences of sin cause terrible things to happen, God's mercy and grace ensure that His kids *don't* get the eternal death we deserve. No matter what hard times you might be in, you can always run to God to find hope. He's where the joy is!

JOB 14–16

ZOOM IN

You have decided the length of our lives. You know how many months we will live, and we are not given a minute longer.

Job 14:5

Job's friends are back with their terrible advice, and this time he is told his grief means he doesn't trust God. This isn't true at all! Grief and mourning are a part of life, and they don't mean that the person who is grieving lacks faith. When we get to the New Testament, we'll learn that even Jesus (who *is* God—remember the Trinity?) grieved and mourned.

Job is mourning, and some of what he says in his speech is hard to read. When someone is going through a really hard time, they might spend more time thinking about how short life is, and how death will come to everyone. If you're not also going through a hard time, it's tempting to want to rush them to find a "silver lining," or something good in spite of all of the bad. Be patient with Job here. His suffering might be lasting longer than you want it to; it's certainly lasting longer than he wants it to. God knows this, and as always, He has a plan.

TODAY'S GOD SHOT

God is worthy of your trust. He's in charge of everything, and He knows exactly how long we will all live. Even when we don't understand why someone has died, and even when we don't think it was the right time for someone to die, God is still in charge. Even in death, we can trust that He has the best plan for all of us, because He's where the joy is!

SEVEN-DAY ROUNDUP

ZOOM OUT

So far, we've read eleven chapters of Genesis and sixteen chapters of Job. (Since we're reading the Bible in **chronological**—or time—order, we'll skip around like this.) We've seen God's very good creation and we've seen the fall, when people first sinned against God. We've seen Noah and his family protected by God's first named covenant and we've seen Job's faith in hard times. And on every page, we've seen that God is both powerful and personal.

WORDS TO REMEMBER

- Chronological—time order. We'll read through the Bible in chronological order, or the order in which the events happened.
- Covenant—a relationship with a promise
- Grace—when you get what you don't deserve
- Mercy—when you don't get what you deserve
- Sin—anything we say, think, or do that displeases God
- Sovereign—having power and authority over someone or something. God has ultimate power and authority over everyone and everything He's created.
- Trinity—three persons in one God: God the Father, God the Son, and God the Spirit. The word *trinity* isn't used in the Bible, but there are many, many passages that explain the meaning of the word.

APPLICATION

There is a lot of information in the Bible that's hard for us to understand today. And while this information can be confusing or even frustrating, remember this: Every time you read the Bible, you'll learn a little more about who God is, what He's doing, and how much He loves His kids.

What have you learned so far about who God is? About what He's doing? About how much He loves His kids? As you read the Bible, pray and ask God to help you understand now what He wants you to. And trust that God will help you understand more when He wants you to. You'll keep learning more about God every time you read the Bible!

DAY 8

JOB 17–20

ZOOM IN

As for me, I know that my Redeemer lives, and he will stand upon the earth at last.

Job 19:25

As Job's friends continue to insist that he's responsible for the bad things that have happened in his life, Job continues to tell them things about God, even pointing out some eternal truths.

Job knows that God is alive, and in 19:25, Job calls God his Redeemer. This is a **prophecy**—a message God speaks to people through a person (we call them **prophets**). Prophecies are often about the future, like this one. In Old Testament times, a **redeemer** pays a price to get something (or someone) back. Thousands of years after Job said this, God sent Himself, as Jesus, to live on earth and pay the ultimate price to get us back, becoming our Redeemer.

TODAY'S GOD SHOT

God is our Redeemer. When Job's entire life is falling apart, he speaks these beautiful truths: God lives, God is Job's Redeemer, and God will live forever! When you read the Bible and learn more about God, that knowledge gets stored in your brain and your heart. And when you're going through hard times, what's stored in your brain and your heart comes out. Put in as much truth as you can so that even in hard times, you'll remember that He's where the joy is!

ZOOM IN

He will do to me whatever he has planned. He controls my destiny.

Job 23:14

Job's friends—like a video on loop—keep telling Job that his sin is the reason for his hardship. It's easy to look at Job's friends now and roll our eyes at how wrong they were. But we are guilty of this same kind of thinking today. When we see someone doing evil things, we expect bad things to happen to them. And when nothing seems to happen, we ask God why. And sometimes, when we do the things we know God wants us to do, we expect a reward from Him (even if we don't say it out loud).

Job is mourning, and he's discouraged that he can't find God. Job can't see what God is doing, but he doesn't doubt that God is there. In the middle of his mourning and discouragement, he longs to see God. Job wants to make his case, like someone on trial would make their case to a judge. Even when Job is grieving and wondering what God is doing, he doesn't curse God. He holds on to the truth, knowing God is in control.

TODAY'S GOD SHOT

God is always at work. Even when we can't see what He's doing, He is still completely powerful. Whether you're scared, heartbroken, wondering, or doubting, you can still trust that God is at work to bless you. He can be trusted, and He's where the joy is!

JOB 24–28

ZOOM IN

God alone understands the way to wisdom; he knows where it can be found, for he looks throughout the whole earth and sees everything under the heavens.

Job 28:23–24

Most of today's passage is Job responding to his friends. He reminds his friends that good things can happen to wicked people, and that bad things can happen to righteous people. This is still true today. Just because someone has lots of money and blessings that doesn't mean they're living righteously. And if someone is poor or is in the middle of hard times, that doesn't mean they're living wickedly.

When talking about the great power of God, Job prophesies again, saying, "By his power the sea grew calm" (26:12). Does this sound familiar? If you've already heard the story, you know that God the Son—Jesus—will do that one day!

Even when his friends insist that he's done something wrong, Job knows his own heart, and he knows the heart of God. Even though he doesn't have answers for what's happening to him, he knows that God isn't punishing him. He's confused and angry and sad about all that has happened to him, but he still trusts God. Job is wise because God gave him wisdom.

TODAY'S GOD SHOT

God is wise, and He is where all wisdom comes from. He gave you His Word so you can learn more about Him. And as you learn about Him, you'll grow in wisdom too. He's where the wisdom is, and He's where the joy is!

ZOOM IN

When I was in my prime, God's friendship was felt in my home.

Job 29:4

Today we hear the end of Job's defense speech. He misses his life before all the tragedy began, and he misses when his friends didn't push him to believe lies about himself.

During the speech, Job remembers a time when he was happy. He says that during that time, he felt like God was his friend who lived with his family. This memory is the opposite of how he feels now, which is the lowest point of his grief and mourning.

Job isn't to blame for the bad things God allowed to happen to him, but Job is still a sinner. God used the bad things that happened to show Job the sin of pride in his heart. Job says that God has acted cruelly toward him and is persecuting him. Job's pride makes him think that God owes him an answer as to why all these bad things occurred. God didn't make tragedy come to Job's life, but He does use it to teach Job more about Himself. Because God is Job's friend and wants Job to understand Him better, God will soon help Job understand what's true about Him.

TODAY'S GOD SHOT

God is so near to you that you can call Him your friend. A friend is someone you can have fun with and share things with, but most of all, a friend is someone you trust and spend time with. As you spend time with God and learn to trust Him more, your friendship with God will grow too! He is worthy of your trust, and He's where the joy is!

JOB 32–34

ZOOM IN

God rescued me from the grave, and now my life is filled with light.

Job 33:28

A new man, Elihu, shows up, and he is angry. He tells Job's friends that their advice has been bad, and that wisdom comes from God, not from age. Since he's younger than them, he's not-so-subtly telling them that he's wiser than they are. Elihu seems wise and has some true things to say about Job's friends and about God. But then, just like Job's friends, he messes up and tells Job a lie. He says that Job claimed he hadn't sinned. This can't be true, because Job gave **offerings** to God, which meant he knew he had to pay a price for his sin.

Job is exhausted. He's mourning and grieving, and his body aches with sickness. On top of that, his friends keep accusing him of doing wrong. He might be in the dark now, but as Elihu says in a moment of truth, God rescues us from darkness and can fill Job's life with light again.

~ TODAY'S GOD SHOT ~

God loves you and knows what's best for you. Even when He allowed Job to go through such a dark time, God never stopped loving Job, and He never stopped knowing what was best for Job. When you go through dark times in your life, remember these truths: God loves you, and He knows what's best for you. Hold on to those truths even in the dark, and rejoice when you can see the light again. He is the light, and He's where the joy is!

DAY 13

By means of their suffering, he rescues those who suffer. For he gets their attention through adversity.

Job 36:15

The longer Elihu talks, the more self-righteous he becomes. He's mean to Job, telling him, "You are talking nonsense, Job. You have spoken like a fool" (35:16). And he brags about himself, even calling himself "a man of great knowledge" (36:4).

While Elihu goes on and on, Job stays silent. Job could be too weary to speak, or he could be practicing humility. And while Elihu says a lot of things that are cruel toward Job, he also shares some truth about God.

In 36:15, Elihu says God "rescues those who suffer. For he gets their attention through adversity." This is true. It's easy to feel like we don't need God when things are going well, when we're healthy, and when we have the things we want. But when we're in darkness, it's easier to realize the truth of how much we need God.

~TODAY'S GOD SHOT~

God is provident. He protects and cares for us now, and He prepares for the future. God's **providence** kept Job alive, and He even used all the darkness Job went through for His plans. God's providence is often far too great for us to understand, but you can rest knowing that He's always working for His glory and for your good. He's where the joy is!

JOB 38–39

ZOOM IN

Where were you when I laid the foundations of the earth?

Job 38:4

The moment Job has been waiting for—and that *we* have been waiting for—is here. God speaks! The Bible uses God's personal name, YHWH, here, because God is talking to Job on a deeply personal level. When He starts speaking, God doesn't directly answer Job's questions about his suffering or explain why Job's troubles happened. But He does remind Job who He is.

God reminds Job that Job wasn't around at the beginning, but God was. He's putting Job in his place, but He's not angry with him. In fact, God is patient with Job as He reminds him of the truth. God asks Job a lot of questions like "Who makes the rain fall?" (38:26) and "Who kept the sea inside its boundaries?" (38:8) and "Who is wise enough to count all the clouds?" (38:37). God is the Creator, the Commander, and the Keeper. He made everything. He's in charge of everything. And He holds everything in His hand.

TODAY'S GOD SHOT

God personally came near to speak to Job. God doesn't answer Job's questions directly, but He does respond to them. By reminding Job who He is, He's letting Job know that He cares about what's happened to him. The God who put the stars in the sky and who gives birds food to eat is the same God who came near to Job, even after Job questioned Him. He is all-powerful, He is always personal, and He's where the joy is!

SEVEN-DAY ROUNDUP

ZOOM OUT

We spent the last seven days in the middle of Job's tragedy. For six of those days, God didn't speak to Job, even though Job was in the deepest places of darkness and despair. While Job had strong faith throughout his trials, he also struggled and questioned God. God is so kind that in spite of Job's questioning, God comes near and speaks to him.

WORDS TO REMEMBER

- Offering—a gift of value (often money) offered as a gift to God
- Prophecy—a message of truth that God speaks to people through a person, often about the future
- Prophet—a person who speaks a prophecy
- Providence—God's protective care and His preparation for the future
- Redeemer—someone who pays a price to get something back

APPLICATION

When you read the Bible, you learn about who God is. In the past seven days, we've learned that He's our Redeemer, our Creator, our Commander, and our Keeper. We've also learned that He's so personal with us that we get to call Him our friend.

Job remembered feeling God's presence as his friend when everything was going well. Job needed God to remind him of His power as God when everything went badly. How have you seen God's presence in your life as your friend? How have you seen His power as God?

When you go through hard times in your life, remember that God's responsibility is to know and protect and provide. Yours is to trust your Friend.

JOB 40–42

ZOOM IN

Job replied to the LORD: "I know that you can do anything, and no one can stop you."

Job 42:1–2

When God speaks to Job, He asks questions. And Job's answer is pretty close to *I'll stop talking now.* Like we learned a few days ago, Job did stay faithful and true to God during his trials. But he is still a sinner, and now God is pointing out to Job his sin of arrogance in thinking God owed him an explanation for his troubles. When Job sees that this is true, he **repents**, or turns away, from his sin.

Then, God moves on to talk to Job's friends. He tells them how wrong they were: "I am angry with you and your two friends, for you have not spoken accurately about me, as my servant Job has" (42:7). God instructs them to give an offering to Him, and He accepts a prayer on their behalf from Job.

As Job finishes praying, God sends rich blessings back to Job, twice as much as he had before! God blesses Job with riches, livestock, children and grandchildren, and a long life.

TODAY'S GOD SHOT

God loves to **restore**, or return, people and things to what they were like before. In Job's case, God first restores Job's relationship with Him. Then He restores Job's relationships with his friends. And then? He restores Job's blessings—twice what they were before! God loves to restore, and He's where the joy is!

ZOOM IN

Abram believed the LORD, and the LORD counted him as righteous because of his faith.

Genesis 15:6

Today we're back in Genesis, so here's a little refresher. Adam was the first man, and Noah is from Adam's family line. Noah had a son named Shem, and a man in Shem's family line is named Abram. God has a special relationship with this family, and God tells Abram that He's going to bless him so that Abram may be a blessing. This won't be completely fulfilled in Abram's lifetime, but someone from his family line—many, *many* years later—will be Jesus. So Abram doesn't quite get it yet, but because he knows that what God says is true, he knows he and his family will somehow be used to bless every family on earth, for all time—including yours!

Because there's no food in their land, Abram and his wife, Sarai, move to Egypt. But they still face all kinds of problems: Sarai is kidnapped, the animals run out of food, there's a war, and Abram's nephew Lot is kidnapped.

And then God makes Abram a promise: He's going to have a son! Abram believes God, and God graciously gives him a sign that his belief is right.

TODAY'S GOD SHOT

God always keeps His promises. Even when they seem impossible or are hard for us to understand, if He says it, He'll do it. God promised Abram land, even though his enemies are living there now. God promised Abram children, even though he and his wife are getting old. Abram knows that his job is to trust in God, and God calls him righteous for it! God is a promise keeper, and He's where the joy is!

GENESIS 16–18

ZOOM IN

[Hagar] said, "You are the God who sees me."

Genesis 16:13

Sarai is now at least seventy-five years old, and she doubts what God promised to Abram. She wants her husband to have the blessing God promised but doesn't trust that God will do it. So she decides to ignore God's ways and take matters into her own hands. She sends her servant Hagar to Abram so that Hagar will have Abram's baby. Sarai's sinful plan is to then take the baby as her own. Sarai abuses Hagar, and Hagar runs away into the wilderness.

In the wilderness, the Angel of the Lord comforts Hagar and tells her to return to Sarai. **Angels** are God's messengers, so this angel speaks God's words to her. Many Bible teachers believe Jesus is the messenger God sends to speak to her in the wilderness, appearing as this angel!

Hagar has a son, and Abram names him Ishmael. God changes Abram's name to Abraham, and Sarai's name to Sarah. God again promises that Abraham—*and Sarah*—will have a son. Abraham and Sarah both laugh at this promise.

TODAY'S GOD SHOT

God sees us and cares for us. Even though He made a promise to Abraham and his family, He sees how they abuse Hagar. God doesn't leave her alone to suffer. When she's alone and scared, God sends her a message of comfort. It doesn't mean her life, or her son's life, will be easy or full of blessing, but it does mean that He shows her mercy. He's where the joy is!

ZOOM IN

Abraham prayed to God, and God healed Abimelech.

Genesis 20:17

Abraham's nephew Lot, who lives close to two cities full of wicked people, welcomes two visitors into his house. The visitors are angels—God's messengers—and the people nearby want to do terrible things to them. The angels make those men go blind, but they tell Lot's family that God will spare them. Because of the unimaginable evil in the two cities, God destroys both cities. Lot's wife disobeys God's angels, and when she looks back at her old home, she dies too.

It's important to remember that in the Bible, there are examples of righteous living, and there are examples of unrighteous living. Even the people God blesses richly still have sinful moments of unrighteous living. These stories don't show us how to live, but rather how *not* to live. And ultimately, they remind us that we're all sinful, and they point us to the only One who is perfect.

Abraham and Sarah have a familiar scene happen again: Sarah is kidnapped by King Abimelech. But God is in charge—He made a promise, and He can't be stopped. God appears to King Abimelech in a dream, and Sarah is returned to Abraham.

Abraham and Sarah finally have a son. They name him Isaac.

~TODAY'S GOD SHOT~

God loves forgiveness, and He wants His kids to forgive each other. God tells Abraham to pray for King Abimelech after Sarah's kidnapping, just like God told Job to pray for the friends who said such unkind things to him. God instructed these men to pray for the guilty ones who had wronged them. Later, in the New Testament, Jesus will pray for all of us—the guilty ones who wrong Him. God *loves* us, the guilty ones. He's where the forgiveness is, and He's where the joy is!

DAY 19

GENESIS 22–24

In the Old Testament, God's people were instructed to **sacrifice** something valuable to pay the price for their sins. They would offer these sacrifices to God and ask Him to forgive their sins. God tells Abraham to offer his son, Isaac, as a sacrifice. This doesn't sound like something God would do, but because of Abraham's great faith, he's willing to obey. God had promised Abraham he would have a family, so Abraham knows God will either *not* allow the offering or bring Isaac back to life. But Abraham is willing to do what God asks.

When they arrive at the top of Mount Moriah, God provides a different sacrifice—a ram. Abraham calls God "the LORD who provides." When someone in the Bible says one of God's names, it teaches us about who God is and what He's doing. God does provide. He provides Abraham with a sacrifice, and one day, in the same mountains, He provides His Son, Jesus, as a sacrifice for all of us.

Sarah dies and Abraham buries her in Canaan, which is the land God promised them. He prays that Isaac will find and marry a woman who loves God. God provides again, and Isaac and Rebekah meet.

TODAY'S GOD SHOT

God reveals His plans to us one step at a time. Even though we sometimes want the entire map and the whole set of directions, God knows that 1) we can't be trusted with it, and 2) having it would make us not trust *Him*! He wants you to stay with Him on the journey, and He'll show you exactly where to go next. He's where the joy is!

ZOOM IN

"I am the God of your father, Abraham," he said. "Do not be afraid, for I am with you and will bless you."

Genesis 26:24

After having six more kids with his second wife, Abraham dies at 175 years old. He leaves everything he has to Isaac. Isaac hears from God, who reminds him of the promise He made to Abraham. But right away, Isaac sins by lying about Rebekah.

God doesn't go back on His promise because Isaac sins. In fact, He blesses Isaac. Isaac gains land and wealth and power. And after many years of waiting, Rebekah gives birth to twin boys.

Through a tangled-up mess of sin, Jacob (the second-born son) will **inherit** what Esau (the firstborn son) should. So far in the Bible, we've seen a number of times that the younger son inherits what the older son would typically get. God's plans were usually different from what the culture said was right, and we'll see this upside-down theme over and over again. The Bible calls Jesus our older brother, which means He should get all of God's inheritance. But just like Abel, Isaac, and Jacob, we share in His inheritance!

TODAY'S GOD SHOT

God always keeps His promises, and His promises are always right on time. God promised Abraham that He would bless their family with a great number of children and that they would come through Isaac's family line. So even though Isaac's first baby isn't born until Isaac is sixty, God made it happen at the right time. When you pray to ask God for something, He always answers you! God answers with yes, no, or wait. And if He's promised it? Then He always answers yes. His answer is always best, because He's where the joy is!

GENESIS 27–29

ZOOM IN

I am with you, and I will protect you wherever you go.

Genesis 28:15

Following the customs of the time, Isaac has a special blessing in mind for Esau, his oldest son. But Rebekah loves their younger son, Jacob, more, and she tricks Isaac into blessing Jacob instead of Esau. Esau is so angry that Jacob is scared for his safety, so he goes to live with his uncle Laban. As he leaves, Isaac tells him to search for a wife who loves the Lord.

On his journey, Jacob has a dream. He dreams that God connects Himself to the earth with a ladder. (Who do you think the ladder will turn out to be? Read John 1:51 to check your answer.) In the dream, God reminds Jacob of two promises: 1) He'll give the enemy's land to Jacob's family, and 2) He'll use Jacob's family to bless all the families on earth.

Laban tells Jacob that he can marry his youngest daughter, Rachel, but Laban tricks Jacob into marrying Rachel's older sister, Leah. Jacob is upset, and he takes it out on Leah. He treats her terribly. But just like God saw and cared for Hagar, God pays special attention to Leah. He gives her four sons, and she begins to learn that God is enough.

TODAY'S GOD SHOT

God is sovereign; even sin can't mess up God's plan. In today's reading, we saw sin after sin after sin: lies and deceit and hatred. God knew all these sins would happen, just like He knows all the sins that will happen for the rest of time. And He's still in charge. He works every single thing together for His glory and good plan. He's where the joy is!

SEVEN-DAY ROUNDUP

ZOOM OUT

We've finished a book of the Bible! We also returned to Genesis, where we followed the story of Abraham. We were reminded that no one but God is perfect. And we saw how God always keeps His promises.

BIG PICTURE: JOB

The book of Job answers two questions: Is God in charge? And is God good? Through Job's story of going from light to darkness to light again, we learn that even though hard times will come to us all, we can answer "Yes!" to both questions. God is in charge. And God is good.

WORDS TO REMEMBER

- Angel—a messenger of God
- Inherit—to receive something valuable when someone else dies
- Repent—to turn away from sin
- Restore—to bring something or someone back to how it was before
- Sacrifice—to give something up as a price for our sin

APPLICATION

In addition to YHWH, God has *lots* of names, and as we read the Bible together, you'll learn more of them. Read the list of some of His names below. As you read each definition, ask yourself if any of the names remind you of a story in the Bible we've read so far.

El Shaddai	God Almighty
El Roi	The God who sees me
Elohim	Creator

Think about things God has done in your life. What names from the Bible could you call God? Even if we studied every name the Bible gives for God, we wouldn't even come close to understanding how powerful and wonderful He is. Praise God!

GENESIS 30–31

ZOOM IN

God remembered Rachel's plight and answered her prayers by enabling her to have children.

Genesis 30:22

Leah keeps having sons, and Rachel is jealous of her. So Rachel does what Sarah did many years ago and tells her servant to get pregnant with Jacob's baby. Then Leah tells her servant the same thing. Do you notice a pattern? When Sarah's, Leah's, and Rachel's prayers were answered with God's "wait," they all sinned, deciding to take matters into their own hands.

Rachel finally has a baby boy, Joseph. Then Jacob and his family decide it's time to go to the land God promised Isaac. Before they leave, Jacob tricks Laban into giving him many of his animals. And Rachel steals from Laban. Laban chases them down, and Jacob and Laban make amends, agreeing to keep peace with each other.

TODAY'S GOD SHOT

God is kind to sinners. Over and over again, we see that Jacob's family doesn't follow God's rules. You know who else doesn't follow God's rules? We don't. But just as God was kind to the sinners in Jacob's family, He's kind to us today. God doesn't like your sin or approve of it, but He does love you and forgive you. He gives you mercy so that you don't get the punishment you deserve, and He gives you grace so that you get blessings far beyond what you deserve. He's where the joy is!

ZOOM IN

I am not worthy of all the unfailing love and faithfulness you have shown to me, your servant.

Genesis 32:10

Jacob and his family continue their journey back to Canaan, and Jacob starts to get scared. He remembers how badly he treated his older brother, Esau, and he's worried Esau might try to hurt him. Though he's scared, Jacob trusts in God and praises God for taking care of him.

At night Jacob wrestles with God. This wrestling isn't a dream or vision, because Jacob ends up with an actual physical injury from the wrestling. When morning comes, God gives Jacob a new name. We've seen this before in the Bible, and we'll see it again: When God renames someone, it usually means He's giving them a new job or direction. God renames Jacob *Israel*. (Eventually, all of Jacob's **descendants** will be known by this name too, but we'll get to that later.)

When Esau meets Jacob, he seems happy to see him. Jacob's fears didn't come true! But Jacob's daughter, Dinah, is attacked and abused by a man from another land. Jacob's sons decide to get revenge on *all* the men of that land, but they do this without God's permission or instruction.

～TODAY'S GOD SHOT～

God changes hearts. Even though Jacob's life has been full of lies and tricks, God doesn't give up on Jacob, and He keeps doing the work He promised He would do. When Jacob is scared and alone, God comes near to Jacob, wrestles with him, and gives him a new name. God always keeps His promises, and He finishes what He starts. He's where the joy is!

GENESIS 35–37

ZOOM IN

Reuben was secretly planning to rescue Joseph and return him to his father.

Genesis 37:22

Jacob moves his family back to Bethel, where he had the dream about the ladder to heaven. His family builds an altar to God, and again God renames him Israel.

Even though God had already given Jacob his new name, the Bible goes back and forth, sometimes calling him Jacob and sometimes Israel. This is probably to keep it clear in our minds, since all the descendants who come after Jacob will also bear the name Israel.

Jacob's wife Rachel dies while giving birth to a son named Benjamin, and Jacob's dad, Isaac, dies not too long after. Joseph—Rachel's first son with Jacob—is Jacob's favorite. Everyone knows Joseph is the favorite, including Joseph himself and all his brothers. Let's just say his brothers don't like that very much. They plan to kill him. The oldest brother, Reuben, steps in to save Joseph's life, and Joseph is sold into slavery instead of killed. Joseph's brothers make their dad believe that Joseph is dead, and Jacob is heartbroken.

~TODAY'S GOD SHOT~

God saves. When Reuben thought of a rescue plan for his younger brother Joseph, he planned to return him to their father. This reminds us of how God sent Jesus, our older brother, to save our lives and to return us to the Father. When we absolutely could not save ourselves, God sent Jesus to bring us back to Him. He's where the joy is!

ZOOM IN

The LORD was with Joseph, so he succeeded in everything he did as he served in the home of his Egyptian master.

Genesis 39:2

Our reading today opens with one of Joseph's brothers, Judah, who gets himself into a giant mess. Judah arranges a marriage for his oldest son with Tamar. When the oldest son dies, Judah gives Tamar to his second son. Then when the second son dies, Judah tells Tamar to wait around until his third son grows up. Tamar decides she doesn't want to wait, and she takes matters into her own sinful hands. As we've seen when other people in the Bible have taken matters into their own hands, it doesn't go well. Long story short, Tamar gets pregnant and has Judah's (not his son's) babies. They name the twin boys Perez and Zerah.

During this same time, Joseph is a slave in Egypt. But he's not alone. The Bible tells us four times that "the LORD was with Joseph." Potiphar, the Egyptian official who bought Joseph, notices that everything Joseph does is successful. Potiphar's wife wants Joseph for herself, but when he refuses to sin, she tells a lie about him that sends him to prison. But even there, God is with Joseph, and Joseph proves himself to be wise and trustworthy.

TODAY'S GOD SHOT

God keeps His promises. God promised Abraham—Judah's and Joseph's great-grandfather—that He would bless Abraham with descendants like the stars. Over and over again we see that when people doubted God, they decided to take matters into their own hands. Even in spite of the sinful messes people get themselves into, God is still at work on His plan. In fact, Judah, Tamar, and Perez are even listed as **ancestors** of Jesus! When we are broken and unfaithful, God is whole and faithful. He keeps every promise He's ever made, and He's where the joy is!

GENESIS 41–42

Pharaoh (the title for the leader of Egypt) needs some dreams interpreted. Joseph tells Pharaoh that his dreams mean there will be seven years of feasting and **abundance** in Egypt, followed by seven years of famine. Joseph warns Pharaoh that they need to prepare for the famine years during the feast years, so Pharaoh puts Joseph in charge of this.

After thirteen years in slavery and prison, Joseph is free! Pharaoh gives Joseph riches, an important job, and even a wife. During the seven years of abundance, when there is more than enough, Joseph prepares the people of Egypt for the upcoming famine, and he also has two sons.

When the famine comes, Joseph's dad and brothers don't have enough to eat. His brothers travel to Egypt to buy grain. The man in charge is their brother Joseph, but they don't recognize him. Joseph puts one of the brothers in prison and sends the rest back to get their other brother, Benjamin, who had stayed back with their father. Joseph overhears the brothers confessing their guilt and regret to each other, and he secretly takes the money they paid him for grain and puts it back in their bags.

TODAY'S GOD SHOT

God is so generous. He is with Joseph and takes care of him during his time in slavery, and He is even with Joseph's sinful brothers during the famine. Joseph grows to be respected in the country that made him a slave, then he gives free grain to his brothers who sent him there. God was generous with Joseph, He was generous with Joseph's brothers, and He's generous with us today. He's where the joy is!

ZOOM IN

> But don't be upset, and don't be angry with yourselves for selling me to this place. It was God who sent me here ahead of you to preserve your lives.
>
> Genesis 45:5

When Joseph's brothers return to Egypt with Benjamin, Joseph invites them over for a feast. As they leave, Joseph again sneaks money into the brothers' bags and a silver cup into Benjamin's bag. Then Joseph sends his servants after the brothers. The servants find the items and accuse the brothers of stealing before taking them back to Joseph.

Judah makes a speech and admits that ten of the brothers are in fact guilty, just not of stealing the silver cup. He seems humbled, perhaps remembering his sin and the tragedy in his own life: selling Joseph into slavery, losing two sons and a wife, and having children with Tamar. God has brought Judah to repentance, and (because Judah might think Benjamin stole Joseph's cup) Judah offers to take Benjamin's punishment for the crime.

Joseph is overcome with emotion and finally tells his brothers who he is. He forgives them, offers them the best land in Egypt, and invites them to move there so he can take care of them.

TODAY'S GOD SHOT

God forgives us and helps us forgive others. When Joseph tells his brothers that he forgives them, he also tells them that God was at work all along. Even though the brothers tried to hurt Joseph, they didn't ruin his life or God's plans. When we remember how much God has forgiven us, and how He is always at work for our good, we can be ready and willing to forgive others. He's where the joy is!

GENESIS 46–47

ZOOM IN

I will go with you down to Egypt, and I will bring you back again.

Genesis 46:4

Jacob and his sons pack up to make the journey to Egypt. Stopping along the way, Jacob offers a sacrifice to God and says an emotional goodbye to his home. Egypt wasn't just a foreign land; it was known as a place that was terrible for God's people. But God gives Jacob a vision and tells him that He'll be with him in Egypt. And more than that, God promises to make his family a great nation while they're there.

Pharaoh allows Jacob's family to live in Goshen, which has fertile land for their animals. Even as the famine around them gets worse, Jacob's family has more than enough. As Jacob grows closer to dying, he makes Joseph promise that they'll move his body out of Egypt. God promised He'd be with Jacob in Egypt, and He promised He'd bring Jacob out of Egypt. Jacob wants to make sure this happens, even though he won't be alive.

～ TODAY'S GOD SHOT ～

God brings abundance. He provides not only what we need, but *more* than what we need. God brought Joseph to a place of importance in Egypt, and God provided a way for Joseph's family to be reunited with Joseph in Egypt. Once they were there, God gave them not only what they needed to live, but so much more! He brings abundance, and He's where the joy is!

SEVEN-DAY ROUNDUP

ZOOM OUT

In the last seven days, we've followed Jacob's family through feast and famine. We've seen God keep His promises to this family, even when they sinned against Him and each other. And we've seen God bless this family over and over again. God has been at work since the beginning, and His work not only kept this family alive and protected, but it provided more than they needed. God had a special plan in mind for this family—a child who would be born many generations in the future. And this child wouldn't be a blessing just for His own family, but for every family on earth.

WORDS TO REMEMBER

- Abundance—having more than enough blessings
- Ancestor—someone before you in your family line (a parent of a parent of a parent . . .)
- Descendant—someone after you in your family line (a child of a child of a child . . .)

APPLICATION

Did you notice the ways God provided abundantly for Jacob's family? He was generous by not only giving them what they needed, but by giving them much, *much* more. God gives abundantly to us today too. Can you think of some of the ways He's blessed you? As you notice abundance in your life, pause to thank God for being who He is and for giving you *more* than enough.

GENESIS 48–50

ZOOM IN

You intended to harm me, but God intended it all for good. He brought me to this position so I could save the lives of many people.

Genesis 50:20

Before Jacob dies, he remembers the promises God made and kept. God gave his family land and many descendants. Jacob blesses Joseph's two sons before he dies. And he blesses them as if they were his own children, making sure that they are heirs to the land God gave them and the promise He made their family.

Then Jacob gathers his own sons and gives a final blessing, and Judah gets a special blessing. All of Jacob's sons have sins recorded in Genesis. Judah gets a special blessing, but not because he's been perfect. Instead, it's because of God's promise: One of Judah's descendants will be Jesus. (Remember the word *grace*? This is grace—getting a good thing we don't deserve!)

Jacob-Israel has twelve sons, and each of those sons has many more children. Each family becomes a "tribe," making up the *twelve tribes of Israel*. We'll come back to this later, so remember this idea.

When Jacob dies, Joseph's brothers panic, thinking he'll get revenge on them now, but Joseph has already forgiven them! Before Joseph dies, he says (like his father did) that he doesn't want his bones left in Egypt. He wants to go to the land God promised.

TODAY'S GOD SHOT

God has been working His plan from the beginning. Have you heard Jesus called "the Lion of Judah"? When God blessed Abraham and Isaac and Jacob, He wasn't only blessing their families. When Jacob gave a special blessing to Judah's family line, he blessed the family line that Jesus would be born into. And through Jesus, God blesses every family on earth. You and your family are blessed because of Jesus! Jesus is the Promised One, and He's where the joy is!

ZOOM IN

Now go, for I am sending you to Pharaoh. You must lead my people Israel out of Egypt.

Exodus 3:10

Four hundred years after Genesis ends, Exodus begins. Joseph is dead, but his family who came to live in Egypt stayed there. The old pharaoh who let them live in Goshen is also dead, and now there is a new pharaoh. He hates the Israelites because he's convinced himself they're going to start a war against him.

Remember how God renamed Jacob "Israel"? Here we see how Jacob's descendants bear the same name. They're called Israelites. And because of Pharaoh's fear and hatred of them, he makes them his slaves. Pharaoh doesn't stop there, though. He orders the midwives to kill all newborn Israelite boys. How terrible and scary!

One Israelite mom hides her baby boy in a basket. Pharaoh's daughter finds him, names him Moses, and raises him in the palace. When Moses grows up, he gets angry about how his people, the Israelites, are treated in Egypt. One day, he sees an Egyptian abusing an Israelite and he kills the Egyptian. He's scared of what might happen to him, so he runs away to live in the desert.

God appears to Moses in the desert, in the form of a burning bush, and tells him to go back to Egypt to save the Israelites from slavery under the cruel pharaoh.

TODAY'S GOD SHOT

God uses broken and scared people to accomplish His plans. When God tells Moses that he's the man who will rescue the Israelites, Moses tries to convince God that he's the wrong choice! God made a plan, and that plan includes Moses. If God promises it, it will happen! He's where the joy is!

EXODUS 4–6

ZOOM IN

Now go! I will be with you as you speak, and I will instruct you in what to say.

Exodus 4:12

God reminds Moses of His power and gives Moses some signs to prove himself in Egypt. Even after seeing signs of God's power, Moses is still scared to go back to Egypt. Honestly, he's scared in general: When God turns the staff into a snake—yikes!—Moses runs away from it! But God reassures Moses. He doesn't tell him that his job will be easy or that everything will go great. Instead, God tells Moses He'll speak for him, and that He'll send someone to help him.

God sends Aaron, Moses's older brother, as his helper. When they get to Egypt, Aaron makes a speech to the Israelites while Moses shows them the signs from God. The people are thrilled! Moses and Aaron request a chance to talk to Pharaoh, who says no. When they ask again, Pharaoh gets angry and makes life even harder for the Israelites.

The Israelites are angry with Moses. They wanted to believe that the promise Moses told them was true, but then life got even harder. They feel hopeless, and they doubt everything Moses told them.

TODAY'S GOD SHOT

God is powerful *and* patient. When Moses gives God a list of reasons why he shouldn't be God's choice to free the Israelites, God responds by showing Moses His power. He warns Moses that the job will be difficult but promises Moses that His power will get him through. He's the source of power, He's the giver of patience, and He's where the joy is!

ZOOM IN

I have spared you for a purpose—to show you my power and to spread my fame throughout the earth.

Exodus 9:16

God reminds Aaron and Moses that Pharaoh is not going to listen to them, and that He will harden Pharaoh's heart against them. When Aaron and Moses show Pharaoh signs of God's power, he is not convinced.

So then the plagues begin. Each plague directly attacks one or more of the false gods the Egyptians worship, showing the people that their false gods are weak and powerless and that the LORD has all the power.

A few times during the plagues of blood, flies, gnats, frogs, and hail, Pharaoh says he'll let the Israelites go. But he never keeps his word, so more plagues come. At one point, Pharaoh asks Moses to pray for him but still doesn't repent of his sin.

TODAY'S GOD SHOT

God knows everything, so He knew that Pharaoh would harden his heart against the Israelites. In fact, God is at work in all of this, because He has a plan. He wants to show His power as the one true God to everyone so that His name would be known! He wants His name to be known so well that people turn to live His way, which is the best way. He's where the joy is!

EXODUS 10–12

ZOOM IN

On that very day the LORD brought the people of Israel out of the land of Egypt like an army.

Exodus 12:51

As Pharaoh's heart remains hard, the Israelites remain slaves in Egypt. God sends a plague of locusts—worse than grasshoppers—and a plague of darkness, but Pharaoh does not repent.

Before God sends the final plague, He tells His people to eat a special meal together. They eat lamb, bitter herbs, and bread without yeast. This meal is called **Passover**, and it's still celebrated by Jewish people all around the world today. Following God's instructions, they paint the blood of the lamb on the sides and tops of the doorways of their homes. They gather their valuables—including the valuables they got from the Egyptians—they stay dressed, and they wait.

God sends the final plague, and an angel passes through Egypt striking down the firstborn son of every Egyptian, but passing over the Israelites' homes that are marked with blood. Realizing their sons are gone, the Egyptians drive the Israelites out.

In the middle of the night, between two and three *million* Israelites leave the land where they have been slaves. They are free!

TODAY'S GOD SHOT

God saves! Even after four hundred years of slavery, when His people had lost hope, God was working out a plan of salvation. The people of Israel walk out of Egypt like an army because God is with them and protecting them. He brings freedom and celebration when He gives salvation, and He's where the joy is!

ZOOM IN

The LORD is my strength and my song; he has given me victory. This is my God, and I will praise him—my father's God, and I will exalt him!

Exodus 15:2

God tells the Israelites to have a seven-day party—the Feast of Unleavened Bread—every year, in order to remember what He did at Passover. This way, the Israelites will remember to tell their children what God did for them.

God is in charge, and He appointed Moses to speak for Him to the Israelites. God leads them through the desert by appearing as a cloud during the day and a fire at night. As they follow God, the Israelites see Pharaoh's army coming after them, and they're terrified. They don't trust Moses, and they don't put their faith in God. They start thinking that their lives were better when they were slaves in Egypt!

But God has a plan, and when the Egyptian army closes in on the Israelites, God wins by parting the sea. The Israelites cross through on dry ground; and when they've made it to the other side, the sea closes and the Egyptian army is defeated. Led by Miriam and Moses, the Israelites worship God by singing, playing instruments, and dancing.

TODAY'S GOD SHOT

God is worthy of our praise. He loves us, He created us, He cares for us, and He fights for us. When the Israelites sing a song of praise, it's the first worship song in the Bible. God wants you to sing songs of praise to Him today too! He wants you to remember everything He's done for you, and He loves to hear your praise. What can you praise Him for today? He's where the joy is!

EXODUS 16–18

ZOOM IN

He told them, "This is what the LORD commanded: Tomorrow will be a day of complete rest, a holy Sabbath day set apart for the LORD."

Exodus 16:23

Only forty-five days after God delivered them, the Israelites start grumbling and complaining. They wish for the days when they were slaves, because . . . the food was better. Instead of punishing the Israelites for not trusting Him, God makes Himself known to them through the cloud they've been following. He promises to give them bread in the morning and meat in the evening.

God tells them to gather food every day except on the **Sabbath**, when they should rest. He also tells Moses to hit a rock with his staff, and when he does, water pours out! God wants His people to rest, and He wants them to trust that He'll provide what they need.

When an enemy army attacks the Israelites, Moses tells a man named Joshua to put together an army, and God brings Joshua's army victory. Moses builds an altar and gives God a new name: The LORD Is My Banner. A banner is like a flag—something visible that marks a victory. So this name means not only that God is victorious, but also that Moses wants everyone to know He is!

TODAY'S GOD SHOT

God gives rest. The Israelites aren't used to days off, so when God instructs them to rest, they may feel confused. Rest reminds us that we can't work our way to God. God gives Himself to us as a gift, and nothing we could ever do would make us worthy of that gift. As we learn to rest in Him, we'll realize more and more that He's where the joy is!

SEVEN-DAY ROUNDUP

ZOOM OUT

You've finished reading a second book of the Bible! As we finished Genesis, we saw God's faithfulness to fulfill His promises. We started Exodus this week, where we saw that God protects and provides. And we were reminded how good it is to praise God!

BIG PICTURE: GENESIS

Genesis is the story of creation, sin, and God's good plan. Through the lives of Adam, Eve, Noah, Abraham, Sarah, Isaac, Rebekah, Jacob-Israel, and many more, we see over and over that God's plans cannot be stopped—not even by our sin. We also see that God's promises always come true. And we are left with the promise that God's plan is a blessing not just for Abraham's family, but for all of us.

WORDS TO REMEMBER

- Passover—a feast celebrated by Jewish people every year that reminds them of when the destroying angel passed over every home marked by the blood of a lamb, leaving the children inside safe
- Sabbath—the seventh day of the week, set aside for rest and worship

APPLICATION

In Exodus, we begin to see a pattern of God saving the Israelites and the Israelites quickly forgetting about it. You would think that millions of Israelites would remember being freed from slavery and walking through a sea while God held the water up like walls, but we are guilty of forgetting too. When things are going well for us, it's easy to forget how much we need God. And when things are going badly, we may doubt that He cares about us at all.

Think of some of the ways God has protected and provided for you and your family. Make a list and put it somewhere you'll see it as a banner to remember and praise God for what He has done!

EXODUS 19–21

ZOOM IN

"Don't be afraid," Moses answered them, "for God has come in this way to test you, and so that your fear of him will keep you from sinning!"

Exodus 20:20

God leads the Israelites to Mount Sinai and tells them He wants to meet with them. So first, they make themselves clean to prepare to meet with Him.

When God arrives, there's a storm and the blast of a trumpet. As God comes down as fire, smoke covers the mountain and there's an earthquake. Then God tells Moses to climb the mountain, and God gives him ten rules to live by. We call them the Ten Commandments.

He reminds Moses of His great love for them and tells Moses (while the people listen in) that He is YHWH, who brought them out of slavery. God saves them and provides for them and gives them His laws; these laws not only honor Him but bless them. The first five laws point us upward: They teach us how to love God. The last five laws point us outward: They teach us how to love each other.

God gives Moses some additional rules too. And all of these laws, as well as the Ten Commandments, teach us God's way to live—which is, of course, the best way to live.

~ TODAY'S GOD SHOT ~

God wants us to fear Him, but not to be scared of Him. What's the difference? Being scared of someone means you don't trust them to treat you well. But *fearing God* means to be in awe of who He is and what He's doing. Being scared moves us far away from God. But fearing God moves us closer to Him. And moving closer to Him helps us remember that He's where the joy is!

ZOOM IN

You must not exploit a widow or an orphan. If you exploit them in any way and they cry out to me, then I will certainly hear their cry.

Exodus 22:22–23

God gives His people more laws that teach them how to live best as a group, how to keep each other safe, and how to treat each other.

Many of God's rules protect the people in society who need the most protection: orphans, widows, the poor, and outsiders. Because of the customs at the time, these people are the most **vulnerable**, or the most likely to be taken advantage of. God deeply loves these vulnerable people, and He makes sure to tell His people how to treat them well.

God even ensures that there are laws that protect the Israelites' enemies. He wants Israelites to remember the mercy and kindness He showed them so that they'll show mercy and kindness to others—even their enemies!

God tells Moses to come up to the top of Mount Sinai, where He'll give him stone tablets with the Ten Commandments on them. Moses goes up on top of the mountain and stays for forty days and forty nights.

TODAY'S GOD SHOT

God cares for everyone, especially the vulnerable. Vulnerable people often become victims of other people's sin, even today. God's heart for them can be seen in so many of the laws He gave the Israelites. He wants the people who have more than enough to make sure that the people who have less are taken care of. His way is the best way for everyone, and He's where the joy is!

EXODUS 25–27

ZOOM IN

Have the people of Israel build me a holy sanctuary so I can live among them.

Exodus 25:8

God gives His people a lot of detailed instructions today. He wants them to build a **tabernacle**—a moveable tent—where He will live among them. He tells them to use beautiful fabrics and valuable metals to build His home. You might be wondering where a bunch of former slaves, who are now living in the desert, got these items. Remember their last night in Egypt when God told them to gather their valuables? And remember how some of those valuables used to belong to the Egyptians? God had a plan for it all along.

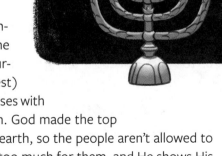

God also gives the Israelites instructions for building the ark of the covenant. This is a small piece of furniture (kind of like a treasure chest) that holds the tablets God gave Moses with the Ten Commandments on them. God made the top of the ark serve as His throne on earth, so the people aren't allowed to touch it. God knows His power is too much for them, and He shows His kindness by protecting them from it!

TODAY'S GOD SHOT

God wants to live with His people. Even after all of their sin separated them from Him, He makes a way to be near to them. And through Jesus, He made a way to be near to you too! He restores relationships, and one day—when Jesus returns—He'll restore the whole earth. He wants to be close to us, which is great news for us, because He's where the joy is!

DAY 39

ZOOM IN

This is the ceremony you must follow when you consecrate Aaron and his sons to serve me as priests.

Exodus 29:1

Remember that Jacob-Israel had twelve sons, and each one was the head of one of the twelve tribes of Israel? Moses and Aaron are descendants of Levi, one of Jacob-Israel's sons. Their tribe is called the Levites, and God has a special plan for them. They're set apart by God to be priests—the people who are in charge of the tabernacle.

God gives the Levites a lot of very specific details about the clothes (also called "garments") they should wear. These garments are what they wear when they go to serve God on behalf of the people. Each piece of clothing has a special job, and God gives certain people the ability to make them.

The priests also have to go through a seven-day **consecration** ceremony to set them apart before they're allowed to do their work for God.

TODAY'S GOD SHOT

God is **holy**, which means "set apart." For the Levite priests to be close to Him, they have to follow a lot of instructions. But once they do, they're allowed to go near Him. Today, we don't need priests to go near to God for us. We get to be near Him ourselves, because Jesus is our priest who did the work of consecration for us! He's where the joy is!

EXODUS 30–32

ZOOM IN

How quickly they have turned away from the way I commanded them to live!

Exodus 32:8

God gives Moses and Joshua more instructions, including to take a count of and collect a tax from all the people. God has been giving them directions for work, and He also gives them directions for rest. He tells Moses more about the Sabbath, that it's "Holy to the LORD."

The Israelites get really anxious waiting for Moses to come down from Mount Sinai; he's been there for six weeks! They want something to worship, so Aaron, the man who God made a high priest . . . makes a golden cow for them. What a terrible, wicked plan! Then the people give it credit for delivering them from Egypt, and they worship it. Can you imagine?

God is angry. Moses asks God to have mercy on the people, which He does. But Moses is also angry. When he sees the mess they've made, Moses breaks the tablets God gave him, destroys the golden calf, and reprimands the people. The people who turn away from their sin and turn back to God live.

TODAY'S GOD SHOT

God has perfect timing. When the Israelites feel like God is taking too long, they look for something else to worship. And while we might think that we'd never worship something as silly as a gold cow, we're also guilty of giving our praise and devotion to ridiculous things—especially when we feel like God has disappointed us or is taking too long. But God is always working things out for your good. He hears your prayers and answers with *yes, no,* or *wait.* The next time He answers your prayer with *wait,* ask Him to give you patience and to help you trust that His plan is the best. He's where the joy is!

ZOOM IN

Moses said, "If you don't personally go with us, don't make us leave this place. How will anyone know that you look favorably on me—on me and on your people—if you don't go with us? For your presence among us sets your people and me apart from all other people on the earth."

Exodus 33:15–16

God tells Moses it's time for the people to start moving toward Canaan, the promised land, but that He won't be going with them. God's people had hurt Him deeply with their sin, and He tells Moses He'll send His angel to go with them instead of Himself. Moses talks to God just like we talk to our friends, and he begs God to come with them, or to let them stay there with Him. He remembers the promises God made to His people and tells God that they need Him there with them to guide them. God agrees to go with them.

Moses asks God to show him His **glory**, and God does—on top of Mount Sinai, again. God rewrites the Ten Commandments on new tablets and gives them to Moses. Moses goes back down to the people, and his face is actually shining from being with the LORD! Wow! The people are afraid, so Moses covers himself with a veil. He reminds the people of God's laws and collects an offering to provide for the needs of the tabernacle.

~TODAY'S GOD SHOT~

God gives us our identity, and He makes us His. Moses knew that if God didn't go with them, they would sin again and again. When we live like God is with us, we become who He really made us to be. God uses His people to show others His power and kindness, and He's where the joy is!

EXODUS 36–38

But the people continued to bring additional gifts each morning.

Exodus 36:3

God's people's hearts have been so moved by His mercy that they bring offering after offering for the tabernacle. Moses even has to tell them to stop giving things, because they've given more than enough to build the tabernacle. God's people—who had just sinned against Him by worshipping the golden calf—have repented and turned back to Him. They work to follow all of God's precise instructions for building the tabernacle very carefully.

Every part of the tabernacle has a special meaning and represents—or stands for—some piece of our relationship with God. The brass altar represents Jesus's sacrifice. The washbasin represents being washed clean of our sins. The menorah (lampstand) represents the light of the Holy Spirit in us. And the ark represents God's presence with us.

TODAY'S GOD SHOT

God shows Himself to us in so many ways. Even though they don't fully understand it, when they build the tabernacle God's way, the Israelites are building symbols that point to Jesus. Even tabernacle furniture is helping us see more about who Jesus is—it's laid out in the shape of a cross! He wants us to learn more about Him, because He's where the joy is!

SEVEN-DAY ROUNDUP

ZOOM OUT

We spent seven days reading a lot of rules and instructions that God gave to His people. We also saw that when they had to wait for Him, they quickly turned away and worshipped a false god that they made out of their own jewelry! God gives us instructions and rules and laws because He loves us. He made us, and He knows the best ways for us to live.

WORDS TO REMEMBER

- Consecrate—to set apart for sacred use
- Fear (of God)—to be in awe of who God is and what He's doing
- Glory—magnificence, splendor, and beauty
- Holy—set apart
- Tabernacle—a moveable tent where God lived
- Vulnerable—people who are the most likely to be taken advantage of

APPLICATION

When you read God's Word, you learn more about who God is, what He's doing, and how much He loves His kids. Even when you read about tabernacle furniture and ark measurements and family trees, you're learning about God!

Write down some words that describe who God is. Beside each word, write a story from the Bible that shows God in this way. Then challenge yourself to think of a story in your own life that shows God in the same way.

EXODUS 39–40

ZOOM IN

Moses could no longer enter the Tabernacle because the cloud had settled down over it, and the glory of the Lord filled the Tabernacle.

Exodus 40:35

One year after the Israelites left Egypt, they complete the tabernacle just as God instructed, and Moses blesses it. This points back to God blessing creation when He completed it. Why? Because God is working to restore what was broken in the garden almost three thousand years earlier. God is making a way to be with His kids because He loves them so much.

God tells Moses to anoint the furniture in the tabernacle with oil. Oil represents the Holy Spirit, so putting oil on something symbolizes dedicating it to God and making it holy. The furniture will serve a special purpose, and it can only be used for the tabernacle—where God dwells. Like He said He would do, God sets up Aaron, from the tribe of Levi, and all of his descendants as a family of priests.

TODAY'S GOD SHOT

God's glory is so strong that it *fills* the entire tabernacle! There isn't even room for Moses to go inside because God's presence fills every single space. His presence is powerful and His glory is great. He's where the joy is!

ZOOM IN

If you present an animal from the herd as a peace offering to the LORD, it may be a male or a female, but it must have no defects.

Leviticus 3:1

God is holy and perfect, and He wants to be near to His people, even though they're sinful. The book of Leviticus explains how this can be possible. It's important to remember that the Bible teaches us about who God is, what He's doing, and how much He loves His kids. Ask God to help you remember this as you read parts of the Bible that may be confusing or difficult.

Almost everything in Leviticus is God speaking to Moses. He's outlining extra rules that the Levites need to follow. Why are there extra rules for them? Because—as we learned in Exodus—their tribe (family) is set apart to be priests. Priests go between the sinful people and the holy God, so they have to follow a special set of rules.

God sets up a system of offerings and sacrifices. Offerings are gifts given by the people to God, and sacrifices are animals used to **atone** for sin. *Atone* comes from a word that means "to cover," and it refers to paying a penalty. Hebrews 9:22 tells us that our sin, which separates us from God, demands death in order to be forgiven. So God gave the people a *sacrificial system* to use until it was time for the real solution: Jesus.

TODAY'S GOD SHOT

God is merciful. Our sin separates us from Him, because He is perfect and we aren't. But instead of leaving us, God gave a solution for atonement—to cover our sins! In the Old Testament, He set up a system of sacrifices that led to the people's forgiveness. But this wasn't the plan forever. He knew that Jesus, the ultimate sacrifice for all our sins, was coming. He made a way for us to come back to Him, and He's where the joy is!

LEVITICUS 5–7

ZOOM IN

Through this process, the priest will purify you before the Lord, making you right with him, and you will be forgiven for any of these sins you have committed.

Leviticus 6:7

God gives the people laws around being clean and unclean. Being unclean isn't sinful, but it does require a process to become purified and clean again. A lot of these laws are symbolic, but many of them are also about health and safety. By telling His people what they can and can't touch, God is showing them how to stay as healthy as possible.

As we just read, sin requires sacrifice. God makes it clear that His sacrificial system *must* be honored. God also makes sure that poor people have a way to participate in the sacrificial system He set up: Their sacrifices can be smaller than those of people who have more.

TODAY'S GOD SHOT

God isn't afraid of our sin. You might have heard people say that God can't be in the presence of sin; this isn't true. In the garden, God went to Adam and Eve when they sinned. In His own throne room, fallen angels came to talk to God about Job. In the desert, God chose to dwell among His people, who were all sinners. We all *have* sinned, and we all *will* sin, and when we do, we don't need to hide from God! He knows that only He can fix our sin problem, so He gave us Jesus. He paid the price for our sin. What a blessing! He's where the joy is!

ZOOM IN

Moses said, "This is what the LORD has commanded you to do so that the glory of the LORD may appear to you."

Leviticus 9:6

In a seven-day ceremony, Moses sets apart Aaron and his four sons as priests. On the eighth day, God's people have their first service at the tabernacle. Offerings and sacrifices are made, and Moses and Aaron bless the people. Then, the glory of the Lord comes down! Fire from heaven burns up the offering. The people shout for joy in praise to God, as they should!

Sadly, Aaron's two oldest sons decide to ignore all of God's instructions because they think their way will be better. God won't stand for this, and the two oldest sons die right away. God talks to Aaron directly and gives him specific instructions about being a priest.

Moses tells the two sons who are left to make an offering and eat it. They make the offering, but they don't eat it, because they're sad about losing their brothers. At first, Moses is angry about it, but when Aaron reminds Moses of the great loss he suffered, Moses is understanding.

TODAY'S GOD SHOT

God shows **compassion**. Over and over in Exodus, God was compassionate when Moses asked Him to be. Today, when Aaron asks Moses for compassion, Moses shows it to him. The more time Moses spends with God, the more he reflects God's character. Have you noticed that in your own life? In what ways are you reflecting more of who God is? You're here, reading through a really tough book of the Bible, because you love God and you want to know Him more. He's where the joy is!

LEVITICUS 11–13

ZOOM IN

For I, the LORD, am the one who brought you up from the land of Egypt, that I might be your God. Therefore, you must be holy because I am holy.

Leviticus 11:45

God tells Moses what foods they're allowed to eat and what they're not allowed to eat, making sure they only eat things that God has declared clean. There's a big, detailed list here, and it includes all kinds of animals—from the sea to the ground to the sky.

God gives Moses more instructions about the different processes unclean people have to follow to become clean again. The instructions in chapter 12 are for women who have given birth.

Then God tells Moses what to do when people are sick and dying. These instructions can be really tough to read, especially if you're not super comfortable with sickness or injuries. So why is this in the Bible? One reason is that Moses wasn't a doctor, and most people back then didn't know about infections or contagious diseases. So Moses had to know what to do when people got sick so that they could take care of each other and get better. God's instructions always have a purpose, and that purpose is always for our good!

TODAY'S GOD SHOT

God is holy, and He wants us to be holy. Because His holiness sets Him apart, His people have to follow His laws and obey Him in order to be consecrated. *Consecrate* means "to set apart for sacred use." So even though following God's laws may be difficult, it means we get to be set apart. And since *He's* set apart, it means we get to be closer to Him! He's where the joy is!

ZOOM IN

If the priest finds that someone has been healed of a serious skin disease, he will perform a purification ceremony.

Leviticus 14:3–4

Today, God keeps going with more rules about being clean and unclean. So let's review before we recap. God is perfect and holy, and we are not. We are sinners who live in a broken world. And in a broken world, there are sickness and infections and even mold. At the time God was speaking to Moses, there were no antibiotic medicines or bleach. So God is being kind by telling His people how to keep themselves and their homes healthy.

God also gives lots of instructions for offerings. Why an offering? It requires a cost from the person making it. People give something to take the place of their debt of sin. And it helps the person making the sacrifice draw near to God, because they have to go to the entrance of the tabernacle. God wants sinners to draw near to Him. And again, God makes sure to note here that poor people should give a less-costly offering. This shows His heart for *all* His people.

TODAY'S GOD SHOT

God heals and God makes us clean. In 14:3–4, after the man with a serious skin disease called leprosy is healed, there is still a cleansing process. This is a picture of what's to come through Jesus: **justification** and **sanctification**. *Justification* is when God declares us righteous because of what Jesus did for us. It's a one-time thing, like the healing of a man with leprosy. *Sanctification* is the process of God making us more like Him. This is a lifelong process. God heals and justifies, then God cleans and sanctifies. He's where the joy is!

LEVITICUS 16–18

ZOOM IN

This is a permanent law for you, to purify the people of Israel from their sins, making them right with the LORD once each year.

Leviticus 16:34

God gives instructions about the Day of Atonement, which will happen once a year. It's the only time the high priest will enter the Most Holy Place in the tabernacle, where he'll offer sacrifices as a penalty for the sins of the priests and the sins of the people.

On the Day of Atonement, the priests bring two goats to the tabernacle. One goat takes the people's sins and is allowed to escape into the wilderness. The other goat is sacrificed to the LORD. As we've seen over and over in the Old Testament, this points *forward* in God's plan. The first goat is the *scapegoat*, and it represents Jesus, who takes all the people's sins. The second goat is the sacrifice, and it also represents Jesus, who was sacrificed to God on our behalf.

God also tells His people how to be set apart in their relationships. For example, they're not allowed to marry anyone they're related to, or act like someone else's wife is their own, or marry someone of their own gender. These were all things that were happening among other groups of people, but God wants His people set apart, like He is.

TODAY'S GOD SHOT

God atones. The Day of Atonement points forward to Jesus, who would come from the Most Holy Place to take all our sins and sacrifice Himself to God. He would atone—or pay the penalty—for our sins. And not just for the Israelites, but for *everyone* who would believe. He would atone for our sins not just for one year, but *forever*. He's where the joy is!

SEVEN-DAY ROUNDUP

ZOOM OUT

We've finished Exodus and started Leviticus, and we've seen how God's been good to the Israelites through their enslavement and their freedom, through their sin and their obedience. He's promised them a home that they don't get to go to yet (the promised land). But even in the desert, He's provided for them with miracles. And He's protected them and set them apart with laws and rules. His way is the best way!

BIG PICTURE: EXODUS

Exodus means "exit." Most of the book was likely written by Moses. The whole book tells a story of how powerful God is, and how He wants to be near to His kids. It teaches us that even when we sin and are unfaithful to Him, God always keeps His promises.

WORDS TO REMEMBER

- Atone—to cover; to pay a penalty
- Compassion—kind concern for others when they're suffering
- Justification—when God declares us righteous because of what Jesus did for us
- Sanctification—the lifelong process of God making us more like Him

APPLICATION

God has led His people on a journey, and He's been with them every step of the way! He sent plagues, parted the sea, sent water from a rock, led them as a cloud by day and fire by night, gave Moses the Ten Commandments, and instructed the Israelites on how to build the tabernacle.

Think about times and places in your own life that you've seen God's power and provision. Draw a map—on paper or in your mind—and mark the places where you've seen God working.

LEVITICUS 19–21

ZOOM IN

You must be holy because I, the LORD, am holy. I have set you apart from all other people to be my very own.

Leviticus 20:26

God keeps giving His people laws that will help them build the best society. He prohibits abuse. He warns against letting selfish emotions take over. He tells His people to be reasonable. And He makes sure that rich people provide for poor people. (Remember this when we get to the book of Ruth!)

God also tells them more about the laws they must follow to honor Him. He gives them civil laws, ceremonial laws, and moral laws. Civil laws list appropriate punishments for behavior that harms their society. Ceremonial laws teach God's people about cleanliness and how to make sacrifices. Moral laws explain what God says is right and wrong.

When Jesus came, it wasn't to get rid of God's laws, but He did accomplish their purpose (Matthew 5:17). Today, God's people live all over the world, in all kinds of nations, so the civil laws and punishments for Israel don't apply to us today. And because Jesus was the perfect and ultimate sacrifice, and He paid the price for *all* sins, we don't follow ceremonial laws now either. He fulfilled the purpose those laws served. *What a relief!* And while Jesus perfected all moral laws, these are still laws that shape and sanctify us and show us what God values. So we follow these today.

TODAY'S GOD SHOT

God sanctifies. We can't make ourselves more holy; only He can make us more holy. It can be really overwhelming to read a long list of rules and expectations, but remember that God is the one who does the hard work! He has already done the work of justification by sending His Son, and He's also the one who does the work of sanctification by making us holy like Him. He's right here with us, and He's where the joy is!

ZOOM IN

You must faithfully keep all my commands by putting them into practice, for I am the LORD.

Leviticus 22:31

God wants His people to be clean, and only He can make them clean. Whenever His people go through the process of becoming clean, they have to follow a series of steps that God requires of them. And during this process, they remember God's holiness and His goodness. They're spending time thinking about Him, which is good!

God also wants His people to remember His goodness to them, and He wants His people to celebrate. So He gives directions for a weekly feast and for six annual feasts. How great is it that God commands His people to feast?

TODAY'S GOD SHOT

God is perfect. When we read Leviticus, we see that we couldn't possibly keep all God's laws, and we won't ever be perfect. The good news is that Jesus has already done it for us! If you start to feel bad when you read God's laws because you know you've already broken them, pray and thank God for sending Jesus for you. Then read Romans 5:20: "God's law was given so that all people could see how sinful they were. But as people sinned more and more, God's wonderful grace became more abundant." Praise God for His grace! He's where the joy is!

LEVITICUS 24–25

ZOOM IN

If you want to live securely in the land, follow my decrees and obey my regulations. Then the land will yield large crops, and you will eat your fill and live securely in it.

Leviticus 25:18–19

God keeps telling His people how they should treat each other. Until God freed them, they were slaves their entire lives, so they don't know how to live outside of Egypt. They also don't really know much about God yet. It's only been a year since He freed them, and they're still learning to trust Him. So God makes sure His people can see His heart in the laws He gives them. He wants the rich to be helpers. He wants the vulnerable to be protected. He wants the poor to have enough. And He wants everyone to rest.

God had already given His people a commandment to rest on the Sabbath, the seventh day of the week. In the Bible, the number seven symbolizes perfection, and God gives His people another rule related to the number seven. He wants them to let the fields and gardens rest on the seventh year, and to trust Him to provide enough food for them. God also sets up a year of Jubilee (every seven "weeks of years," or fifty years), when debts are forgiven and debtors are set free!

TODAY'S GOD SHOT

God is generous. His laws make sure everyone is cared for. His laws make sure everyone gets rest. And His laws make sure everyone has enough. No matter how much money we have or how many things we buy, they won't make us safe or happy. Only God can make us safe and happy. He's where the joy is!

ZOOM IN

I will walk among you; I will be your God, and you will be my people.

Leviticus 26:12

God tells His people that if they keep their covenant with Him, He will bless them greatly: He'll give them peace and safety and abundance. He also warns them about what will happen if they break their covenant promises: He'll send five phases of curses. Each phase of curses is worse than the one before it, but His people can repent and turn back to Him at any point, and when they do, God says that the curses will stop.

These curses aren't punishment—they're a form of discipline. It may be hard to tell the difference, but God's discipline is meant to bring people back to Him. He disciplines us because He loves us and because He knows that living His way is the best way.

God also instructs His people to give a **tithe**, or ten percent of their income. For the Israelites, this could've been money, food, or animals. This will support the work of the tabernacle and help the priests—the Levites—continue to do their jobs.

～TODAY'S GOD SHOT～

God forgives. In ancient Israel, if one party broke the terms of a covenant, then the covenant was void and gone. But here, God tells His people that He won't withdraw His covenant if the Israelites break their part of it. Instead, He'll give them a chance to repent from their sins. Even in His discipline, He's always gracious and merciful. He's where the joy is!

NUMBERS 1–2

ZOOM IN

So the people of Israel did everything as the Lord had commanded Moses.

Numbers 2:34

We started a new book today, and even on days when reading Numbers seems like . . . reading a bunch of numbers . . . we'll learn something more about who God is, what He's doing, and how much He loves His kids!

We've followed the same family since we started reading the Bible together. One of Adam's descendants was Noah. One of Noah's descendants was Abraham. Then there were Isaac, Jacob-Israel, Joseph and his brothers, and eventually, Moses. Remember all those people?

God meets with Moses again and tells him to count all the men ages twenty and up from the twelve tribes. Judah's tribe is the biggest—double the size of some of the other tribes. God tells Moses not to count the Levites, since their work is all about the tabernacle.

God also instructs the tribes on how to arrange themselves in camps around the tabernacle and what order to place themselves in when they move through the desert.

TODAY'S GOD SHOT

God keeps His promises. He has been at work since He first promised a childless Abraham that He would make him a great nation. And by the time we hit the book of Numbers, Abraham's descendants number into the millions! No matter how many times His people have sinned against Him, God has been keeping His promise. And He's not done yet. He's where the joy is!

ZOOM IN

The LORD said to Moses, "Look, I have chosen the Levites from among the Israelites to serve as substitutes for all the firstborn sons of the people of Israel. The Levites belong to me."

Numbers 3:11–12

God has given His people instructions on how to live together, and He's told them how to organize themselves. Now He's giving them instructions for the tabernacle—His home with them in the wilderness. Remember that God has set apart the Levites as keepers, caretakers, and protectors of the tabernacle. He tells His people that because an entire tribe is dedicated to His service, every other family doesn't have to send their firstborn son for God's service.

There are three clans of the Levite tribe, and God gives each a special job. The Gershonites work with fabric in the tabernacle: the curtains and coverings. The Merarites handle the structure of the tabernacle: the poles, pillars, and pegs. And the Kohathites guard the holy vessels, such as the ark and the lampstand.

～ TODAY'S GOD SHOT ～

God sees everyone and uses all His people to accomplish His plans. The largest tribe—Judah—has a special place in the arrangement God set up for them. And the Levites are the smallest tribe, but God set them apart for special service. Whatever job God has for you in His kingdom, it's important. He may call you to serve in a place that's seen by many, or in a place that's seen by few. But remember that God always sees. Serve Him wherever He's placed you to serve, because He's where the joy is!

NUMBERS 5–6

ZOOM IN

May the LORD bless you and protect you. May the LORD smile on you and be gracious to you. May the LORD show you his favor and give you his peace.

Numbers 6:24–26

God reminds His people that they are to live holy lives and uphold the covenant they made with Him. He gives instructions on living holy lives, both on the outside and the inside. He sets up rules for when they sin against God and each other: They should confess, repent, and—when needed—pay the consequences to the people they harmed.

God also outlines the vows that Nazirites must take. These are people who are set apart, even among God's people, for service, and must follow special rules. Some of these rules are even stricter than the ones priests follow! They can't eat, drink, or touch certain things. Most Nazirites only serve a set amount of time, but some serve for life. (We'll meet a few later in the Bible!)

Then God tells Moses how the priests should bless His people and promises that when Aaron and his sons bless the people, God Himself is the one blessing them.

TODAY'S GOD SHOT

God blesses His people. Today's reading ended with a beautiful blessing that you may have heard before. Go back to the top of this page and read it again. God blesses His people, He blesses *you*, and He's where the joy is!

SEVEN-DAY ROUNDUP

ZOOM OUT

You've finished four books of the Bible! You've followed a family through times of blessing and times of struggle. You've learned that God gives rules because His way is the best way. And you've seen how God loves His kids and always keeps His promises.

BIG PICTURE: LEVITICUS

The book of Leviticus lists a lot of laws, rules, and instructions. For most of the book, God talks to Moses. He tells the Israelites how to live as God's free people. And as He does this, we see that the holy God wants to be close to His sinful people.

WORD TO REMEMBER

- Tithe—"one tenth," an offering of income (money, food, or animals) made by God's people

APPLICATION

God keeps His promises! Make a list of the promises God made to the Israelites in Genesis, Exodus, and Leviticus. If you need some reminders, look up Genesis 12:2, Exodus 6:6, and Leviticus 26:12.

Then make a list of promises that God has made to us today. If you need a preview of these, look up Hebrews 13:5, James 1:5, and Luke 12:40.

Praise God for always keeping His promises!

NUMBERS 7

ZOOM IN

Whenever Moses went into the Tabernacle to speak with the LORD, he heard the voice speaking to him from between the two cherubim above the Ark's cover—the place of atonement—that rests on the Ark of the Covenant. The LORD spoke to him from there.

Numbers 7:89

When Moses finishes setting up the tabernacle, he anoints it with oil. During a twelve-day dedication period, each tribe sends a leader to bring offerings to the tabernacle.

The Levites are responsible for taking care of the tabernacle, but they need the help and support of the other tribes. So each tribe brings valuable gifts to show their support. These gifts not only help the Levites, but they help everyone. When people give their gifts, it helps them feel connected to the tabernacle and to all the people who God told to take care of it. He uses the gifts of one to bless all!

TODAY'S GOD SHOT

God speaks to us. After twelve days of dedication, Moses goes into the tabernacle and God speaks to him. The fabric and the furniture and the metal would mean nothing if God wasn't using them to speak to His people through His servant Moses. Moses knew then what we know today: that He's where the joy is!

ZOOM IN

Of all the people of Israel, the Levites are reserved for me. I have claimed them for myself.

Numbers 8:16

God instructs Moses how the Levites should be purified (made clean), that the people must be clean to celebrate the Passover, and that the people can invite outsiders, like the Egyptians who left their country with the Israelites. God is so kind and welcoming! They celebrate the Passover, and then a new season begins for the Israelites. They start moving through the wilderness toward Canaan.

Canaan is the land God promised them way back in Genesis (12:1–3, 15:13–21). A person could walk from Egypt to Canaan in about eleven days, but so far God hasn't led them there. Remember, He's shown Himself to them as a pillar of cloud and fire, and they have followed where He's led and waited where He's stayed.

God teaches two trumpet players some tunes that mean different things, like praising God and asking Him for help. And then? After almost a year in the wilderness, they pack up, line up, and walk.

TODAY'S GOD SHOT

God makes us holy. He chose to consecrate the Levites, even though they doubted Him. He set them apart for special service. He turned a bunch of doubters into people who lived and worked closest to Him. He made them holy for Himself! He's where the joy is!

NUMBERS 11–13

ZOOM IN

Soon the people began to complain about their hardship, and the LORD heard everything they said.

Numbers 11:1

As we've seen before, it doesn't take long until God's people start grumbling. God is angered by how quickly they've forgotten all He's done for them, and He sends fire. The fire kills some people, and when Moses prays, God stops the fire.

After this, the people start talking about how much they miss all the food they used to eat in Egypt. That's right—*in Egypt . . . where they were slaves.* Moses is frustrated with the hard job God gave him and talks to God about it. Moses seems mad at God, but it's the people who are the cause of his anger. God hears Moses, He knows what the problem is, and He has a solution. God sends His Spirit to seventy other people who will support Moses in leading the Israelites. It doesn't stop the problems—there are still grumbling and gossip—but it gives Moses helpers to deal with them when they happen.

God tells Moses to send twelve spies (you guessed it—one from each tribe) to check out the promised land. They spy for forty days and report back about how beautiful it is and how easy it would be to grow crops there. But out of the ten leaders, only two believe that the Israelites can actually take the land: Caleb and Joshua.

TODAY'S GOD SHOT

God is with His people, even when they grumble and gossip. He dwells in the Most Holy Place, He leads them with a pillar of cloud and fire, and His Spirit rests on Moses and the other leaders He chooses. He's where the joy is!

NUMBERS 14–15; PSALM 90

DAY 60

ZOOM IN

Let us, your servants, see you work again; let our children see your glory.

Psalm 90:16

When the Israelites hear the reports from the ten spies, they are scared. They decide they want a new leader to bring them back to Egypt. The people rebel against Moses and Aaron. Meanwhile Joshua and Caleb tear their clothes apart and try to convince everyone to trust God. And the people respond by wanting to throw stones at them. It's total chaos!

God shows up angry. And as you can imagine, it's not good news for the Israelites. He's so angry that He wants to kill everyone and start over. Moses begs God for mercy, and God agrees to give it. The ten spies who convinced the rest of the people to be scared die. And God tells everyone that they'll stay there in the desert for forty years. Everyone over the age of twenty, except for Caleb and Joshua and their children, will die before they see the promised land.

God warns the people to go south because their enemies are nearby, but they don't listen. They go north and lose the battle. Moses prays a prayer, recorded in Psalm 90, asking for God's goodness.

TODAY'S GOD SHOT

God keeps His promises. When His people rebelled against Him, He didn't kill them or start over with a new people or turn away from them. He forgave them and let them know He would keep His promise. In the beginning of Numbers 15, God gives instructions to the Israelites, saying, "When you finally settle in the land I am giving you . . ." They're still His! And He's still giving them the promised land. He's where the joy is!

NUMBERS 16–17

ZOOM IN

He stood between the dead and the living, and the plague stopped.

Numbers 16:48

A few hundred people form a group to rebel against Moses and Aaron because they want to take over and be the leaders. Moses asks them to prove their leadership by offering incense to God. Two of the rebel leaders refuse. God sends a sinkhole to swallow them up and sends fire to consume the rest of the rebels. Their incense holders are made into a cover for the altar so that everyone will remember God is holy and powerful; He's the one who gets to appoint leaders.

But still, the people wake up mad and accuse Moses of killing everyone. God is angry again and wants to wipe everyone out with a plague, but Moses has an idea. He tells Aaron to stand in between the living and the dead and burn incense to atone for their sins.

God makes Aaron the high priest and shows His choice by making an almond flower grow and bloom on Aaron's staff overnight. A miracle! The people repent, and Aaron's staff is stored in the ark of the covenant for future generations.

TODAY'S GOD SHOT

God the Son **intercedes** for us. When Aaron came in between the living and the dead, it was risky. High priests weren't supposed to be near dead bodies because they were unclean. But Aaron risked his life to save others' lives. Jesus is our ultimate High Priest, and He intercedes by facing death and defeating it to save our lives. Romans 8:34 (ESV) says, "Christ Jesus is the one who died—more than that, who was raised—who is at the right hand of God, who indeed is interceding for us." He's where the joy is!

ZOOM IN

The LORD said to Moses, "You and Aaron must take the staff and assemble the entire community. As the people watch, speak to the rock over there, and it will pour out its water. You will provide enough water from the rock to satisfy the whole community and their livestock."

Numbers 20:7–8

God talks directly to Aaron, telling him how the priests and Levites are supposed to take care of the tabernacle. God reminds Aaron that He provides for the Levites through the tithes from the other tribes. They won't inherit land or animals, but they'll be taken care of, because God has promised it.

The Israelites need water, so God tells Moses and Aaron to take a staff, gather everyone in front of a rock, and talk to it; then it'll give water. But Moses doesn't talk to the rock; instead, he hits it with the staff. Twice. Whether he made a purposeful decision to disobey God or just wasn't listening fully, Moses still sinned against God. God provides water for the people, but also lets Moses know that he and Aaron won't be going to the promised land with the people.

TODAY'S GOD SHOT

God never changes. He makes the rules. His people break them. We have to deal with the consequences of our sin, and sometimes those consequences are difficult, but God is still merciful. Adam and Eve were sent out of the garden, but He gave them clothes to wear and food to eat. Moses won't get to enter the promised land, but God still allowed him to lead His people out of slavery. God's mercy and grace are always so much more than we deserve. He's where the joy is!

NUMBERS 21–22

ZOOM IN

The Lord told him, "Make a replica of a poisonous snake and attach it to a pole. All who are bitten will live if they simply look at it!"

Numbers 21:8

The Israelites are getting closer to the promised land, and they need more food and water. By this point, they should know that all they have to do is ask God to provide for them, because they've seen Him do it over and over again. But they don't. They complain about God and about Moses.

Of course, God hears them. So He sends poisonous snakes that kill them. More of them die and won't get to go to the promised land, just like God told them. When the people see what's happening, they confess their sins and repent. Moses prays for them. God tells Moses to make a fake snake and put it on a pole. Anyone who has been bitten can simply look at the snake and they'll live.

They need to pass through two other kings' lands next, but the kings send men to attack them. God gives Israel the victory and a lot of land! Another king hears about this and is scared, so he hires Balaam to put a spell on the Israelites. But God's plan to bless His people will not be stopped, and God even makes Balaam's donkey talk to make sure everyone knows that God is in charge. Wow!

TODAY'S GOD SHOT

God saves. When the people who looked at the snake lived, the snake didn't save them—*God* did. They were given longer life on earth because of their faith to do what God said. He's where life is, and He's where the joy is!

SEVEN-DAY ROUNDUP

ZOOM OUT

Over and over again, we've seen the Israelites complain, doubt, and rebel. God has always provided for them, but they've continued to sin against Him. Still, God has given mercy and let them live.

WORD TO REMEMBER

- Intercede—to advocate or mediate between two people or groups

APPLICATION

Through Leviticus and Numbers, we've seen that God spoke to Moses a lot. He gave Moses commandments and laws and rules. He explained the consequences of sin. And He also gave Moses mercy, promises, and blessings.

God speaks to us today too. One of the ways He speaks to us is through His Word, the Bible. As you've been reading the Bible, what has God told you about Himself? (Read Leviticus 26:11–12 and Deuteronomy 4:31 if you need a reminder.) What has God told you about you? (Read 2 Corinthians 7:1 to see how Leviticus 26:11–12 applies to us.)

NUMBERS 23–25

ZOOM IN

No misfortune is in his plan for Jacob; no trouble is in store for Israel. For the LORD their God is with them; he has been proclaimed their king.

Numbers 23:21

The Canaanites—who are living in the land God promised to the Israelites—believe that if you say something, it becomes true. So they hire Balaam (yep, him again!) to curse the Israelites. But God gives Balaam a word to speak about Israel, and it's actually a blessing instead!

Meanwhile, the Israelites are up to their usual business: worshipping idols, Baal in particular. Because of their sin, God sends another plague and twenty-four thousand people die. The plague stops when Phinehas—Aaron's grandson—honors God and intervenes.

TODAY'S GOD SHOT

God isn't limited by time. When He talks through Balaam and says things like "No misfortune is in his plan for Jacob" and "No trouble is in store for Israel," you might wonder what God means. His people have sinned against Him again and again, and He's gotten so angry that He's wanted to wipe them all out! But because God is outside of time, He knows not only what they've done, but what will be done *for* them. And through Jesus's death, their sins—and ours—are paid for. Praise God! Because God isn't limited by time, He sees our sin, our forgiveness, and our **redemption**! He's where the joy is!

ZOOM IN

The LORD replied to Moses, "The claim of the daughters of Zelophehad is legitimate. You must give them a grant of land along with their father's relatives."

Numbers 27:6–7

Many people have died and many people have been born since the last time God told Moses to count everyone, so He tells them to count again. For the Israelites to enter the promised land, no one from the first count can still be alive, except for Caleb's and Joshua's families. Once they confirm this, God tells Moses and Eleazar (Aaron's son, who is the new high priest) how to divide the land among the tribes.

One man, Zelophehad, had five daughters but no sons. So these women ask Moses if they can inherit the land their father would've given to sons. Moses asks God, and God says the women are right. He tells Moses to give them the land.

God tells Moses that he will die soon; he'll get to see the promised land from the top of the mountain, but he won't get to go in. God instructs him to appoint the next leader, Joshua.

TODAY'S GOD SHOT

God is fair. We've seen how He's merciful, sparing us from what we deserve. And we've seen how He's gracious, giving us far more than we deserve. We also see through His response to the daughters of Zelophehad that He's fair. He cares about what's right and fair, and He acts accordingly. He's where the joy is!

NUMBERS 28–30

ZOOM IN

On the eighth day of the festival, proclaim another holy day. You must do no ordinary work on that day.

Numbers 29:35

God sets out the guidelines for the religious calendar they'll observe once they get to the promised land. They'll be spread out around the land, so He's coordinating their schedules now. Each day will begin and end with worship: a sacrifice at sunset and at sunrise, with twice that number required on the Sabbath. This may seem like a lot of sacrifices to us today, and it would've felt like a lot of sacrifices to the Israelites then. But the sacrifices remind them that God is in charge of providing for them, and He always will.

We don't have to offer sacrifices to God today, but we still need to be reminded that He provides for us. We have the opportunity to do that by giving to the church (tithing) and by resting and spending time with God on the Sabbath.

TODAY'S GOD SHOT

God wants us to spend time with Him, and He wants us to rest. In all the rules and instructions He's giving to His people, He talks about two of them repeatedly: to have no other gods before Him, and to rest. Most of the things that we make into "gods" today require more work from us: being popular requires more work; having nice things requires more work; getting better jobs requires more work. God wants us to stop and to rest and to trust Him to provide what we need. He's where the rest is, and He's where the joy is!

ZOOM IN

The LORD said to Moses, "On behalf of the people of Israel, take revenge on the Midianites for leading them into idolatry."

Numbers 31:1–2

God tells Moses what his last assignment before he dies will be: wipe out the Midianites. They led the Israelites into sin, which caused the deaths of twenty-four thousand of God's people. So God will have His justice. After the battle, the Israelites count their men; not a single one died. Incredible!

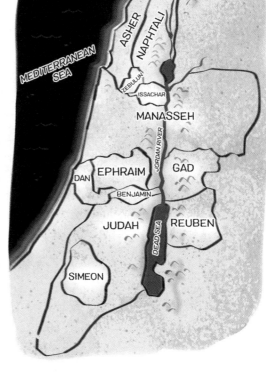

The land God promised to the Israelites is on the west side of the Jordan River. Right now, they're all on the east side of the river, on the land they won earlier. The tribes of Reuben and Gad make their living through agriculture, and they love this land. They ask Moses if they can stay there. After they promise to fight for Canaan with the other tribes, Moses agrees.

TODAY'S GOD SHOT

God fights for our hearts. He knows that sin destroys, and He wants any temptations to sin to be destroyed. Do we obey God and get as far away from temptation as we can? Or do we downplay the temptation and act like we can overcome it? The next time you find yourself battling with a temptation to sin, remember that God fights for your heart. Ask Him to fight the battle for you! He's stronger than we'll ever be, and He's where the joy is!

NUMBERS 33–34

ZOOM IN

You must drive out all the people living there. You must destroy all their carved and molten images and demolish all their pagan shrines.

Numbers 33:52

After Moses makes a list of all the places they camped over the last forty years, he gets more directions from God. God tells Moses they have to drive out all the people in Canaan—the land God has promised the Israelites. They also have to destroy the altars and every item used to worship false gods.

God explains to Moses where the promised land's boundaries are: from the Mediterranean Sea to the Jordan River and the Salt Sea (Dead Sea), and from Mount Hor to Kadesh-barnea. Nine and a half tribes (Manasseh's tribe split in half) will settle inside these boundaries, and two and a half will settle in the fertile land east of the Jordan River.

~~TODAY'S GOD SHOT~~

God is the King of kings, LORD of lords, and God of gods. He knows there are false gods that people worship, but He's not threatened by them. Other gods are limited, but God is limitless. He is all-powerful and He defeats His enemies, including those false gods. By defeating His enemies, He's keeping His people safe. He protects His kids, and He's where the joy is!

ZOOM IN

This is what the LORD commands concerning the daughters of Zelophehad: Let them marry anyone they like, as long as it is within their own ancestral tribe.

Numbers 36:6

The Israelites continue to make plans for the promised land based on God's instructions. The Levites won't get their own land (they're set-apart priests, remember?), so God's plan is that each tribe gives a little bit of the edges of their land to the Levites.

Some people in the tribe of Manasseh realize that if the five daughters of Zelophehad marry outside of their tribe, then those tribes would get their land. So they ask Moses for help, who asks God, and God tells them they're right. Zelophehad's daughters must marry within their tribe so that the land stays how God arranged it. So that's what all five daughters do. Everyone is provided for in God's plans!

TODAY'S GOD SHOT

God pays attention to each one of us. He cares for the whole group and gives them what they need to live abundantly. He also cares for each person and makes sure they have what they need too. Twice in the book of Numbers, we see how God makes sure Zelophehad's daughters—five women out of three million Israelites—are treated fairly. Just like these women did, God wants you to bring your questions and problems to Him—because He cares for all of us *and* for each of us individually. He's where the joy is!

DEUTERONOMY 1–2

For the LORD your God has blessed you in everything you have done. He has watched your every step through this great wilderness. During these forty years, the LORD your God has been with you, and you have lacked nothing.

Deuteronomy 2:7

Deuteronomy may seem like a review of what you've already read, and that's good! If you're reading something and say, "Wait a minute, I've already read this," *you're right!* Stop to thank God for giving you a strong memory, and ask Him to teach you something new too!

Moses knows the time is coming close for him to die, because God told him. For forty years, he has taught the Israelites, fought for them, prayed for them, walked with them, and loved them. He knows that God will keep His promises, but he's also nervous that the Israelites will fall back into sin. So Moses has some final things to say (okay, *a lot* of final things to say) to the people.

Moses reminds the people of the highlights of what's happened since they left Egypt, including what went wrong because of their sin. And because the people are afraid about the battles that are coming up, Moses also encourages them.

TODAY'S GOD SHOT

God blesses anyone He chooses to bless. He blesses His kids and He blesses others too! For a time, the promised land was in the hands of other people. It's a good land, and those people were blessed by it because God allowed them to be. But even in the wilderness, God was with His people, and that is the greatest blessing of all. He's where the joy is!

SEVEN-DAY ROUNDUP

ZOOM OUT

We've followed the Israelites to the edge of the promised land, and we've seen how God has protected and provided for them. They've gotten instructions on sacrifices, cleanliness, land divisions, and celebrations. And Moses has begun his final speech to the people.

BIG PICTURE: NUMBERS

We finished Numbers this week! In Hebrew, the title for the book of Numbers is In the Wilderness, and the book follows the Israelites over forty years, through the wilderness, to the edge of the promised land. We continue to see how—even when His people sin against Him—God keeps His promises.

WORD TO REMEMBER

- Redemption—salvation that comes because of a redeemer who paid a price

APPLICATION

Using God's math, a little bit can become a lot. Giving a small offering to the Levites helped to support an entire tribe. Today, giving a small offering can help support an entire church. Then and now, dedicating a day for rest and time with God gives us enough energy to make it through six days of work.

Want to see it in action? For a month, challenge yourself to give an offering to your church and take a real Sabbath for resting and spending time with God. After the month is over, ask yourself what you notice about how the rest of your week feels.

DEUTERONOMY 3–4

ZOOM IN

Be careful never to forget what you yourself have seen. Do not let these memories escape from your mind as long as you live! And be sure to pass them on to your children and grandchildren.

Deuteronomy 4:9

In chapters 1 and 2, Moses talked mostly about things these people's parents had seen and done in the wilderness. Now he reminds them about what they've lived through. He reminds them that their victories over King Og and King Sihon were in spite of high walls, gates, and bars. Even cities fortified with the best protection can't stop God!

God tells Moses that he needs to encourage and build up Joshua because Joshua will be the one who leads the people into the promised land. This is really hard for Moses. He wanted to go into the promised land himself, but because of his sin, God told him no. Now God gives him a difficult task: preparing someone else for the job he wants.

Moses focuses on the future, calling the people to obey God's laws and be set apart. He warns them that if they worship idols, they'll either die or be sent away. Moses remembers all that God has done and praises Him for it.

TODAY'S GOD SHOT

God is worthy of our trust. By reminding the Israelites of everything God has done for them and their ancestors, Moses reminds them that God can be trusted. By reminding ourselves of everything God has done for us, we also remind ourselves that God can be trusted. He's worthy of trust, and He's where the joy is!

ZOOM IN

Listen, O Israel! The LORD is our God, the LORD alone. And you must love the LORD your God with all your heart, all your soul, and all your strength.

Deuteronomy 6:4–5

Moses tells the people that God's covenant didn't die when their fathers died. God's covenant is with them too; they have their own relationship with God. When God rescued their parents and grandparents, He rescued them too.

God is going to punish His enemies for their wickedness and drive them out from the promised land, but not all at once. He has a plan and a process, so Moses warns them that even when it seems like the land will never be all theirs, they should keep trusting God.

In chapter 6, there's a prayer called the **Shema**, which means "hear." Jesus quotes it in the New Testament, and today religious Jewish people still pray this prayer twice a day. The Shema teaches that God's Word should fill our hearts, minds, and souls. When we wake up, when we eat, when we go out, when we go to bed, we should remember God's words.

⁓TODAY'S GOD SHOT⁓

God is generous. He's going to give the Israelites land, cities, vineyards, and wells. And what did the Israelites do to earn these things? Nothing. He wants them to always remember that it was God who gave them their home, and it was God who chose them to be His. He's generous, and He's where the joy is!

DEUTERONOMY 8–10

Look, the highest heavens and the earth and everything in it all belong to the LORD your God. Yet the LORD chose your ancestors as the objects of his love. And he chose you, their descendants, above all other nations, as is evident today.

Deuteronomy 10:14–15

Moses tells the Israelites that the promised land will be good, but not perfect. They are sinners living in a fallen world, and they will continue to face the consequences of sin.

Moses warns the people twice against pride. Pride makes us look to ourselves for power or answers, instead of looking to God. We can fight against pride the same way Moses told the Israelites to: by remembering who God is and what He's already done.

Moses also reminds the people that God doesn't just want them to obey His laws. He wants their love! God's laws don't take away freedom and joy; they give *more* of it. He created freedom and joy, and living His way means we get more of both!

TODAY'S GOD SHOT

God owns everything, and even so, *you* have His heart. You didn't do anything smart enough, funny enough, impressive enough, or good enough to earn His love. He just loves you. As we learn about how much He loves us, we'll love Him more and more. He's where the love is, and He's where the joy is!

DEUTERONOMY 11–13

ZOOM IN

There you and your families will feast in the presence of the LORD your God, and you will rejoice in all you have accomplished because the LORD your God has blessed you.

Deuteronomy 12:7

God gives a command to the Israelites—and us—to love Him. To love someone, you have to know them, and to know them, you have to pay attention. Moses tells the people to pay attention to their hearts so that they can make sure they're not drifting away from God and toward **idolatry**.

God explains the shifts that will happen around offerings and sacrifices once they get to the promised land. God will dwell in the middle of the land. The Levites will be spread out among each tribe, on the perimeter (the edge) of each section of land, like God instructed. But the tabernacle is the only place where they can give burnt offerings to God. Everyone will travel to give their offerings and sacrifices.

Then Moses warns people that even false prophets can sometimes say truthful things. He warns that God's people shouldn't seek information from them, because most of what they say is lies. God is protecting them.

TODAY'S GOD SHOT

God says to be joyful! Three times in today's readings, He tells His people to bring Him offerings and sacrifices, and then to rejoice. When people make sacrifices to false gods, they usually hope the gods will give them something in return. When God's people make sacrifices and offerings to Him, it's because He's already given us so much. We can rejoice in everything—even in giving offerings—because of what He's already done. He's where the joy is!

DEUTERONOMY 14–16

ZOOM IN

In honor of the LORD your God, celebrate the Passover each year in the early spring, in the month of Abib, for that was the month in which the LORD your God brought you out of Egypt by night.

Deuteronomy 16:1

Moses continues with his final speech to the Israelites before he dies and they go into the promised land. He explains rules about hair and food. Remember: God gives rules for a lot of reasons, such as keeping His people safe and setting them apart for Himself.

God tells His people again to take care of the poor. Giving to the poor brings blessing. In fact, God tells them that He'll bless them so richly that other nations will have to borrow from them. Not bad for a people who were slaves forty years ago!

Moses reminds them of their celebration calendar. When they get to the promised land, they'll have to travel to the tabernacle to make sacrifices. This will help them remember God and what He's done for them.

TODAY'S GOD SHOT

God has done so much! God the Son (Jesus) came, and He's coming again! When we look back at Jesus's **resurrection**, we also look forward to when He'll come again. Many Bible teachers call the time we live in now "the already and the not yet" because Jesus has already come once and will come again. When people whose ancestors are from Israel look back on the exodus, they are filled with joy. When we look back at the resurrection and forward to Jesus's second coming, we are filled with joy! Since the beginning of time and for forever, He's where the joy is!

ZOOM IN

Listen to me, all you men of Israel! Do not be afraid as you go out to fight your enemies today! Do not lose heart or panic or tremble before them. For the LORD your God is going with you! He will fight for you against your enemies, and he will give you victory!

Deuteronomy 20:3–4

Today, Moses gives laws about worship in the promised land. If someone is caught worshipping false gods, they will have to go on trial for their life. Because these are serious crimes with serious consequences, God sets up a court system with priests and judges whose wisdom will guide them. Moses also knows that one day, the Israelites will decide they want a king, just because all the other nations around them have kings. So he says that the future king must have his own book with God's laws written in it.

God tells His people how to deal with the cities outside of the promised land. If they are peaceful, then the Israelites will take over the city peacefully. If they fight, then the Israelites will wipe them out. God is using the Israelites to fulfill His promise of land to them, to get rid of temptations to idolatry, and to bring justice to wicked nations.

∼ TODAY'S GOD SHOT ∼

God made a way for us to be with Him. When the Israelites were scared or doubting, God wanted them to know that He was with them. Our sin means that we deserve to be separated from God forever. But He loves us, and He made a way for us to be with Him, by giving Jesus to take every punishment for every time we have ever sinned—or will ever sin! Praise God. He's full of mercy and grace and love, and He's where the joy is!

DEUTERONOMY 21–23

ZOOM IN

But the LORD your God refused to listen to Balaam. He turned the intended curse into a blessing because the LORD your God loves you.

Deuteronomy 23:5

Moses gives a lot of laws today that have to do with adults' relationships with each other. It's important to remember two things when we think about these laws. First, the Israelites lived during a very different time from ours, with very different cultural traditions. And second, if God gives a law about something—like slavery, for example—it doesn't mean He approves of that thing. He is talking to a specific group of people who are living at a specific time. So He's giving them laws that apply to the situations they're already in. As we've seen since the beginning, God's heart is for the vulnerable, and He is both powerful and kind.

Some of God's laws have to do with mixing things together: different kinds of seeds, plowing animals, and fabrics in a piece of clothing. These serve practical purposes, but they also remind the Israelites that they themselves are separate from those around them, set apart as God's people.

TODAY'S GOD SHOT

God reverses the future we earned. When King Balak tried to get Balaam to curse the Israelites, the curse turned into a blessing. Because of our sin, we deserve the curse. But because Jesus redeemed us from the curse, we get His blessing. God turned the Israelites' curse into a blessing, and He turns our curse into a blessing too. He's where the joy is!

SEVEN-DAY ROUNDUP

ZOOM OUT

Moses has been giving a final speech to the Israelites. He's reminding them of some of the laws they already know about the promised land and explaining some new ones too. Over and over, we see how God keeps His promises, protects His people, and sets them apart.

WORDS TO REMEMBER

- Idolatry—worshipping idols or false gods
- Resurrection—coming back to life from the dead
- Shema—from a Hebrew word meaning "hear"; an important Jewish prayer made up of Old Testament Scriptures

APPLICATION

Are you ready for the Israelites to get to the promised land already? They were too! For forty years, God kept them in the wilderness. But He didn't leave them there. He was with them all along, leading them, protecting them, and providing for them. While they waited, they learned about who God is. Are you waiting for something big to happen in your life? God answers all our prayers with yes, no, or wait. If He's told you to wait, there's a very good reason. Make a list of the ways He's led you, protected you, and provided for you. What can you learn about God as you wait?

DEUTERONOMY 24–27

ZOOM IN

You will be a nation that is holy to the LORD your God, just as he promised.

Deuteronomy 26:19

Moses gives the people more laws, including the only law in the Old Testament about divorce. Because our culture today is so different from the ancient Israelites', there are a few different beliefs about what the law means. But the important thing to know is that this law made sure that someone—the husband or the wife—was being protected from bad intentions.

There are also more laws that show us again how much God has always cared about vulnerable people. God disapproves of slavery and kidnapping. And He won't let a lender accept a poor person's coat or millstone as collateral to a loan, because they need these things to stay warm and grind grain for food. He wants the poor people to be warm and fed!

Moses also tells the Israelites what to do when they enter the promised land: Six tribes will climb Mount Gerizim and six tribes will climb Mount Ebal, where God will explain the blessings and curses of the covenant.

TODAY'S GOD SHOT

God *treasures* His people. He called Israel *His*—putting His name on them. How beautiful it is to be made, chosen, protected, loved, and treasured by the God of the universe. He treasures all His kids! And He's where the joy is!

ZOOM IN

The LORD our God has secrets known to no one. We are not accountable for them, but we and our children are accountable forever for all that he has revealed to us, so that we may obey all the terms of these instructions.

Deuteronomy 29:29

Moses reminds the people that if they obey God and keep the covenant, He'll bless them richly. He'll give them victory and command His blessing on them!

If the people don't follow God, the curses will come. Covenant curses are the opposite of covenant blessings; so as wonderful as the blessings of God sound, the curses of God sound terrible in equal amounts. Be careful not to assume something about God here that goes against everything we've learned about Him so far. He doesn't *want* to harm His people. He pursues them again and again, even when they've betrayed Him. But when we sin, He allows discipline so that we'll be protected from ourselves and turn back to Him.

Moses encourages the Israelites to keep this covenant; it's not just for the priests or the leaders. This covenant is for every single Israelite, and all the Israelites who will be born.

TODAY'S GOD SHOT

God reveals some things to His people, and He keeps some things hidden. The things He shows us are meant to draw us closer to Him, and so are the things He keeps hidden. We can't know everything God knows, and that's good. We don't have to know what He knows, because we know *Him*. And one thing we can always be sure of is this: He's where the joy is!

DEUTERONOMY 30–31

ZOOM IN

So be strong and courageous! Do not be afraid and do not panic before them. For the LORD your God will personally go ahead of you. He will neither fail you nor abandon you.

Deuteronomy 31:6

Moses tells the people the bad news and the good news. The bad news is that they're going to break God's covenant. God knows this, Moses knows this, and the people know this. The good news is that when they repent and turn back to God, He won't abandon them. He'll welcome them and restore their blessings.

Moses wants the people to want God, not just what God gives them. Moses isn't going to get the blessing of the promised land; God's already told him this. But he's gotten the blessing of knowing God, which matters even more. Moses wants the people to know God too.

Moses tells the people not to be afraid, but to remember that God is near. Then Moses calls Joshua over, and God makes him the next leader of the Israelites and tells Joshua that He will be with him.

TODAY'S GOD SHOT

God already knows all the times we're going to ignore His laws, and He still loves us. He knows every time we'll walk away from Him, and He still loves us. He knows that we will forget Him, doubt Him, and even blame Him. And He still loves us. No one else loves like God does. He's where the joy is!

ZOOM IN

The LORD says, "I will rescue those who love me. I will protect those who trust in my name."

Psalm 91:14

Because God told him to, Moses sings a song he wrote about Israel's past, present, and future. It tells Israel to pay attention to how great God is. Because a song is like a poem, there is some symbolic language here that exaggerates a bit to make a point. But the main theme is that when Israel rejects God, God will bring other nations into His family, but He'll show compassion to Israel.

Moses gives a final blessing to eleven of the twelve tribes. (Simeon doesn't get a blessing, but they'll eventually spread out and become part of Judah.) Then, he goes up on the mountain that God told him to, sees the promised land, and dies, old and strong. God buries Moses in the valley, in a place that no one knows.

Psalm 91 records Moses's words from Deuteronomy 32 into the Bible's songbook.

TODAY'S GOD SHOT

God wants us to know Him and love Him. He wants us to spend time with Him and to trust Him. When we spend time with Him, we'll go to Him when we're joyful, excited, or peaceful. And when we trust Him, we'll go to Him when we're scared, hurt, or lonely. You can always go to Him—no matter what! He's where the joy is!

JOSHUA 1–4

The book of Joshua is the first history book of the Bible we'll read together. And while it does teach us about history, of course, its main job is to teach us about God: who He is, what He's doing, and how much He loves His kids. Look for Him on every page!

Joshua sends two spies to Jericho, which is the first city in the promised land. They want to get a good view of the city, so they stay in the house of a woman named Rahab. Rahab doesn't live by God's laws, but she's heard about God and what He's done for the Israelites. And she knows that God is powerful, so she protects the spies when they're in her home.

The spies report back that they believe God will give them the land. Joshua gathers everyone together to cross the river. And as they do, God calls them not just a people, but a *nation*. He tells them to set up twelve stones to remember His provision.

TODAY'S GOD SHOT

God wants Joshua to be strong and courageous, but He doesn't expect Joshua to do it on his own. Every time God tells Joshua to be brave, God also tells him that He will be with him. We can't force ourselves to be strong or courageous, and God doesn't ask us to! Real bravery comes from knowing that God is with us. You can be brave, because He's with you. He's where strength is, He's where courage is, and He's where the joy is!

When the people heard the sound of the rams' horns, they shouted as loud as they could. Suddenly, the walls of Jericho collapsed, and the Israelites charged straight into the town and captured it.

Joshua 6:20

Today the nation of Israel steps into the promised land! Their enemies are still there, so they have instructions for how to drive them out. They are going to take down Jericho first and have to follow God's instructions to prepare for battle. God's instructions aren't to run sprints or practice using weapons; His instructions are to walk and blow trumpets. (This is a *terrible* battle strategy by human standards.)

Joshua runs into a man with a sword who says He has come as a commander of the LORD's army. Joshua believes he's in God's presence, so he bows down in worship. Joshua and his men follow the instructions God gave: They march around the city with the ark, once a day for six days, blowing trumpets. On day seven, the people shout, the walls fall down, and the Israelites take the city. Everyone except Rahab and her family—who are now protected by the two spies she protected—is defeated.

TODAY'S GOD SHOT

God is always at work. As the Israelites walked around Jericho the first six times, they probably thought they were wasting time and energy. But even if it's work we can't see, we can trust that God is working. When we follow God's directions, we grow in our obedience to Him. Obeying God is always the best place to be, even if we don't see or understand what He's doing. He's where the joy is!

JOSHUA 9–11

ZOOM IN

For the LORD hardened their hearts and caused them to fight the Israelites. So they were completely destroyed without mercy, as the LORD had commanded Moses.

Joshua 11:20

The Gibeonites have heard that Israel shows mercy to people outside of Canaan. So they lie to Israel and pretend they don't live in Canaan. They ask Israel for a protective covenant. Joshua doesn't ask God about it but agrees to it anyway. The Israelites assign the Gibeonites to do manual labor in the promised land.

God hardens the other nations' hearts, and no one besides the Gibeonites makes peace with Israel. So God uses miracles—even making the sun stand still so the battle day is longer—to help Israel win battle after battle. Wow! They defeat six more cities.

TODAY'S GOD SHOT

God shows mercy on whom He shows mercy (Exodus 33:19). When we read in 11:20 that God hardened the enemies' hearts, it can seem really unfair. Remember that we are all sinners, and our sin means we deserve death and separation from God forever. So what's actually unfair is that we *won't* get that; we get God's mercy instead. These are hard parts of God's character to understand, and you can ask Him to help you trust His good heart, even when you don't understand all of Him. He's where goodness is, and He's where mercy is, and He's where the joy is!

SEVEN-DAY ROUNDUP

ZOOM OUT

You've finished the **Torah**, or the **Pentateuch**, the first five books of the Old Testament! We also started the first of the history books in the Bible: Joshua. Before Moses died, we saw him bless the people and appoint Joshua to lead them.

BIG PICTURE: DEUTERONOMY

Deuteronomy means "second law," and for most of the book, Moses addresses the people, encouraging them to follow God's commandments, laws, and rules. In all these instructions, we see that God wants His people's obedience in what they do *and* what they think and feel.

WORDS TO REMEMBER

- Pentateuch—Greek for "five books," the first five books of the Bible, also called the Torah
- Torah—the first five books of the Bible, also called the Pentateuch

APPLICATION

In the New Testament, Jesus quotes from Deuteronomy often. Read the two passages below, and ask yourself how Jesus explained the Old Testament law. What does it mean for us today?

- Deuteronomy 6:5
- Matthew 22:37–38

JOSHUA 12–15

ZOOM IN

I myself will drive these people out of the land ahead of the Israelites.

Joshua 13:6

The Israelites obey God and follow His instructions, and they keep winning battles and gaining more land inside Canaan. But the tribes that settled east of the Jordan River don't obey God when they let some of the people who are there stay. *Uh-oh.* This act of disobedience will cause lots of trouble over the years.

Joshua and Caleb—the two spies who believed God's promise would come true—are old now, but they trust that God still has work for them. Caleb and his men get Joshua's blessing and follow God's instructions to fight against the giants, and they win! (By the way, Caleb is probably eighty-five at this point—you're never too young or old for God to use you!)

Judah gets the most land, and even though it's mostly the desert, they also get the land close to the Dead Sea, where the soil is rich with minerals.

TODAY'S GOD SHOT

God wants our obedience. Joshua 13:13 says the tribes that settled east of the Jordan didn't drive out the people of the land, and it sounds like they didn't try. And Judah can't drive out the Jebusites, even though they tried. God hasn't given up on them or gone back on His promise, but He *does* want their obedience. Still, He is with them, even in their sin. Even in the waiting, He's at work shaping their hearts. Even in failure, He's strengthening their faith and joy. He's where the joy is!

JOSHUA 16–18

DAY 86

ZOOM IN

So Joshua gave them a grant of land along with their uncles, as the LORD had commanded.

Joshua 17:4

As the Israelites divide up the promised land—even though God had given *very* specific instructions on how to do this—drama unfolds. When Jacob-Israel adopted two sons (Ephraim and Manasseh), those sons and their descendants had rights to become tribe leaders and landowners. And since Manasseh split in half, they don't feel like they're getting their fair share.

Then the daughters of Zelophehad—remember them?—come back. They remind Joshua about the land Moses had promised them, and Joshua follows God's orders.

On top of the drama, seven tribes still haven't received their land, so they're getting impatient. And the Israelites aren't fully obeying God: Most of them are letting the Canaanites, the people living in their land, stay in their land.

~TODAY'S GOD SHOT~

God marks His valuables. In Hebrew, the letter *shin* is viewed as God's initial, because it's the first letter of His name *Shaddai*, which means "God Almighty." Jerusalem is surrounded by three valleys that look like a *shin*. God marked Jerusalem. And He chose the Israelites, called them His, and marked them as His own. And because of Jesus, we get to be marked by the same name! He's where the joy is!

The letter *shin*

JOSHUA 19–21

ZOOM IN

Not a single one of all the good promises the Lord had given to the family of Israel was left unfulfilled; everything he had spoken came true.

Joshua 21:45

The Israelites continue dividing up the land. God wants this to be their home, as long as they keep their part of the covenant. The land is small, but so different from place to place. There are mountains and valleys and deserts and seas. Where each tribe lives has a big impact on the food they will eat and the work they will do.

Because Joshua believed God's promise about giving them this land, he gets to choose where he wants to live first. But he kindly lets everyone else choose first. He gets a hilly area in Ephraim's land. It's quiet and there aren't a lot of people, so it's a good place to spend the end of his life.

The Levites are spread out among the tribes, and God also sets up cities of **refuge**. These are places where people who accidentally kill someone can live safely, without fear of revenge.

TODAY'S GOD SHOT

God is generous and faithful. He promised the Israelites—who were slaves in Egypt and then waited for forty years in the wilderness—a home. Because of God's power and strength, the Israelites get their home. And because of God's love, they also get God. He's where the joy is!

ZOOM IN

Deep in your hearts you know that every promise of the LORD your God has come true. Not a single one has failed!

Joshua 23:14

The promised land has been mostly conquered, and the tribes who settled east of the Jordan finally fulfill their promise. They helped the other tribes fight, and now they return home when Joshua sends them.

Joshua reminds the leaders of Israel that God is responsible for every good thing that's happened for them. And he tells them they *have* to drive out the remaining Canaanites. He assures them that God has given them everything they need to obey Him and keep their part of the covenant. Joshua asks the people if they want to serve YHWH or false gods. The people proclaim that they want to follow YHWH, the one true God.

Eleazar, the high priest, dies and leaves his son Phinehas in charge. Joshua dies and he's buried in the promised land. And remember how Joseph didn't want his bones left in Egypt? Well, the people have been carrying them all these years! Finally, they bury Joseph's remains in the promised land too.

TODAY'S GOD SHOT

God keeps His promises! God promised Abraham three things about His people: that they would be a great nation, that they'd have a blessed relationship with YHWH, and that they'd live in the promised land. All those things are coming true! He's where the joy is!

JUDGES 1–2

ZOOM IN

So the LORD burned with anger against Israel. He said, "Because these people have violated my covenant, which I made with their ancestors, and have ignored my commands, I will no longer drive out the nations that Joshua left unconquered when he died."

Judges 2:20–21

When you hear the word *judge*, you probably think of someone who's in charge of a courtroom. But in the book of Judges, each judge was a leader of God's people. God is in charge and makes the rules, but He gives the people judges to help lead them.

Remember the last instruction Joshua gave the leaders of Israel? To drive out the remaining Canaanites? They didn't do it. And as the Israelites see the things the Canaanites have—fancy buildings and art and exciting cities—they want to be like them instead of like God.

God shows up as the Angel of the LORD to **rebuke** them. He tells them that their sin will make them turn to worshipping idols.

TODAY'S GOD SHOT

God wants His people's hearts. Even though He's all-powerful, He doesn't force our obedience. In the Bible, we see a pattern of God's people promising they'll never forget what He's done for them, quickly turning away from Him, and then facing the consequences of their sin. And over and over, we see God's patience and compassion when they call out to Him and He forgives them. The more we understand and experience God's great love for us, the more we'll want to obey Him. Obeying Him brings us joy because He's where the joy is!

ZOOM IN

Israel's leaders took charge, and the people gladly followed. Praise the LORD!

Judges 5:2

Today we meet four of Israel's judges, and they're pretty good at their job. Because the Israelites worshipped other gods, they become slaves for eight years. They turn back to God, and God gives them Othniel. He's a military leader and a judge, and God gives him victory. There is peace for forty years. But then . . .

The Israelites rebel against God again, and their enemies take back Jericho. They become servants again, this time for eighteen years. They cry to God for rescue, and He gives them their second judge, Ehud. He's left-handed, which at that time meant people thought something was wrong with you. But God uses Ehud's left hand to defeat King Eglon, and

the Israelites have peace for eighty years. Then Shamgar, who is probably a Canaanite turned YHWH worshipper, leads them to victory and more peace, until . . . the Israelites fall into sin again.

After twenty years of slavery for Israel, God raises up Deborah. She's the judge who honors God the most. She and her military leader Barak sing a song of praise when God gives them the victory.

TODAY'S GOD SHOT

God uses unlikely people to accomplish His purposes. So far in Judges, He's used a left-handed man, a Canaanite, and a woman. He uses unlikely people not only so that His power will be seen, but also so that His heart for the vulnerable will be seen. These victory stories with unlikely leaders bring God glory and bring us joy. He's where the joy is!

JUDGES 6–7

ZOOM IN

The angel of the LORD appeared to him and said, "Mighty hero, the LORD is with you!"

Judges 6:12

Deborah leads the people in peace for forty years, and then (do you already know what's coming?) the Israelites fall back into sins. The Midianites **oppress** the Israelites, fighting them and eating their food. So the Israelites hide in caves. After seven years of this, they cry out to God.

God tells a man named Gideon that he will be the one to save Israel from the Midianites, but Gideon doesn't believe it. He asks for a sign, which God gives him. So he gets rid of the Israelites' idols like God told him to. (But he does it in the middle of the night because he's scared.)

Gideon asks God for more signs, and God patiently gives them. After reducing the size of the Israelite army down to three hundred men (1 percent of where they started!) God gives the Israelites the victory. Whew!

～TODAY'S GOD SHOT ～

God is patient with our questions and our doubts. Gideon doubts God a lot, but God doesn't get angry with him. He answers Gideon's questions and encourages him with the truth: that Gideon is a warrior hero not because of himself, but because of God. God is *the* Warrior Hero, and He's with Gideon, and if God says Gideon will have the victory, then he will! He's where the joy is!

SEVEN-DAY ROUNDUP

ZOOM OUT

The Israelites are finally settled in the promised land! We saw Joshua and Caleb serve God until the end of their lives. And we met the first five judges God appointed to lead His people. We saw Israel choose sin many times, and we saw God welcome them back every time they turned back to Him.

BIG PICTURE: JOSHUA

Joshua shows us that God keeps His promises: Like He promised Abraham, they become a great nation, having a blessed relationship with YHWH and living in the promised land. In the book of Joshua, God gives His people victory, a home, and rest.

WORDS TO REMEMBER

- Oppress—to treat someone in a powerless position cruelly and unfairly
- Rebuke—to express sharp disapproval
- Refuge—a safe place to live

APPLICATION

God kept His promises to Israel, and He keeps His promises to us too. Read John 14:27–28. What does Jesus promise? How does this help us to not be afraid? Any time you are afraid, pray and ask God to remind you of His promises.

JUDGES 8–9

ZOOM IN

They forgot the LORD their God, who had rescued them from all their enemies surrounding them.

Judges 8:34

Gideon wins a few more battles and quickly moves from scared to arrogant. He decides that he should be the king of Israel, even naming one of his sons Abimelech, which means "my father is king." Pretty bold, Gideon. But God didn't make Gideon a king, so deciding this himself is a sin. And as we've seen over and over, when God's people sin against Him, there are consequences.

Abimelech is even more selfish and scheming than his dad, and pretty soon he decides that it's his turn to be king. Abimelech kills his brothers and declares himself king. But Abimelech doesn't know that his youngest brother, Jotham, got away. Jotham climbs up to the top of Mount Gerizim and tells the people a story about trees and a thornbush.

Abimelech is, of course, the thornbush in the story, and he brings death and destruction everywhere he goes. Eventually, a woman drops a giant stone from a rooftop, and it kills him.

TODAY'S GOD SHOT

God is protective. When we love something or someone, we do everything we can to protect it. God—who loves us more than we can imagine—loves His people and is fiercely protective of them. Even though they forget Him again and again, God still loves His people and brings justice to protect them. He's where the justice is, and He's where the joy is!

ZOOM IN

Then the Israelites put aside their foreign gods and served the LORD. And he was grieved by their misery.

Judges 10:16

There are six more judges today, and Israel keeps spiraling into more and more sin. It seems like they'll worship anything except God. So God lets them spiral all the way down to rock bottom, and the Israelites are conquered by the Philistines and the Ammonites. Finally, the Israelites turn away from their idols and back to God. They seem repentant.

But when the Ammonites attack them again, the leaders of Israel appoint Jephthah as their military leader without consulting God. Jephthah is desperate and in a hurry, and he makes an unwise vow to God in an effort to win the war. When the time comes for him to follow through with his vow, the result is that his daughter will have no children, and Jephthah's family name will end with him.

TODAY'S GOD SHOT

God is grieved when His kids are suffering. In 10:16, when Israel is once again dealing with the consequences of their idolatry, they cry out to Him in their despair. Even though they keep choosing sin over God, His heart aches at their misery. If you feel heartbroken—because of sin or other circumstances in your life—cry out to God. He promises to be near you! And when we remember how close He is, we also remember that He's where the joy is!

JUDGES 13–15

ZOOM IN

His hair must never be cut. For he will be dedicated to God as a Nazirite from birth. He will begin to rescue Israel from the Philistines.

Judges 13:5

Guess where we find the Israelites at the beginning of today's reading. Yep, deep in sin again. In order to turn their hearts back to Him, God lets the Philistines oppress them—for forty years! Sound familiar? But then the Angel of the LORD tells a childless woman she'll have a son who'll help rescue Israel. She is instructed to raise him as a Nazirite, so he can't get a haircut, drink alcohol, or touch dead things. (We saw God's instructions for Nazirites in Numbers.)

The child is named Samson. God gives him surprising, superhuman strength, and he doesn't use an army to fight. He *is* the army. But Samson secretly breaks every rule he's supposed to follow as a Nazirite. He drinks alcohol. He kills a lion with his bare hands, and a few days later he . . . eats honey out of its dead body. And he's *so* arrogant. In a whole mess of sin that came from him feeling embarrassed by a riddle, people are murdered, animals are killed, and homes are destroyed.

TODAY'S GOD SHOT

God uses sinful people—sometimes even sinful people with wicked motives—to accomplish His plan. This doesn't mean their sin is okay. It means God is bigger than their—and our—sin. Even our most selfish and hateful motives aren't big enough to mess up God's good plan. Praise God! He's where the joy is!

ZOOM IN

Samson prayed to the LORD, "Sovereign LORD, remember me again. O God, please strengthen me just one more time."

Judges 16:28

Samson's sin costs him. He has a big weakness for women and marries a Philistine named Delilah. Samson doesn't know she's being paid by her people to find out the secret to his strength (it seems like he might not even have big muscles!).

Samson finally tells Delilah that he's strong because of God's calling on his life. But he refers to God as *Elohim*, which is not God's personal name. This probably means he didn't take his vows to God very seriously—like it was more of an *arrangement* than a relationship.

Then, Samson's sin catches up to him. Delilah hires a man to shave his head, and his strength is gone. Samson is blinded by the Philistines, and they put him in prison. Finally, Samson calls out to God and calls Him YHWH—God's personal name—and God gives him strength. Samson pushes down two pillars in the Philistines' **pagan** temple, and everyone inside dies.

Then, Israel falls into more and more sin as everyone does whatever they want.

TODAY'S GOD SHOT

God answers our prayers. Samson spent most of his life being arrogant and breaking God's rules. But at the end of his life, he cries out to God, calling Him YHWH. God hears Samson and gives him the strength he asks for. Even in prisons and at last breaths, God hears our prayers. And even after a lifetime of sin, God answers our prayers. He's where the joy is!

JUDGES 19–21

ZOOM IN

In those days Israel had no king; all the people did whatever seemed right in their own eyes.

Judges 21:25

Israel is an absolute mess of sin and misery. Their greed, hatred, and selfishness take over, and horrible and heartbreaking things happen as a result. When the Israelite army learns of some of the things that have been happening because of their people's sins, they decide something needs to be done.

Israel goes to war against one of their own tribes, Benjamin. This is the first time they've fought among themselves. Israel asks God to guide them, and in three days, He gives them the victory.

But Israel continues to make decisions without asking God, and they work themselves into a bigger and bigger mess of sin.

TODAY'S GOD SHOT

God is joy. There wasn't a lot of joy in today's reading because the people turned away from God. The book of Judges ends with the Israelites' sin growing and growing. Sin might lead to small moments of satisfaction or even happiness, but it won't lead to joy. Living God's way means that we can have real, lasting joy. He's where the joy is!

ZOOM IN

The neighbor women said, "Now at last Naomi has a son again!" And they named him Obed. He became the father of Jesse and the grandfather of David.

Ruth 4:17

At some point during the time of the judges—when people do whatever their sinful hearts want—a man named Elimelech takes his wife, Naomi, and their sons to Moab. Elimelech and his sons die, leaving three widows—Naomi and her two daughters-in-law—behind.

Naomi goes back to Israel, and Ruth, one of her daughters-in-law, goes with her. Her heart is with Naomi; and even though she's a Moabite, she knows and worships the one true God. In Leviticus, God gave His people laws to ensure that poor people were provided for by rich people; they had to leave the crops around the edges of their field for the poor. This is how Ruth came to the field of Boaz, a wealthy Israelite landowner, where Naomi told her to go gather food. Boaz sees her working tirelessly and asks about her. He's impressed by her devotion to God and her love for Naomi. He treats her with extra kindness.

Naomi realizes what's happening and plays matchmaker for Ruth and Boaz. Boaz marries Ruth and they have a son named Obed.

TODAY'S GOD SHOT

God brings people into His family. Ruth was a Moabite, not an Israelite. And Boaz's mom was Rahab, who protected the Israelite spies in her home in Jericho. The son of an outsider marries an outsider; one of their descendants is King David. And one of his descendants is King Jesus. God welcomes the outsider and makes them part of His family. He's where the joy is!

1 SAMUEL 1–3

ZOOM IN

I asked the LORD to give me this boy, and he has granted my request. Now I am giving him to the LORD, and he will belong to the LORD his whole life.

1 Samuel 1:27–28

The Israelites—wrapped up in their mess of sin—have decided that things would go better for them if they had a king.

Meanwhile, Hannah is devastated because she hasn't been able to have a child. One day she goes to the tabernacle, crying out to God. Because she's praying so passionately, the priest, Eli, comes to see what's going on. Soon after, Hannah and her husband have a son, Samuel. Hannah had promised God that she'd give Samuel back to Him, and she does. She brings Samuel to Eli, who agrees to raise him in God's house. Hannah worships God with a song. The song says that God values humility, that God is at work, and that God will anoint a future king.

Samuel humbly serves God in the tabernacle. God speaks to him—out loud—but Samuel doesn't understand what's happening. Eli tells Samuel how to respond to God, and Samuel delivers a hard message back to Eli. Eli says the LORD should do what is best.

TODAY'S GOD SHOT

God can be trusted with our hearts. When Hannah is heartbroken over not having a child, she prays. She doesn't turn away from God, take matters into her own hands, or demand a child from Him. Instead, she brings her sorrow to the one who hears her. He always hears us, and He's where the joy is!

SEVEN-DAY ROUNDUP

ZOOM OUT

We covered a lot in the last seven days! You've now finished *nine* books of the Bible, and in those books, we saw God keeping the promises He made to Abraham. We saw that even when His people sin against Him, He never stops loving them. And we saw God's care and kindness for the vulnerable: providing for them and even using them to fulfill His plan of salvation.

BIG PICTURE: JUDGES

In Judges we see again and again the consequences of sin. The Israelites have seasons of peace, then they turn away from God, then they face the consequences of their sin, then they cry out to God, and then God rescues them. Through all of their unfaithfulness, we are reminded that God is always faithful.

BIG PICTURE: RUTH

In Ruth, God's kind plan of redemption shines. Even in tragedy, God is kind to the brokenhearted and is working to accomplish His plan.

WORD TO REMEMBER

- Pagan—having to do with false gods

APPLICATION

God showed such kindness to Naomi and Ruth. At a time when widows were among some of the most vulnerable people in a society, God provided them with food, a home, and a family. Make a list of the ways God showed His kindness to some of the people we've read about together so far: Hagar, Job, Joseph, Moses, and Joshua. Then make a list of some of the ways God has shown His kindness to *you*.

1 SAMUEL 4–8

Israel loses a battle to the Philistines, and they blame God for their loss. Instead of asking Him for help, they decide—without God's permission—to bring the ark of the covenant with them to battle next time. Eli's sons are killed in battle—which fulfilled the message that the LORD told Samuel to give to Eli—and the ark is stolen. When he hears the tragic news, Eli dies.

Following Samuel's instructions, the people fast, pray, make sacrifices, and ask God for forgiveness. God gives them victory over the Philistines, and Samuel sets up an "Ebenezer"—a stone of remembrance.

But the people aren't satisfied, and they want a king. Because God knows everything, He knows that this king will break God's commands and the people will beg Him for help. God warns them through Samuel, but they ignore the warning.

～TODAY'S GOD SHOT～

God set Israel apart and made them His. He hasn't given them a king because *He's* their King. They don't want to be different, and they keep rejecting the ways He's set them apart. Even when the people say that they'll remember God and all He's done for them, they let fear take over, and they wind up forgetting. If you ask God, He'll help you remember that He's where the joy is!

ZOOM IN

The Lord will not abandon his people, because that would dishonor his great name. For it has pleased the Lord to make you his very own people.

1 Samuel 12:22

Even though He knows this won't go well, God tells Samuel to appoint Israel's first king and makes it clear who that king should be. Samuel tells a Benjamite named Saul that God has a plan for him to rescue His people. Samuel proves it by telling Saul three things that will happen to him on his way home. (And of course, all three things happen.)

God the Spirit (remember the Trinity?) comes upon Saul, and people can tell that he's been changed by God. God gives Saul an incredible first victory over the Ammonites, who were oppressing the Israelites.

Samuel isn't a judge anymore—he's getting pretty old—but he's still a prophet. He reminds Israel that if they obey God, things will go well for them. He also warns them that if they sin, things won't go well. He tells them that even though they sinned by begging for a king, it's not too late to turn back to Him!

TODAY'S GOD SHOT

God delights in His people. *Delights!* After all the times they've disregarded God, Samuel still tells the Israelites that it has pleased God to make them His own. And after all the times we've disregarded God, He is pleased to make us His own because of Jesus's sacrifice. He rejoices over His kids, and He's where the joy is!

1 SAMUEL 13–14

ZOOM IN

But now your kingdom must end, for the LORD has sought out a man after his own heart. The LORD has already appointed him to be the leader of his people, because you have not kept the LORD's command.

1 Samuel 13:14

Saul's big weakness is fear. Did you catch where Saul was when Samuel was going to anoint him in front of the people? He was hiding. So it's not really a surprise that when the Philistine army gathers around Saul and his men at Gilgal, he panics. Saul is supposed to wait for Samuel's instructions, but instead he hastily offers a sacrifice to God. Only the priests are allowed to do this, and Saul isn't a priest. When Saul has the opportunity to repent, he insists his actions were right. He's fearful and he's prideful, and Samuel tells Saul that God will raise up his replacement.

Meanwhile, Saul's son Jonathan is brave and busy winning battles against the Philistines. When he sins, even accidentally, he repents and turns back to God.

TODAY'S GOD SHOT

God is sovereign (remember that word?), and He can use anything and anyone to move His plan forward. The people wanted a king, and even though this wasn't God's best plan for them, He allowed it and used it. Saul is fearful and prideful, and God still uses him to move His plan forward. Nothing any of us do—or don't do—can ruin God's plan. He is in charge of every moment, and He's where the joy is!

ZOOM IN

But the LORD said to Samuel, "Don't judge by his appearance or height, for I have rejected him. The LORD doesn't see things the way you see them. People judge by outward appearance, but the LORD looks at the heart."

1 Samuel 16:7

Samuel tells Saul that God wants him to wipe out all of the Amalekites. But Saul disobeys. He wins the battle but lets the king—and a lot of animals—live. Saul even sets up a monument praising himself and calls YHWH "your God" (not "my God" or "our God") when he talks to the people. And he lies. A lot.

God tells Samuel that David is the new king of Israel, and Samuel anoints David privately but doesn't announce him as king yet. God the Spirit leaves Saul and comes to David to empower him for the job ahead.

The Israelites are at war with the Philistines again, and they have a giant soldier named Goliath. No one wants to fight this guy, but David says he'll do it. With one swing of his slingshot, he kills Goliath. Saul decides he wants to get to know this David guy.

TODAY'S GOD SHOT

God is outside of time, but He's inside time too, experiencing things *with us* as they happen. We see this when the Bible tells us His emotions. He's angry when His people are abused. And He's sad when His people disobey Him. He's not distant or detached. He's with all of us at every moment. He's who we can turn to in our anger, sadness, and happiness. He's where the peace is, and He's where the joy is!

1 SAMUEL 18–20; PSALMS 11, 59

ZOOM IN

But Lord, you laugh at them. You scoff at all the hostile nations.

Psalm 59:8

Saul doesn't just want to get to know David—he wants to kill him. When David killed Goliath, he became a local hero, and the people give David—not Saul—the credit for winning the war against the Philistines. Saul becomes extremely jealous of David and feels threatened by him too. He tries at least sixteen different times to kill David.

David marries Saul's daughter Michal, and he becomes friends with Saul's son Jonathan. Both Jonathan and Michal work to save David's life. When the murder attempts won't stop, Jonathan helps David escape to safety.

David writes two psalms while his life is being threatened, remembering God's past faithfulness, trusting in God's present protection, and putting his life and future in God's hands. He's preaching to himself and to all of us!

TODAY'S GOD SHOT

God laughs, but the Bible only mentions that He laughs at His enemies. His laughter should be a comfort to His kids, because it means that He's not worried! Even the fiercest army or the biggest problem doesn't make God scared. He's already defeated His and our enemies. He can laugh because He knows that nothing can get in the way of His good plans. He's victorious, and He's where the joy is!

ZOOM IN

May the LORD therefore judge which of us is right and punish the guilty one. He is my advocate, and he will rescue me from your power!

1 Samuel 24:15

Saul is hunting David to kill him, so David goes to many different places, including Nob, Judah, and Moab. Some people try to earn favor with the king by telling Saul where David is, but just when Saul catches up to David, Saul gets word that the Philistines have attacked Israel. So Saul has to leave and go back to war. David is safe again!

When Saul goes out looking for David again, he brings three thousand men with him. David and his men are waiting in a cave—the very cave Saul chooses to use for a bathroom break. Saul is by himself in the cave, right in front of David. But David doesn't kill him; he only cuts Saul's robe. Even though Saul has tried again and again to kill David, David shows faith in God and respect for the king. David trusts God's sovereign timing for his own life and Saul's.

TODAY'S GOD SHOT

God's timing is amazing. God leads everyone's movements—from a surprise enemy attack to a bathroom break—to deliver Saul right into David's hands. It's all so perfectly timed that it almost seems like a dance. God guides His kids in a dance today too, leading everyone's movements to fulfill His plans. Will you follow His lead? He's where the joy is!

PSALMS 7, 27, 31, 34, 52

ZOOM IN

Those who look to him for help will be radiant with joy; no shadow of shame will darken their faces.

Psalm 34:5

David wrote about half of the psalms in the Bible, and today we read a few that he wrote during his time on the run from Saul.

Psalms 7, 27, 31, and 52 are psalms of **lament**. The laments express sadness and even doubts. They teach us that we can go to God with all of our emotions and thoughts, even the hard and uncomfortable ones. In these psalms, David cries out to God, grieves enemies' actions, maintains his innocence, and asks for God's mercy, protection, and nearness.

Almost all of the psalms, even the psalms of lament, end with praise. They remind us that it's good to bring our sadness to God and it's good to bring our praise to God. By remembering who God is and what He's done, we're able to praise Him, even when we're sad.

Psalm 34 is a psalm of thanksgiving. David praises God for rescuing him and invites others to trust Him too. He reminds us that God not only saves us from the *things* we fear, but from fear itself. Life won't be without its troubles or worries, but God can be trusted.

TODAY'S GOD SHOT

God is joy, and God gives joy. David says in Psalm 34 that those who look to God for help will *shine* with joy. Every day that you pray and read your Bible, you look to God for help. You're shining because of His faithfulness. Keep looking to Him for everything! He's where the joy is!

SEVEN-DAY ROUNDUP

ZOOM OUT

Over the last seven days, we met Israel's first king, Saul. We saw David defeat a giant and followed him on a run for his life. Through the psalms he wrote, we also got a glimpse inside David's heart and mind during his trials. We learned that we can bring *all* of our feelings and thoughts to God, and we were reminded that we can trust Him with everything!

WORD TO REMEMBER

- Lament—an emotional expression of grief or sorrow

APPLICATION

What's happening in your life right now? Are you having feelings of joy, sadness, doubt, or frustration? Take those feelings and write your own song of lament or thanksgiving. It doesn't have to be perfect; just tell God how you're feeling and what you know to be true about Him. Read it out loud to God and ask Him to be near.

PSALMS 56, 120, 140–142

ZOOM IN

Then I pray to you, O Lord. I say, "You are my place of refuge. You are all I really want in life."

Psalm 142:5

Today we read more psalms, and while they do include lament, they also include a lot of hope. David rightfully remembers the one he's praying to and reminds himself of what's **eternal**.

In Psalm 56, David fixes his eyes on God in the middle of his trials. Remember that David knows he's going to be king of Israel, but he's been running from Saul, who's trying to murder him. It's easy to think God has forgotten about us when we're going through troubles, but David reminds us that God always sees us.

Psalm 120 is an honest and personal song of heartbreak. It's written from the perspective of someone who has been living away from their home, and it doesn't end in praise or joy. On days when you are heartbroken and don't feel like you can pray a moving or beautiful prayer, remember Psalm 120. God wants your prayers no matter what they sound like.

Psalm 142 has deep pain as well, but also beautiful hope. David feels alone, and even though things aren't better yet, he knows that God is for him.

TODAY'S GOD SHOT

God delights when His children come to Him. In these psalms, David brings God his worship and his tears. Sometimes we bring Him offerings from the abundant blessings He's given us. Sometimes we come to Him empty-handed. Sometimes we bring Him our praise. Sometimes we come to Him with our fears and questions. God delights when we come to Him, no matter what we're bringing with us. He's where the joy is!

ZOOM IN

Thank God for your good sense! Bless you for keeping me from murder and from carrying out vengeance with my own hands.

1 Samuel 25:33

Saul has acknowledged that David will be Israel's next king, and Samuel—the priest and prophet—dies. In the meantime, David and his workers are protecting flocks of sheep for a rich man named Nabal while he's traveling. They ask Nabal for some food and supplies since it's a time of celebration. Nabal not only refuses, but mocks David and his men.

Abigail, Nabal's wife, finds out about Nabal's rudeness. She takes food and wine to David and accepts blame for her husband's sins. From the way she speaks to David, it seems like she remembers that David killed Goliath, and like she somehow knows he's going to be king. David realizes that his anger would've overtaken him if it weren't for her visit, and he's thankful.

Nabal dies from a sudden illness, and David marries Abigail. (David's first wife, Michal, was taken from him without his permission, and her father, Saul, gave her to another husband.) Even though David had already spared Saul's life, Saul is still hunting down David. David has an opportunity to kill Saul in his sleep, but he doesn't. Instead, he takes his spear and water jar. Then David seeks protection from King Achish in Philistia.

TODAY'S GOD SHOT

God works through Abigail to calm down a situation that would've otherwise ended in many deaths. The Bible tells us that Abigail was sensible. God gave her wisdom and humility, and because she used those gifts well, she saved lives! God gives people beautiful gifts and opportunities to use them to accomplish His plans. He's where the joy is!

PSALMS 17, 35, 54, 63

ZOOM IN

I will praise you as long as I live, lifting up my hands to you in prayer.

Psalm 63:4

Since Samuel anointed David as king, David's life has gotten much more difficult. But he trusts that God will keep His promises and make him the king. David knows that meaning and purpose aren't found in a job—even in the job of being king—but in knowing the LORD personally.

David uses imagery of battles and war to ask for God's salvation. David preaches to himself, knowing that God pays attention to the needy and weak. He asks for God's rescue. His prayers are both respectful and bold, which shows David's trust in who God is.

And David longs for the days when he won't live in the wilderness anymore. He wants to return to the tabernacle so he can worship God there. He doesn't know when that will happen, but he's confident God will deliver.

TODAY'S GOD SHOT

David clings to God and His promises. Even when he's being chased down in a foreign land, away from his people, David knows that God is upholding him. David knows he'll be king, because God promised it. And David also knows that in the end, God—who is worthy of trust and praise—will bring justice. He's where the joy is!

1 SAMUEL 28–31; PSALM 18

ZOOM IN

I love you, LORD; you are my strength.

Psalm 18:1

King Achish and the Philistines want to attack Israel. Since they've been giving David protection—and since they believed his lies when he told them he attacked Israel—they think David will help them.

Saul doesn't know what he should do about the upcoming attack, and he asks God for direction. But God doesn't answer him. (You might be thinking, *Wait. God always answers when we pray!* But Saul isn't living God's way, and he doesn't repent of his sin. Saul should pray a prayer of confession and repentance, but he doesn't. He just wants to know how to win a battle.) So Saul goes to talk to a fortune-teller instead, where he hears bad news: He and his sons will die tomorrow, and the Philistines will win.

King Achish and the Philistines are heading to war, but on their way, they decide they don't trust David. They send him away. The Israelites lose, and Saul and three of his sons die. Meanwhile, when David gets back to Philistia, he sees that the Amalekites attacked the city when everyone left for war. They've taken his family away and burned the city. He prays to God for help, and God delivers. David gets everything back, including his family.

TODAY'S GOD SHOT

God is our strength. On the day God saved him from his enemies, David wrote Psalm 18. David says God saved him and protected him. David knows that all his strength came from God, where all good things come from. God is where every good thing can be found. He's where the strength is, and He's where the joy is!

PSALMS 121, 123–125, 128–130

ZOOM IN

My help comes from the LORD, who made heaven and earth!

Psalm 121:2

All seven of today's psalms are in a group of psalms known as the Songs of Ascent (there are fifteen total). Jerusalem is at a higher elevation than the rest of Israel, and you have to walk uphill to get there. The Songs of Ascent were sung by Israelites making their **ascent**—their way *up*—to Jerusalem. They did this up to three times every year, when they went to celebrate together with all the other Israelites.

In these psalms, we're reminded that God never sleeps, that God gives protection, that God pours out blessing, that God keeps His covenant with Israel, and that God forgives sin and redeems!

TODAY'S GOD SHOT

God wants us to remember Him. Over and over in the Bible, we've seen God do great things for His people, only to be quickly forgotten by them. He wanted them to remember Him, and He inspired songwriters to record the Songs of Ascent. Generations of Israelites sang these psalms on their pilgrimages to Jerusalem. He wants us to remember Him too, and He still inspires songwriters to record songs about Him today. Singing praise songs is one of the ways we can remember God every day! He's worthy of our praise, and He's where the joy is!

ZOOM IN

And I was gentle today, though anointed king.

2 Samuel 3:39 ESV

A messenger comes to tell David that Saul is dead. David doesn't rejoice at the news, and when the messenger lies and takes credit for killing Saul, David orders the law-appropriate punishment: The messenger will get the death penalty.

David asks God what to do, and God sends him to the tribe of Judah. Judah makes David king, but only over their tribe. Some of Saul's surviving descendants want to stay in power. One of his sons, Ish-bosheth, is anointed as king over the other eleven tribes of Israel, with Abner as his commander.

Abner gets accused of crimes by his own people, and he's deeply offended. He promises to help David become king over all twelve tribes of Israel, and to prove his loyalty, Abner brings David's first wife, Michal, back to him. Abner and Ish-bosheth are both eventually killed. And when the military captain who killed King Ish-bosheth brags to David, he doesn't rejoice, but orders the law-appropriate punishment again. With almost all of Saul's male descendants gone, everything is lining up for David to become the king.

TODAY'S GOD SHOT

God is the gentle King. David shows us a picture of who God is, and today we read that he did not rejoice when people killed his enemies. Ezekiel 33:11 says God is not pleased when wicked people die—He'd much rather them turn from wickedness and live! God is the King, and the King will have justice, but He's not a King we should run from. He's the King we should run to, because He's good and He's gentle. He's where the joy is!

PSALMS 6, 8–10, 14, 16, 19, 21

ZOOM IN

You will show me the way of life, granting me the joy of your presence and the pleasures of living with you forever.

Psalm 16:11

After asking again and again for God to deliver him from his enemies, David praises God for doing it. When you get God's yes to a prayer you've prayed, remember to thank and praise Him for it! David also teaches us that we have nothing to offer God, and he thanks God for all the good things He's given him.

In the psalms we read today, there was a lot of imagery and exaggeration, which is common in poetry and songs. When reading the Bible, especially tricky passages, it's important to remember what type of literature we're reading and the time when it was written. In Psalm 6, even though he knows God well, David seems to fear that his sin will separate him from God. Because the psalms are songs, David is using some poetic exaggeration here. And so far in the Bible, God has been showing His people how to get to know Him in this life, but He hasn't told them specific things about the **afterlife** yet. What we know now (that David didn't know then) is that because of Jesus, absolutely no sin can separate God from His kids. Not even death can separate us! Praise God!

TODAY'S GOD SHOT

God's presence is joy. God has blessed David greatly, giving him safety and health and power and riches. David is thankful for these things, especially after living in **exile**. But he keeps pointing us back to the biggest blessing of all: God. In 21:6 and 16:11, David calls God's presence *joy*. David knew that He's where the joy is!

SEVEN-DAY ROUNDUP

ZOOM OUT

There was a lot of action in the past seven days of reading! Samuel and Saul both died, along with most of Saul's descendants. David spent some more time in exile, but he became the king of Judah and is prepared to become the king of all Israel. We read more psalms that expressed lament, hope, sadness, victory, and praise.

BIG PICTURE: 1 SAMUEL

In 1 Samuel, we see a **monarchy** established in Israel. Even though God is their true King, He gives His people an earthly king when they ask Him to. Following God's instructions, Samuel anoints Saul, then David. God guides David with His perfect care in His perfect timing to accomplish His purposes.

WORDS TO REMEMBER

- Afterlife—what happens after someone dies
- Ascent—to go up
- Eternal—lasting forever; having no beginning and no end
- Exile—to be sent away from your land, home, and people
- Monarchy—a form of government where a king or queen is in charge

APPLICATION

When we sing songs of praise, we remind ourselves of who God is and what He's done for us. Read Psalm 9:1. On a card, write down three words that describe who God is and two things He's done for you this week. Keep the card in a place where you'll see it a lot, and every time you see it, sing God a song of praise.

1 CHRONICLES 1–2

ZOOM IN

The sons of Israel were Reuben, Simeon, Levi, Judah, Issachar, Zebulun, Dan, Joseph, Benjamin, Naphtali, Gad, and Asher.

1 Chronicles 2:1–2

In 1 and 2 Chronicles, we go all the way back to the beginning. These books **chronicle**—or give a detailed, written record of—Israel's history from the beginning of time. Starting with Adam, we'll get a refresher on who we've met so far. Remember, if something seems familiar as you read, stop and praise God for the strong memory He gave you! Then ask Him to show you something new, even as you read a long list of names. There are details and stories in Chronicles that we don't get anywhere else in Scripture, so be on the lookout!

Today we did read a long list of names, but we got a few unique details about some of the people in God's family: Nimrod was a mighty hunter. Peleg's name meant "division" because he was born when God spread the people out by dividing their languages. And Achan brought disaster by disobeying the Lord.

We also read a lot about the tribe of Judah in chapter two. Do you know why? Because David is from the tribe of Judah, so it's the royal tribe of Israel.

~ **TODAY'S GOD SHOT** ~

God uses every story. It may seem boring to read long lists of names, but each name is a person. And each person has a story, just like you have a story! God can use every single person—and every single story—in *His* story. He is writing the story of redemption, and you get to be a part of it. He's where the best story is, and He's where the joy is!

ZOOM IN

When the LORD registers the nations, he will say, "They have all become citizens of Jerusalem."

Psalm 87:6

When David feels far from God, he reminds himself of the truth. Hundreds of years earlier, Moses told the Israelites that when they felt far from God, they should remind themselves of who God is, what He's done, and how much He loves His kids. David does that now, saying, "Why am I discouraged? Why is my heart so sad? I will put my hope in God! I will praise him again—my Savior and my God!" (43:5).

Psalm 49 reminds us that everyone—no matter who we are or what we have or don't have—will die someday. It reminds us what matters in life, which pushes away fear. We belong to God, and that's what matters!

TODAY'S GOD SHOT

God invites everyone to make their home among His people. In Psalm 87, we see again God's special relationship with Israel. But we also see that He welcomes people from Egypt, Babylon, Philistia, Tyre, and Ethiopia—all of which are evil or far-off lands at the time. God invites outsiders to be a part of His family, and we praise Him for it! He's where the joy is!

1 CHRONICLES 3–5

ZOOM IN

They cried out to God during the battle, and he answered their prayer because they trusted in him.

1 Chronicles 5:20

We read another **genealogy**—list of names in a family line—today, starting with King David. In this list, we meet an honorable man named Jabez. He asks God for blessings, which God gives him.

We also learn that one of the twelve tribes of Israel—Simeon—is shrinking, but Reuben is growing. Reuben settled east of the Jordan River with Gad and some of the people from Manasseh. They work together and protect each other and pray to God for victory when they fight together.

TODAY'S GOD SHOT

God always answers the prayers of His kids. We read two prayers today: The tribes on the other side of the Jordan cried out for victory in battle, and Jabez prayed for the blessing of more land. God answers both prayers with a yes. Some of us have a hard time asking God for victories or blessings for ourselves, because we think it's selfish. But God can be trusted with all our prayers—even our prayers for the things we want—and He can be trusted to answer in the best way. He might say yes; He might say no; He might say wait. But no matter what good answer He gives us, He wants us to talk to Him! He's where the joy is!

ZOOM IN

But as for me, how good it is to be near God!

Psalm 73:28

Asaph—another psalm writer—writes in today's three psalms about the importance of focus and worship. When he's looking at what other people have, and it's what he wants, he thinks they're getting what he deserves. But when he shifts his focus to God, he's left with only praise.

Asaph also reminds us how important it is to bring our honest feelings to God, and to bring them *with* our family. When God's people struggle, we shouldn't struggle alone. Pray first, and then ask others in God's family to pray with and for you. God's family is a place where we should be heard and loved and prayed for, no matter what we're going through. When we have a hard time reminding ourselves, others can remind us who God is, what He's doing, and how much He loves His kids.

~TODAY'S GOD SHOT~

God wants our eyes on Him. In all three of today's psalms, Asaph wrote about our eyes: where we should look, and what happens when we look elsewhere. When we place our eyes on ourselves or others, we quickly forget God. But when we keep our eyes on God, we remember His goodness and faithfulness. He's where the joy is!

1 CHRONICLES 6

ZOOM IN

The LORD sent the people of Judah and Jerusalem into captivity under Nebuchadnezzar.

1 Chronicles 6:15

As we read more of the chronicles of the Israelites, we get another genealogy. In this list of names, there's some new information, and a spoiler.

God promised Israel that if they didn't keep their part of the covenant, He'd send them into exile. So when 6:15 tells us that the LORD sent the people of Judah and Jerusalem into captivity, we know that they don't end up keeping their covenant. This is a little bit of a spoiler, but are you surprised? God told His people exactly what would happen if they broke their covenant. And over and over again, we've seen Israel forget God and live by their own rules instead. And like the good Father that He is, God will follow through with the discipline He warned them about. But don't worry; He also has a plan to get them back. (This shouldn't surprise you either!)

When God brings them back to the promised land, they'll use these genealogies and records to restore each tribe and family to their rightful place. Genealogies are more than just a list!

TODAY'S GOD SHOT

God loves to restore and redeem. He brought His people out of slavery, through the wilderness, and into the promised land. Because of their sin, which breaks God's heart, they'll lose their land. But before the Israelites even knew they'd lose their land, God had already made a way to bring them back. That's what God does for His kids: He made us, we went astray, and He paid the ultimate price to get us back. His plan is for restoration and redemption, and He's where the joy is!

ZOOM IN

But the godly will flourish like palm trees and grow strong like the cedars of Lebanon.

Psalm 92:12

We read another of the (very few) psalms today that doesn't end in praise: Psalm 88. These can be hard to read, but when you're going through a time of trouble or heartbreak, psalms like these will probably bring comfort. Our prayers don't need to be polished or perfect for God. He can handle our pain, frustration, and questions. He wants us to come to Him.

We also read some psalms of praise today. They mention people playing harps, tambourines, and trumpets! God wants people to play instruments to Him! We read that the whole earth—even the stormy sea—knows that God is King. And we were reminded to start and end our days with worship.

TODAY'S GOD SHOT

God makes us godly. Psalm 92 tells us that godly people "will flourish like palm trees and grow strong like the cedars." How do people grow strong and flourish? By becoming godly. How do we become godly? God makes us godly. Remember *justification* and *sanctification*? Justification is when God declares us righteous because of what Jesus did for us. Sanctification is the process of God making us godly, or more like Him. Praise God that He does the work that lets us grow strong and flourish. He's where the joy is!

1 CHRONICLES 7–10

ZOOM IN

So Saul died because he was unfaithful to the LORD.

1 Chronicles 10:13

Remember that one of the purposes of the genealogies in 1 Chronicles is to restore each tribe and family to their rightful place when they return to the promised land. In chapter 9, we learn the order in which the people come back to the land (spoiler, again!) and where they go to live. We also learn a lot about Jerusalem, because it's the spiritual capital of Israel. It takes a lot of people to run the temple after it's built; these workers do everything from mixing incense to guarding gates to leading worship to baking bread. Every worker is called a leader, no matter what their job is. All jobs that serve God are important ones!

We also read about Saul's death, and the sad end of his time as king. He was anointed to lead God's people, but he turned to God's enemies for advice. Saul fell on his own sword in battle, but the Bible says that God killed him. This can be hard to understand, but Saul ignored and betrayed God, so by Saul dying, God protected His people from a very bad leader.

TODAY'S GOD SHOT

God protects His people. When Saul was doing things his own way, ignoring God and His good laws, God put an end to his kingship and his life. God wouldn't let His people be led astray by someone so selfish. Even though we aren't Israelites, God protects us too. Because of sin in our fallen world, bad things may happen to us in this life, but God protects our relationships with Him, and our souls belong to Him. He keeps us forever! He's where the joy is!

SEVEN-DAY ROUNDUP

ZOOM OUT

In the last seven days, we read some of the chronicles of God's people, starting all the way from the beginning. We saw that God keeps His word, even when it means discipline for His people. And through the psalms, we learned more about how to pray to and worship God.

WORDS TO REMEMBER

- Chronicle—to give a detailed, written record of
- Genealogy—list of names in a family line

APPLICATION

In Psalm 92 we read that godly people "will flourish like palm trees and grow strong like the cedars." We've seen this to be true when reading the stories of people like Joshua, Job, Ruth, Samuel, and David. And if you look for it, you'll see it to be true in the lives of godly people you know today too.

Remember the words *justification* and *sanctification* that we learned about in Day 48? On a piece of paper, draw a strong and flourishing tree. If you've already decided to follow Jesus, then God's work of justification is done! Write the word *justification* on the roots of your tree. Sanctification is a process that will last the rest of your life. Write the word *sanctification* on the trunk of your tree. God is going to use all kinds of events and people in your life as He sanctifies you. Can you think of ways He's already sanctifying you? Maybe through your relationships with your family or reading His Word? Write those on some of the branches, and make sure those branches have fruit. When God sanctifies, fruit grows!

PSALMS 102–104

Psalm 102 is a lament for the writer and for Israel. He is confident that God will hear him and asks for a quick response. The psalmist is suffering, but he knows it's temporary, and contrasts that with God's eternal reign. He looks ahead in hope and knows that someday, God will rescue him, help Israel, and bring other nations to God's family.

Psalm 103 looks back at God's goodness to His people throughout time. David wrote this psalm, and in it, he even praises God for things he wasn't around to experience! He understands the big story that he's part of: the story of God and His people. David points out that life is short but God's reign is forever.

Psalm 104 is a song of worship to God the Creator. It teaches us that God created all things and set up systems for their life cycles. It also shows us that He created not only what we need, but blessings as well!

TODAY'S GOD SHOT

God sends the darkness. Sometimes we think of darkness and nighttime as something sad or scary, but God sends it! In fact, He made it (Genesis 1), He's in it (1 Kings 8:12), and it brings Him glory (Psalm 19). The next time you're sad or scared in the dark, remember that God is there with you, and praise Him for it. He's where the light is, He's where the dark is, and He's where the joy is!

2 SAMUEL 5; 1 CHRONICLES 11–12

ZOOM IN

They anointed [David] king of Israel, just as the LORD had promised through Samuel.

1 Chronicles 11:3

In Chronicles, we'll often read a story for the second time, but from a different point of view. Here's where we left off in David's story: He's been the king of Judah—one of the twelve tribes—for about seven years. The other eleven tribes said that Saul's son, Ish-bosheth, was their king, but he and his military commander, Abner, were killed. Right before that happened, Abner told the other tribes they should follow David too.

So David is *finally* king over all of Israel, about fifteen years after Samuel anointed him. Wow! David wants to move the religious capital of Israel to Jerusalem, but the Jebusites live there. They're pretty confident that no one could possibly breach their walls, but David outsmarts them by going into the city through a water tunnel. The Israelites move the capital to Jerusalem and David builds his castle there.

God also gives David victory over the Philistines, who fight him when they realize he wasn't really ever on their team. David obeys God in battle, but his personal life is a different story. He starts collecting new wives and mistresses, even though God forbids it.

TODAY'S GOD SHOT

God makes people great for His sake. David's greatness as king of Israel comes from God. God is the creator of David's life and the holder of his kingship. David's victories—and his flaws—point us forward to our eternal God and perfect King, who makes people great not only for our good but also for the sake of His glory. He's where the joy is!

PSALM 133

And there the LORD has pronounced his blessing, even life everlasting.

Psalm 133:3

Today's psalm is short but full of meaning. It's a Song of Ascent, so it would've been sung by Israelites while they journeyed to Jerusalem.

Whole families and entire tribes would be singing this song together as they traveled from near and far. We can guess that an argument or two would happen along the way, and that the people would need to be reminded that they are united in God. They would also be looking forward to the feast that they'd share in Jerusalem. So it makes perfect sense that this song praises God for **unity** among His people, and for the abundance of the land. In each of this short psalm's lines, we see God's faithfulness to His people.

TODAY'S GOD SHOT

God richly blesses His kids. In Deuteronomy, God promised Israel that He would bless them in the promised land. In this psalm, David writes about the best parts of life on earth: abundance, harmony, peace. But the blessings don't stop there: The last line of today's psalm talks about the best blessing—eternal life! God is preparing a future for His kids when He will restore all things so that we can live, forever, *with Him*. He's where the joy is!

ZOOM IN

Let them praise the LORD for his great love and for the wonderful things he has done for them.

Psalm 107:8

In Psalm 106, the sins throughout Israel's history are summarized, confessing a pattern of unfaithfulness to God. But even though His people have rebelled again and again, God hasn't given up on them. We also have a memory of Moses mediating between man and God. Moses stands in the gap on behalf of the people, showing early psalm readers a picture of what Jesus will do for all people.

Psalm 107 describes four different types of people and their troubles. All four types of people go through a similar cycle: a problem, a cry for help, God's deliverance, and a call to praise. No matter how their problem came to be, God has mercy on each of them. The psalmist tells everyone to thank the LORD for His work and His never-ending love!

~ TODAY'S GOD SHOT ~

God does wonderful things for us. It's so important that we remember what He's done so that we remain obedient to Him. Trying to remember and follow a list of commands, laws, and rules will just leave us angry and frustrated. But remembering God's great love for us and all the wonderful things He's done for us will help us stay close to God and be obedient to Him. He's where the joy is!

1 CHRONICLES 13–16

ZOOM IN

So all Israel brought up the Ark of the Lord's Covenant with shouts of joy, the blowing of rams' horns and trumpets, the crashing of cymbals, and loud playing on harps and lyres.

1 Chronicles 15:28

David is busy making plans to move the ark of the covenant to its new home in Jerusalem. He's so busy, in fact, that he doesn't ask God for instructions on how to move the ark. God made instructions for moving the ark very clear: Only Levites can move it, and it has to be carried on poles. But David decides to move the ark *on a cart*.

The people gather for a parade to celebrate the ark's arrival in Jerusalem. But during the parade, the cows attached to the cart stumble, and Uzzah (who was David's nephew) touches the ark. What happens next is exactly what God warned them about: The man who touches the ark dies.

David is angry, and probably embarrassed, because this is his first big event as Israel's king. After some time, David tries again. This time, he follows God's instructions. The Levites bring the ark into the city, and everyone is thrilled except for Michal, David's first wife. (But as you'll learn in a few days, Michal is not happy with a lot of what David does.)

~TODAY'S GOD SHOT~

God makes His ways known to His kids. Almost every opportunity for obedience has been made clear to us through His Word. And for everything else, He gives us His Spirit to guide and help us. Through Bible reading, prayer, and advice from trusted teachers, we will never be left to figure out what God wants on our own. He shares His ways with us! He's where the joy is!

PSALMS 1–2, 15, 22–24, 47, 68

The LORD is my shepherd; I have all that I need. He lets me rest in green meadows; he leads me beside peaceful streams.

Psalm 23:1–2

We read a lot of psalms today with a lot of different themes. In Psalm 1, we see a wicked man and a righteous man. The righteous man delights in God's Word, and it's the source of his life! In Psalm 15, we see that God is holy and shows so much mercy to us when He draws near.

Psalm 22 is the Psalm of the Cross, a prophecy that points forward to Jesus. He spoke the first words of this psalm with His final breaths: "My God, my God, why have you abandoned me?" It's so important to our faith that we understand that God didn't abandon Jesus on the cross. God and Jesus are two of the three persons of the Trinity, and one person cannot be removed from the others, even for a moment. When Jesus spoke some of the words of this psalm with His final breaths, He wasn't saying that God turned away from Him. Rather, He was letting everyone know that He was fulfilling the prophecy of this psalm: that He is the **Messiah**.

In Psalms 24, 47, and 68, the ark's return to Jerusalem is celebrated. We see God as King, not just of Israel but of the whole earth!

TODAY'S GOD SHOT

God invites us to be still and quiet. It's not easy, is it? We have plenty of opportunities for distraction all the time. Quiet may feel boring or even scary sometimes, especially if we forget God. But when we're still and quiet, God has our full attention. He restores our souls. He's where comfort is. He's where peace is. And He's where the joy is!

PSALMS 89, 96, 100–101, 105, 132

ZOOM IN

His enemies will not defeat him, nor will the wicked overpower him. I will beat down his adversaries before him and destroy those who hate him.

Psalm 89:22–23

Psalm 89 has layers of prophecy, so we see three "firstborns." Israel is the firstborn of a people group, David is the firstborn of the line of kings God established, and Jesus is the firstborn over all creation. The psalmist may not have fully realized all these layers of meaning when he wrote the song, but God inspired his words to show what would be revealed over time.

There are songs of praise and thanks in this group, reminding us it's good to celebrate God. And when we don't feel like celebrating and praising, we should remind ourselves to celebrate and praise anyway.

TODAY'S GOD SHOT

God is in control of the big picture, and He's in control of the details. Psalm 89:22–23 teaches us that God not only guaranteed David's wins, but also arranged the enemies' losses. He sees every outcome for every person, because His plans include all things. The fact that He's in every single detail in every single life is mind-blowing. He's where the joy is!

SEVEN-DAY ROUNDUP

ZOOM OUT

For seven days, we read some beautiful psalms and we followed some of the early days of David's time as king. He moved the capital to Jerusalem and—after a failed attempt that disregarded God's instructions—moved the ark of the covenant there as well. We saw that God is in control of the details and He does wonderful things for us!

WORDS TO REMEMBER

- Messiah—savior; from a Hebrew word meaning "chosen or anointed one"
- Unity—being joined together as parts of a greater whole

APPLICATION

We learned in Psalm 133 that one of the great earthly gifts we have is unity. You have realized by now that the Bible wasn't written during some magical time period when everyone got along. That period ended with the first sin, way back in Genesis 3. Kids in the Bible who sang the Psalms of Ascent with their families weren't too different from you. They argued with their parents and fought with their siblings and felt hurt by their friends too. The next time you find yourself out of unity with a family member or friend, take a moment to read Psalm 133:1. Even better, memorize it so you won't need to read it! Pray for wisdom on how to work toward unity, in this situation and in the future.

2 SAMUEL 6–7; 1 CHRONICLES 17

ZOOM IN

What more can I say to you? You know what your servant is really like, Sovereign LORD.

2 Samuel 7:20

After what happened the first time David tried to move the ark, he's scared to do it again. He's left the ark at someone's house on the way to Jerusalem but knows he needs to bring it into the city. David remembers how God blesses His friends, and he's not afraid anymore. He brings the ark to Jerusalem! His first wife, Michal, is unhappy—about David's dancing and even about what he's wearing. But David keeps celebrating anyway.

David wants to build a house for God, so he talks to Nathan, a prophet, who thinks it's a great idea. But later, when God reveals to Nathan that he was wrong, Nathan has to go back to David and tell him that God says no. The right path isn't following our hearts' desires, even if they're good desires, but in following our God.

God tells David that He has something bigger in store: God's going to build *him* a house through his family. One of David's descendants will build God a house, and one of them will build a Kingdom. David is overwhelmed by God's kindness and wants everyone on earth to see how good God is.

TODAY'S GOD SHOT

God knows everything about us, including every desire we have in our hearts. If He says no to our prayers, it's the best, kindest answer He can give us. He told Moses no, He told David no, and sometimes He will tell you no too. Even if you don't understand why, you can trust that the answer is for His glory and your good. He's where the joy is!

ZOOM IN

In him our hearts rejoice, for we trust in his holy name.

Psalm 33:21

In a few psalms today, we see David confess his sin. This is an important part of life for anyone following Jesus, and it's not something we do just once. It's an ongoing process, part of our sanctification. In Psalm 25:11, David admits his guilt, saying, "For the honor of your name, O LORD, forgive my many, many sins." David wants for-giveness for his sins, of course, and he also wants God to be known as merci-ful and loving.

In Psalm 39, David confesses his sin to God. He knows he's experiencing God's discipline for his sin, but he tells God that he's learned his lesson. He asks God to end the discipline. It's impor-tant to note that he asks God for this in private. He doesn't want people who don't know God to be confused about God's char-acter by his prayer.

~ TODAY'S GOD SHOT ~

God can be trusted, and we can rejoice. It would be hard to rejoice in someone if you didn't trust them. But when you know you're with some-one who you fully trust, you can rejoice. That's what we can do with God. The more you learn about who He is, what He's doing, and how much He loves His kids, the more you can trust Him. Rejoice! He's where the joy is!

2 SAMUEL 8–9; 1 CHRONICLES 18

ZOOM IN

So David reigned over all Israel and did what was just and right for all his people.

2 Samuel 8:15

Today we read a lot about David's battle victories. These don't necessarily happen one right after the other, but they're grouped together here. David wins a lot of battles, but it's not because he's strong. It's because God causes him to win. Three times in the reading today, God is given credit for the battle victories.

God is the hero, not David. David knows this too, because when the defeated kings give him expensive gifts of gold and silver, he gives these gifts to the LORD. He doesn't keep them for himself. Eventually, these items are going to be used by David's son Solomon in the temple he builds for God.

David is a good king. He sets up leaders under him and trusts them to run things well. And he keeps his word. Mephibosheth is apparently Saul's only remaining male descendant. His dad was Jonathan, David's friend and protector. David honors Jonathan—and God—by bringing Mephibosheth to his home to live there with him.

TODAY'S GOD SHOT

God made a way for us to be with Him. Because of His Son, Jesus, we're invited to live in His kingdom and eat at His table forever! David welcoming Mephibosheth to his kingdom because of Jonathan is a picture of what God does for us because of Jesus. Every bit of the work was done for us; all we have to do is accept the gift. He's where the gift is, and He's where the joy is!

ZOOM IN

We thank you, O God! We give thanks because you are near.
People everywhere tell of your wonderful deeds.

Psalm 75:1

In three psalms today, we see a theme of the wrong way to respond to something versus the right way. Instead of seeing sacrifices and offerings as a way to earn God's forgiveness, the people should view them as a way to remember Him and be thankful for all He's provided. Instead of dismissing God like a fool does, we should trust His goodness in our lives. And instead of convincing ourselves that God is angry or rejecting us, we should talk to God about it. He'll give us peace and understanding.

We also see God's people thanking Him for His presence and the great things He has done for them. They know He'll bring justice to their enemies, which is reason to celebrate. There will be an end to wickedness, and the righteous will live!

TODAY'S GOD SHOT

God wants us to think about Him, and one way we can do this is through gratitude. When we think of the things and people we're thankful for, we should thank God! He's the giver of all good gifts. When we thank God, we think about Him. And usually, when we thank Him for one thing, we start to remember *lots* of things to thank Him for. It puts our heart close to Him. He's where the joy is!

2 SAMUEL 10; 1 CHRONICLES 19; PSALM 20

ZOOM IN

May he grant your heart's desires and make all your plans succeed.

Psalm 20:4

The Ammonite king dies, and since he was always kind to David, David sends some of his men to offer their condolences. But the Ammonites are suspicious of David's motives, and they humiliate and abuse David's men.

Then the Ammonites send some hired soldiers and Syrians (who already hate Israel) to attack Israel. In response, David sends his men into battle. An Israelite commander, Joab, encourages his brother Abishai, who is also an Israelite commander, by telling him that they can have courage and faith because God is in control. He knows that no matter what the outcome is, God will take care of them. The Israelites win the battle, and the surviving Syrians become Israel's servants and allies.

Psalm 20 is a song of praise for God's promises to King David. There are specific promises in this psalm that apply only to David, not all followers of Jesus. But what we do get to see is God's heart for all His people: He sees our needs; He meets us there; He rescues us. He is our only hope.

TODAY'S GOD SHOT

God's plan is always best. When David prays in Psalm 20, He knows God will only grant desires and make plans succeed when those desires and plans align with His plan. When our hearts are aligned with God, we pray for what He already has planned. Pray that He will align your heart with His—He's where the joy is!

DAY 132

ZOOM IN

What joy for those you choose to bring near.

Psalm 65:4

Our psalms today begin with a lot of praise. David knows he can't fix his sin by himself, and he praises God for atoning—paying a price—for his sin. As David sees the abundance of the year's harvest, he also praises God for creating and taking care of everything. David praises God even for the trials he's endured.

We also learn about God's attentiveness to all things and all people. He's everywhere, so He hears every prayer, even the selfish ones. Remember that He doesn't have to answer yes to any of us and will only answer yes when it's something that fits in His perfect plan.

The author of Psalm 67 knows that God is big enough to save more than Israel; he prays that God will save other nations, even nations that are Israel's enemies.

TODAY'S GOD SHOT

God chooses and brings people near. If you know God, it's because He chose you and brought you to Himself. He came down from heaven and picked you to be adopted into His family. If that's you, do you realize how beautifully blessed you are? It's the greatest gift of our lives. He's where the joy is!

2 SAMUEL 11–12; 1 CHRONICLES 20

ZOOM IN

I gave you your master's house and his wives and the kingdoms of Israel and Judah. And if that had not been enough, I would have given you much, much more.

2 Samuel 12:8

As the king, David should be with his soldiers in battle, which is where they are now. Instead, he sent them away to danger while he stayed home. And while he's home avoiding battle, he disobeys God's laws in a way that leads to heartbreak and death. He steals another man's wife—Bathsheba—and acts like she's his own. Then, when Bathsheba is pregnant, David tries to cover up his sin, but it doesn't work. So David has Bathsheba's husband killed in a battle.

God sends the prophet Nathan to tell David a story about a great sin. When Nathan points out that the sinner in the story is David, he repents. By law, David has earned the death penalty, but Nathan tells David that God has put away his sin. What great mercy! While there is mercy, there are still consequences. One of the consequences is that David and Bathsheba's child dies. David is heartbroken, and he worships God.

David goes to war with his men, and they win the battle. He and Bathsheba have another child—a son whose name is Solomon.

TODAY'S GOD SHOT

God is abundantly generous. David forgot God's generosity, and in the sin that he committed as a result, lives were lost. Today's story was difficult and sad, but it points us to this reminder: God is a good Father who gives abundant gifts. Our job is to thank Him for those gifts. Focus on His goodness and remember that He's where the joy is!

SEVEN-DAY ROUNDUP

ZOOM OUT

For seven days, we followed David as Israel's king. He made some wonderful and wise decisions and led his people in beautiful songs of praise. He also made some sinful and awful decisions. Yet he repented and left all of us with a model of how to turn back to God when we sin. Through David's obedience and his sin, we saw the real hero: our merciful and generous God.

APPLICATION

God is the giver of all good gifts, and He loves when His people thank Him for His gifts! Before you go to bed tonight, stop and thank God for at least three good gifts in your life. These could be things or people or opportunities. Challenge yourself to do this for at least a week, and pay attention to what happens. The more you make gratitude a habit, the more you'll notice *all* the good gifts in your life!

PSALMS 32, 51, 86, 122

ZOOM IN

The LORD says, "I will guide you along the best pathway for your life. I will advise you and watch over you."

Psalm 32:8

David has sinned again and again, and in the psalms we read today, we can see his heart is full of repentance. When David uncovers his sin before God, confessing the wrongs he has done, God covers it.

This is what Jesus did for us on the cross: paid for our sins. When we follow Jesus and turn to live His way, the Holy Spirit comes to live inside of us, and He helps us to recognize and confess our sin. This is called **conviction**—when God the Spirit leads us to repent from our sin and turn our hearts toward God.

In some of the psalms David wrote, he's so convicted about his sins that his body feels like he's carrying a big weight. This makes sense: David's sins impacted not only him, but other families, and even the entire nation of Israel. When David confesses his sin to God, God forgives him and the weight is lifted.

TODAY'S GOD SHOT

God wants us close to Him. He even shows us how to be close! Psalm 32:8 tells us that He won't leave us to figure things out on our own: He'll watch us and guide us. This takes work on our part. We can't get close to God while holding on tight to the things He doesn't have for us. We have to let go of our own control and follow Him wherever He leads. Wherever He leads will bring us joy, because He's where the joy is!

2 SAMUEL 13–15

DAY 135

ZOOM IN

"If the LORD sees fit," David said, "he will bring me back to see the Ark and the Tabernacle again. But if he is through with me, then let him do what seems best to him."

2 Samuel 15:25–26

Today's reading is full of sin and sadness. It's also pretty confusing, so here are the important details to remember: Amnon, David's oldest son, sins horribly against his half-sister Tamar and ruins her life. Tamar grieves for what's been taken from her and tells her brother Absalom about what happened. Absalom is filled with hatred, and he sins by having Amnon killed.

Now that Amnon is gone, Absalom is the oldest son. He wants to be Israel's king, and he sins by trying to kick his father, David, off the throne. He gets a lot of people on his side, including one of David's closest advisors, Ahithophel.

When David realizes what is being plotted against him, he escapes Jerusalem. He trusts that God will bring him back to Jerusalem if God has more work for him to do there.

TODAY'S GOD SHOT

God is sovereign. Even when His people lie and steal and kill, His perfect plan can't be stopped. God had a plan to bring the Savior, His Son, into the world through David's family. And like only God could, He worked out the timing so perfectly that David was able to stay safe and flee from danger. No matter what the sin is, God is still in control. He's where the joy is!

PSALMS 3–4, 12–13, 28, 55

ZOOM IN

Save your people! Bless Israel, your special possession. Lead them like a shepherd, and carry them in your arms forever.

Psalm 28:9

The psalms we read today fit David's current situation: running away from someone who's trying to hurt him, and waiting on God to deliver him.

In these psalms, we see that David remembers who God is and how good He's been to him. David cries out to God about people who lie, boast, and ignore the poor, and he asks God to bring justice. These psalms teach us that when we're angry, scared, or feeling forgotten, we have to put our trust in God. We'll only find our peace and hope in Him.

TODAY'S GOD SHOT

God is our Good Shepherd, and we are His sheep. Sheep face dangers, such as wolves and thieves, and their shepherd protects them. But sheep's worst enemies are themselves. They can't see well, they forget really quickly, and they tend to run away. Sounds like us, right? When our Good Shepherd takes care of us, He protects us not only from danger but from ourselves. He's where the joy is!

ZOOM IN

For the Lord had determined to defeat the counsel of Ahithophel, which really was the better plan, so that he could bring disaster on Absalom!

2 Samuel 17:14

There is more sin and sadness today. While David is hiding from his son Absalom, who wants to be king, other people also try to hurt David: Mephibosheth (according to his servant Ziba), Shimei, and even his own servant. Meanwhile in Jerusalem, Absalom has convinced a lot of people to be on his side. Hushai is David's friend, and when David escaped from Jerusalem, Hushai promised to keep David informed about what was happening there. So Hushai pretends to be on Team Absalom, and eventually Absalom lets Hushai in on his plans.

Hushai tricks Absalom into listening to his advice over Ahithophel's. Hushai also gets word back to David about what's happening, and David sends his army to find Absalom's army. David tells his army not to hurt Absalom, but when Absalom gets tangled up in a tree, Joab—the commander of David's army—disobeys and kills Absalom.

When David finds out that Absalom is dead, he cries and mourns for him.

TODAY'S GOD SHOT

God is always working. Even with all the people plotting against David, God is at work. He chose David's line to bring Jesus into the world, and absolutely nothing could stop Him from doing that, not even the sins of His enemies. He's where the best plan is, and He's where the joy is!

PSALMS 26, 40, 58, 61–62, 64

ZOOM IN

I take joy in doing your will, my God, for your instructions are written on my heart.

Psalm 40:8

David talks to God about his sin and knows that his righteousness comes from God. David has learned to be patient and wait for the LORD, even when everything around him seems to go wrong. In David's lifetime, Saul tried to kill him, he sinned greatly against Bathsheba and her family, and his son tried to take his place as king. But David thanked and praised God throughout his life, and God continued to bless David.

Throughout the psalms, David teaches us how to pray. He goes to God with his heartbreak and fear and anger. And he asks God for forgiveness, safety, and justice.

TODAY'S GOD SHOT

God wants us to live His way, not because He wants us to follow a bunch of rules or miss out on anything fun, but because His way is the best way. When we remember who He is and what He's done for us, we want to live the way He tells us to. He made us, He knows us, and He knows what's best for us. He's where the joy is!

ZOOM IN

There was a famine during David's reign that lasted for three years, so David asked the LORD about it. And the LORD said, "The famine has come because Saul and his family are guilty of murdering the Gibeonites."

2 Samuel 21:1

With Absalom dead, David returns to Jerusalem. The people can't decide if they want him to be their king or not. David replaces the commander of his army, Joab, with the former commander of Absalom's army, Amasa. He shows mercy toward his enemies by forgiving them.

The people of Israel decide they want David as their king after all, but then the Benjamites—Saul's descendants—decide that Sheba from their tribe should be king instead. Amasa has orders to attack the Benjamites, but he doesn't move fast enough, and Joab kills him. A wise woman stops Joab and his army from attacking the whole city by asking who they're looking for. She and her people give Sheba to the army, and she saves her entire city.

God tells David that the famine in Israel is because of Saul's sin: killing some Gibeonites after he promised to let them live. David inherited Saul's throne, but he also inherited the consequences of the old king's actions.

TODAY'S GOD SHOT

God takes sin seriously. Israel endures a famine because an already-dead king broke a promise. God cares about sin and He can be trusted to do justice. When someone sins against us, we can trust that God will work it together for His plan. And when we sin against others, God will work in our hearts within His plan. He's always working in our hearts and on His plan. He's where the joy is!

PSALMS 5, 38, 41–42

ZOOM IN

Do not abandon me, O Lord. Do not stand at a distance, my God. Come quickly to help me, O Lord my savior.

Psalm 38:21–22

David is a king who calls God *his* King. David knows that even though he's in charge of a whole nation, God is in charge of the whole world, forever! He knows that the reason he gets to be close to God is not because he is good, but because *God* is good.

When David is suffering, he asks God for help. Whether it's physical, spiritual, or emotional suffering, David knows God can bring him peace. He asks God to be near and to be gracious to him.

~TODAY'S GOD SHOT~

God is near, even when we can't feel Him. Each psalm we read today ends with a plea for help and a belief that God *will* help. It can be really hard to wait on God to work when we're scared or lonely or hurting. By praying like David did, we remind ourselves of who God is and that He's where the joy is!

SEVEN-DAY ROUNDUP

ZOOM OUT

David's life was full of extremes, both highs and lows. He was king, but he also had to run for his life more than once. He was wise and sought after God's heart, but he also sinned greatly. But God was always with David, and God used him to lead His people and to teach us how to pray.

WORD TO REMEMBER

- Conviction—when God the Spirit leads His kids to repent from our sin and turn our hearts toward God

APPLICATION

Through the psalms, David teaches us how to pray. Choose one of the verses below, write it on a card, and pray it every day this week. See what God does and praise Him for it!

Finally, I confessed all my sins to you and stopped trying to hide my guilt.

Psalm 32:5

I take joy in doing your will, my God, for your instructions are written on my heart.

Psalm 40:8

Come quickly to help me, O Lord my savior.

Psalm 38:22

So rejoice in the Lord and be glad, all you who obey him!

Psalm 32:11

2 SAMUEL 22–23; PSALM 57

ZOOM IN

You have given me the shield of your salvation, and your gentleness made me great.

2 Samuel 22:36 ESV

David is getting older and knows he won't live too much longer. He thinks back on his life and all the ways God has helped him. David knows it's only because of God that he was made strong, protected from his enemies, and able to serve as Israel's king.

While David reflects, he is **humble**, thinking of himself rightly—as someone who is not the most important. He gives God the praise for all he's accomplished as Israel's king, and he knows that no matter what happens, God is there working out His perfect plan.

TODAY'S GOD SHOT

God's gentleness makes His kids great. David was a mighty warrior, so you might expect him to reflect back on his life and praise God for strength, bravery, or courage. But David praises God for His gentleness. David knew that every time he sinned, God showed him great mercy and gentleness. He's where the gentleness is, and He's where the joy is!

ZOOM IN

Light shines on the godly, and joy on those whose hearts are right.

Psalm 97:11

Today's psalms remind us of some beautiful truths about God. God isn't just the creator; He's the ruler over all His creation. He can show up like a thunderstorm or melt mountains like wax.

Yet God doesn't only rule over all creation; He's also attentive to us and cares for us: "We are the people he watches over, the flock under his care" (95:7).

And God doesn't only care for us, but He's had a plan all along to make us His! In Psalm 98, the writer probably thought of God's salvation as safety from enemies in battle. But God knew all along that He had a plan to save us from bigger things than just earthly enemies—He always had a plan to send Jesus for our ultimate, eternal salvation.

TODAY'S GOD SHOT

God is light, and He shines on those who love Him and live His way. If you're going through something difficult, it may feel dark, but light is still there. Look for the ways God is shining, even in the darkness. It's in the places He shines that you'll remember He's where the joy is!

2 SAMUEL 24; 1 CHRONICLES 21–22; PSALM 30

ZOOM IN

You have turned my mourning into joyful dancing. You have taken away my clothes of mourning and clothed me with joy, that I might sing praises to you and not be silent. O LORD my God, I will give you thanks forever!

Psalm 30:11–12

David takes a census, or an official count, of Israel. Taking a census isn't a sin, but David's *reason* for taking one is. The Philistines have been attacking Israel, and it seems David doesn't trust that God will win Israel's battles for them. He apparently wants to be confident in Israel's number of soldiers, not in their mighty God. Joab knows this is a bad idea, and David is quickly convicted of his sin.

David repents, and God forgives him, but there are consequences. Seventy thousand people die in three days, and David offers himself as a sacrifice to God. But God provides a sacrifice and sends fire to consume it, letting David know that He's accepted the sacrifice, and also that this is where God's new home should be built. David tells his son Solomon that his job will be to build the temple there.

TODAY'S GOD SHOT

God always works for good. Even sin can't stop Him. Even before David sinned—and David sinned a *lot*—God had a plan to redeem the mess David made for good. Whenever you think you've sinned too badly for God to forgive you, remember that even the worst sin can't stop God. He'll forgive your sin when you ask Him, and He'll redeem even the biggest mess. He's where the joy is!

ZOOM IN

With God's help we will do mighty things . . .

Psalm 108:13

David feels like God isn't fighting for them and cries to God for help. When David laments, he doesn't hold back. He tells God exactly how he feels. David takes his anger directly to God and asks God to act. In the psalms of lament, David reminds us that we should go to God with our anger and sadness; God knows how we feel anyway, and He's the one who can do something about it!

In the final psalm we read today, Psalm 110, David writes a prophecy about King Jesus—who has always existed, but who wouldn't be born on earth as a baby until about a thousand years later! This psalm is quoted in at least six books in the New Testament, including three of the gospels. Jesus Himself quotes Psalm 110 and confirms that verse 1 is about Him: Jesus sits at the right hand of God, in the position of honor, having defeated all His enemies.

TODAY'S GOD SHOT

God is our Helper. Without Him, we can do nothing. We can't save ourselves, but He saves us. He is our Creator, Helper, and Savior. He's where the joy is!

1 CHRONICLES 23–25

As he continues to prepare for Israel's future after his death, David makes his son Solomon king. Many years before, God told David that Solomon would be the one to build His temple in Jerusalem.

After the exodus from Egypt, God gave His people lots of instructions for building His temporary, moveable tent home: the tabernacle. Now David gives Solomon lots of instructions for building God's permanent home: the temple. It's hard for us to fully understand how huge of a deal this was for Israel. Today, we have the Holy Spirit, who lives inside of us, but for the Israelites, they were building God's home, the place where He would live among them. And, unlike the tabernacle, they didn't have to move it anymore! So David is very detailed in his instructions to Solomon for building this holy place.

David divides the priests from the tribe of Levi into groups and assigns them special tasks. He also organizes musicians and gives them three leaders: Asaph, Jeduthun, and Heman. Each of these leaders wrote at least one of the songs in the book of Psalms.

TODAY'S GOD SHOT

God gives rest. Think about how amazing this was for the Israelites. They had endured slavery, the wilderness, wars, and more. And God wanted them to build Him a permanent home in Jerusalem so He could live among them! God is the giver of rest and the maker of home. He's where the joy is!

PSALMS 131, 138–139, 143–145

ZOOM IN

The LORD is righteous in everything he does; he is filled with kindness.

Psalm 145:17

When David is confused about why certain things happen to him, he puts his trust in God, and he knows God can be trusted with the outcome. David realizes he is fully known and fully loved by God.

God's greatness is so big and so wonderful that we'll never be able to understand it all. We get to see pieces of it throughout our lives, but the whole of His greatness is more than our human minds could possibly understand.

David says that "the LORD is good to everyone" (145:9). Remember what grace and mercy are? Grace is when we get what we don't deserve, and mercy is when we don't get what we do deserve. There is also *common* grace and *common* mercy, which David is teaching us about here. We all have air to breathe and water to drink and food to eat because of God. That's common grace. And even God's enemies don't usually die the second they hurt God's kids; they have more time. That's common mercy. Common grace and common mercy exist because God is good to everyone, even those who don't know or follow Him. How incredible!

TODAY'S GOD SHOT

God is righteous and filled with kindness. Every answer He gives us to every prayer we pray is right and kind. If He says yes, no, or wait, it's right and kind. He's always right and He's always kind. He's where the joy is!

1 CHRONICLES 26–29; PSALM 127

David continues to make preparations for the temple that Solomon will build for God. David assigns gatekeepers to guard the gates, treasurers to take care of money and gifts, and leaders to help the tribes get along with each other. He organizes them in a big rotation, and there are over 200,000 in all.

David reminds Solomon and the people of Israel to put God first and to obey all His commands. David shows the people how important it is to give to God cheerfully and generously by donating a lot of his own riches toward making the temple. At the end of 1 Chronicles, David dies, but remember his story is written in a few books of the Bible, so we'll see him one more time.

Solomon writes in Psalm 127:1, "Unless the LORD builds a house, the work of the builders is wasted," and teaches us that only the things God builds will last!

TODAY'S GOD SHOT

God is the source of everything, which means everything good is a gift from Him! David tells God in 29:14 that anything he gives to God was given *to* him by God in the first place. That's not just true for money or offerings, but for time and talents. Every single thing we're able to give to God was given to us by Him first! He's where the joy is!

SEVEN-DAY ROUNDUP

ZOOM OUT

This week as we got close to the end of David's life, we saw that he reflected a lot on who he is and what God has done for him. While David made sure his son Solomon would be ready to carry on after him, he also took time to show that he's thankful. David praised God for who He is and all He has done.

BIG PICTURE: 2 SAMUEL

Following David during his reign as king of Israel, we see that even though David is a man after God's own heart, he's not perfect. David's imperfect reign points us toward our need for the perfect King: Jesus.

BIG PICTURE: 1 CHRONICLES

Chronicles shows us a highlight reel of God's covenant with Israel being fulfilled. It's a "big picture" kind of book, so some of the details are left out, but there are still plenty of stories in the two books of Chronicles. In the first book, we see that God's promise is fulfilled through setting up the monarchy.

WORD TO REMEMBER

- Humble—thinking of yourself rightly, as less important; having humility

APPLICATION

David is not our hero, and he wasn't a perfect king. David knew he wasn't perfect, and we can see this in the psalms he wrote throughout his life. Fill in the blanks from these verses that David wrote about our perfect King.

You will show me the way of _____, granting me the _____ of your _____ and the pleasures of _____ with you forever.

—Psalm 16:11

With _____ help we will do _____ things.

—Psalm 108:13

The LORD is _____ in everything he does; he is filled with _____.

—Psalm 145:17

PSALMS 111–118

ZOOM IN

These gates lead to the presence of the LORD, and the godly enter there.

Psalm 118:20

God does amazing things that reveal His greatness! When we remember who He is and what He's done, we'll be filled with delight and awe. And when we're filled with delight and awe, we'll live God's way; He changes our hearts to make us more like Him.

God is the ultimate authority over all people and things, but He doesn't leave us here on earth to fend for ourselves. He bends down to be close to us, to lift us up, and to help us. He does what pleases Him, which is also what's best for His kids!

God loves us with a great, faithful, never-changing love. There is no way we could repay God for how much He loves us and for everything He has done for us, but—as the psalms teach us—the proper response to His goodness is to overflow with gratitude and praise.

TODAY'S GOD SHOT

God made a way for us to get to Him: Jesus. When Psalm 118 was written, the "gates" meant the gates of Jerusalem. But God meant them as the gates of Jerusalem *and* something more. In John 10:9, Jesus calls Himself "the gate" to salvation. Jesus is the only way we get to God. Because of Him, we get to be in the presence of the King forever. He's where the joy is!

1 KINGS 1–2; PSALMS 37, 71, 94

ZOOM IN

Take delight in the LORD, and he will give you your heart's desires.

Psalm 37:4

David is getting old and sick, and his oldest living son, Adonijah, decides he wants to be king. (Solomon is David's oldest son with Bathsheba, but David had other sons before Solomon. Remember that his first two sons, Amnon and Absalom, were both killed. Adonijah was the next oldest.)

Adonijah even rides horses and chariots all through the town, which basically means he's declaring himself to be the king. But God's plans won't be stopped, and Solomon is anointed as the next king of Israel. Right before David dies, he gives Solomon a list of people to kill in revenge for the ways they had hurt David's family and threatened his life. After David dies, Solomon has them killed.

The psalms we read today remind us of different times in David's life: when David delighted in God, when God carried David through hard times, and when God gave David victory over those who tried to harm him.

TODAY'S GOD SHOT

God covers all our sin. When David died, there was still sin in his heart. Does that mean his entire life was wasted or ruined? No. Hebrews 11–12 tells us that David is one of the ancestors of our faith. David couldn't earn his way into God's family no matter how hard he tried; God *put* David in His family. And we can't earn our way into God's family, either. God puts us there by His mercy and grace! He covers all the sins of His kids—past, present, and future—with Jesus's death and resurrection. He's where the joy is!

PSALM 119

Your word is a lamp to guide my feet and a light for my path.

Psalm 119:105

Psalm 119 is the longest chapter in the Bible, and it might've been written by Ezra, a priest and scribe we'll meet later. Whoever the mystery writer is, he loves God's Word and wants to love it even more. The entire poem is an acrostic in which each section starts with the next letter of the Hebrew alphabet. The psalmist took such care in writing this beautiful poem!

The writer points out seven of God's **attributes** (characteristics): righteous, trustworthy, truthful, faithful, unchangeable, eternal, and light. God also changes our hearts, and the psalmist gives us some prayers to pray when our hearts need changing: "open my eyes to see" (verse 18), "help me understand" (verse 27), and "teach me" (verse 33).

And the writer helps us remember that hard times and struggles can bring us closer to God. Loving God doesn't mean we won't feel hurt or pain, but it does mean we have a safe Person who will be with us in our hurt and pain.

TODAY'S GOD SHOT

God gave us His Word. It's a lamp to guide us—one that gives us just enough light to take our next step. And it's a light to lead us, lighting everything as far as we can see. God's Word is big enough to light up the entire world, and it's small enough to show us the next step in our lives. It's infinite and personal, and God gave it to us. He's where the joy is!

ZOOM IN

Give me an understanding heart so that I can govern your people well and know the difference between right and wrong. For who by himself is able to govern this great people of yours?

1 Kings 3:9

Solomon's reign starts off . . . not so great. He had a few people killed because his dad asked him to. Then he marries a woman who's not an Israelite because he wants to make sure her people won't hurt Israel. While this may seem like a smart idea, it shows that Solomon doesn't trust God to take care of His people. Besides, God had given rules for the Israelites about not marrying people from other nations. And now Solomon gives sacrifices to false gods, probably thinking he should cover all his bases just in case the false gods turn out to be real ones.

Solomon also loves the one true God, who comes to him in a dream. He tells Solomon to ask Him for whatever he wants. So Solomon asks God for wisdom. God is happy with Solomon's request and gives him wisdom, riches, and a long life.

Solomon has a chance to prove his wisdom right away, through a story you may have heard before with two women and a baby. The people of Israel see that his wisdom comes from God.

TODAY'S GOD SHOT

God is patient with us. Solomon was worshipping other gods when God showed up and asked Solomon what he wanted. Solomon says he wants God's way, but—spoiler alert—like all of us, he won't always live like it. Solomon will sin and turn away from God and fail. And even still, God won't give up on him. He's where the joy is!

2 CHRONICLES 1; PSALM 72

ZOOM IN

Praise the LORD God, the God of Israel, who alone does such wonderful things.

Psalm 72:18

Today's reading might seem familiar, and that's because it replays Solomon's dream encounter with God. God praises Solomon for not asking Him for his enemies to die.

Did you notice that Psalm 72 says at the beginning that Solomon wrote it, but at the end that David wrote it? Some people think Solomon wrote it and told about David's death at the end. Some people think that David wrote it and told us that it was about Solomon at the beginning. What we do know for sure is that whoever wrote it was a king, and he knew how much prayer a king needs in order to do his job well.

The king asks God for help to do what is right, to be fair to people, and to help those who need it. The king knows that everything good comes from God, and that God does wonderful things.

TODAY'S GOD SHOT

God is generous. We should never be afraid to go to Him and ask Him for things, because He loves to bless His kids. When we remember that all good things are from Him, we remember how needy we are and how generous He is. He's where the joy is!

SONG OF SOLOMON 1–8

ZOOM IN

Love flashes like fire, the brightest kind of flame. Many waters cannot quench love, nor can rivers drown it.

Song of Solomon 8:6–7

Song of Solomon, or Song of Songs, was written either by Solomon or in honor of him during his time as king. This book of the Bible is pretty different from most of the other books, and some of the reading today might have even made you say, "*Ew*." Some people say this book is a picture of God's love for His people, and while that might be true, it makes the most sense to think about it as a book about God's best plan for love and marriage.

The book is a conversation that starts off with the shepherdess talking about how much she loves the shepherd. The shepherd loves her back! So throughout the book, they move from courtship (which some people might compare to dating) to their wedding to their marriage. They celebrate the love for each other that God has given them!

TODAY'S GOD SHOT

God gives love and marriage as a gift to His kids. When God created Eve for Adam, He had good, beautiful things in mind for them. Since He made people and marriage, He knows what's best for us, and He gets to make the rules. As you get older, you'll hear a lot of people say God's rules are too strict or old-fashioned. But remember this: All of God's rules, including the ones about love and marriage, keep us safe and bring us joy. After all, He's where the joy is!

PROVERBS 1–3

ZOOM IN

Trust in the Lord with all your heart; do not depend on your own understanding.

Proverbs 3:5

Proverbs was written by multiple authors, including Solomon, over time. It's wisdom literature, which means we need to think about it a little differently from other books of the Bible. The proverbs are not history or law or prophecy; the proverbs are general pieces of advice about living in the world God's way. Much of the advice is helpful, wise, and true, but because advice from men is not the same thing as a promise from God, we need to remember that wise advice won't always produce the hoped-for results.

There are three main types of people you'll read about in Proverbs: the wise person, the foolish person, and the simple person. The wise person loves and obeys God. The foolish person doesn't listen to or obey God. The simple person doesn't pay attention and is distracted easily. When you read a proverb about a person, ask yourself this: Which type of person is the proverb talking about?

In chapter 1, we see that both the simple and the foolish person die, whether they're choosing wickedness or just ignoring the call of wisdom. In chapters 2 and 3, we see that God gives us wisdom, knowledge, and understanding. These things alone won't bring us peace, but being close to God will!

TODAY'S GOD SHOT

God wants us to talk to Him about everything. He gave us knowledge and understanding, but they're nowhere close to what God knows and understands. He made us; He knows everything. We need His help, and He wants to give it! He's never too busy, and He always cares. He's where the joy is!

SEVEN-DAY ROUNDUP

ZOOM OUT

Since we're reading the Bible in chronological order (the order in which the story happened), we spent the last seven days in a few different books. We read some more psalms of praise. We saw David die (for the second time in our reading!), and we watched Solomon take over as Israel's king. We followed a young couple through their courtship and wedding, and we learned a bit of wisdom from the first few chapters of Proverbs. Finally, we saw the good gifts that God gives: wisdom, love, and most of all, Himself.

BIG PICTURE: SONG OF SOLOMON

Song of Solomon is a love story between a young shepherd and shepherdess. It reminds us that God's design for everything, including love and marriage, brings joy!

WORD TO REMEMBER

- Attribute—characteristic or quality of someone's character

APPLICATION

God gives good gifts such as knowledge and wisdom and love. Think of three gifts that God's given you and thank Him for them!

PROVERBS 4–6

ZOOM IN

There are six things the LORD hates—no, seven things he detests: haughty eyes, a lying tongue, hands that kill the innocent, a heart that plots evil, feet that race to do wrong, a false witness who pours out lies, a person who sows discord in a family.

Proverbs 6:16–19

So far in Proverbs, a dad is giving his son advice for living a wise life, which includes seeing God with delight and awe ("fearing God"). When you know you need wisdom, you try to find it, which gives you more wisdom. It's similar to our relationship with God. When you know you need God, you look for Him and try to find Him, which brings you closer to Him. It's a mystery of life and faith that can be explained like this: God is the source, the supply, and the goal.

The dad also warns his son many times to stay away from evil and to be faithful to his wife. He prays a blessing over their love and marriage. We also get some advice here that reminds us Proverbs isn't a book of God's laws: The dad tells the son not to lend money to anyone. But God had already given His people a law about how to lend money to each other with kindness. So while the dad thinks this is good advice, it's just that: advice. It's not God's law.

TODAY'S GOD SHOT

God hates the things that attack what He loves. Proverbs 6 tells us the things that He hates. So what are the things He loves? Humility, honesty, innocence and justice, purity, righteousness, truth, and peacemaking. These things are beautiful, and they also describe God! When we become more like the things God loves, we become more like Him. He's where the joy is!

PROVERBS 7–9

ZOOM IN

And how happy I was with the world he created; how I rejoiced with the human family!

Proverbs 8:31

Proverbs Dad gives his son advice on how to stay wise and pure. He wants his son to keep away from things and people that tempt him to sin, so he tells him to be careful with these things: what his eyes see, what his hands do, and what his heart loves. This is good advice for us to follow too!

The dad tells his son that he can choose which path to walk: foolishness that leads to death, or wisdom that leads to life. Proverbs Dad ends his advice to his son by reminding him again to chase after wisdom and life.

~ TODAY'S GOD SHOT ~

God delights in wisdom. Proverbs 8 describes wisdom as if it were a person, but some Bible teachers also say it describes Jesus. When creation is described, there are pictures of delight and rejoicing, love and smiling. God feels that way about wisdom and He feels that way about us—His creation! He's where the joy is!

PROVERBS 10–12

ZOOM IN

The words of the godly are like sterling silver; the heart of a fool is worthless.

Proverbs 10:20

Today we get some wisdom for everyone, not just the son. How we live—what we do and say—impacts others, so we should seek truth and live by wisdom. We should also be willing to learn from wise leaders and teachers. Did you recognize two types of people in chapter 10? Fools keep babbling nonsense and slander, but wise people listen to and learn from instruction. Their words are few and righteous.

We also learn that being humble is connected to being wise. When someone is humble, they know that they are nothing without God, and they will walk in His ways. This blesses their life and the lives of those around them!

TODAY'S GOD SHOT

God hates foolishness and He loves wisdom. As you read Proverbs, you might start to feel like it would be impossible to live up to the checklist of wisdom. If you feel that way, you're right. We all sin, and we all fall short on the checklist of wisdom and many other things. The good news—the *best* news—is that Jesus's death covers all our sins. Because of that, we can rest in God's presence as we chase after wisdom, knowing that we're His kids. He's where the joy is!

ZOOM IN

The LORD is far from the wicked, but he hears the prayers of the righteous.

Proverbs 15:29

Wise people won't live lives without suffering. Because of sin, hard times and even suffering will come to everyone. But those who are wise know God is with them during the hard times, and they know suffering gives them a chance to grow closer to God.

Wise people choose to surround themselves with other wise people. They build each other up in truth and wisdom! When we ignore God's ways and choose our own ways, it always ends poorly. Even if we can't see or understand the poor ending right away, it will eventually come. And when we choose our own ways, we don't honor God. That is a poor ending in itself.

God knows our hearts, and He always hears the prayers of the righteous.

TODAY'S GOD SHOT

God always hears—and answers—the prayers of His kids. When we follow Him, we become righteous. This isn't because of us; it's because of who He is and what He's done and how much He loves His kids. So if He's your Father, pray to Him! He'll hear you and He'll answer you. He might give you peace in chaos, hope in sadness, or even patience dealing with an annoying situation. Ask for Him to be near to you; He's where the joy is!

PROVERBS 16–18

ZOOM IN

We can make our plans, but the LORD determines our steps.

Proverbs 16:9

Getting wisdom is never an accident. Wisdom comes when we search for it, and the best place to search for it is in God's Word.

When we are wise, our thoughts and words reflect it. It's really difficult to control the things we think and say, but if we ask God for help, He'll do it! As you study God's Word, you'll probably notice your thoughts and your words changing to become more patient, kind, forgiving, and loving. When you notice this, give thanks to God!

Wise people are humble. They don't assume people owe them things, and they don't think they deserve things. They know in their hearts that without God they're nothing. Their words and actions show the wisdom in this knowledge.

TODAY'S GOD SHOT

God is sovereign. Solomon knows this and spends a lot of time in chapter 16 talking about how God is in charge of everything. We can make all the plans in the world, but God is in charge of what actually happens. This should bring us such peace! We don't want to be in charge of our own lives, because we'd make an absolute mess of them. Recognizing that is *truly* wise and humble. God made us, He loves us, and He does what's best for us. He's where the joy is!

If you help the poor, you are lending to the LORD—and he will repay you!

Proverbs 19:17

Today's proverbs give us advice on relationships and the consequences of sin. Our most important relationship is with God, and knowing Him is worth the time and effort it takes!

When we sin, God offers forgiveness, but there are often still consequences from our own actions. When this happens to us—and it will happen to all of us—we have to remember that God isn't mad at us or punishing us. Instead of blaming Him for the consequences of our sin, we should pray and ask Him to teach us and keep us from sinning more.

The world is full of foolish and simple people who desperately need wisdom. Every time wise people speak the truth, it makes the world more beautiful. But that doesn't mean we should take credit for the wisdom we share; we have to remember that it's all from God.

TODAY'S GOD SHOT

God cares about the poor. Proverbs 19:17 tells us that if you help the poor, it's like you're lending your resources to God Himself. And God will be the one who pays the giver back. If you give money to the poor, you may not see that money come back to you; but you'll get something so much better. God cares about people who have nothing; God cares about people who have a lot. He's generous with all of us, and He's where the joy is!

PROVERBS 22–24

ZOOM IN

Don't rejoice when your enemies fall; don't be happy when they stumble.

Proverbs 24:17

Today's advice includes avoiding sin, keeping our attention fixed on God, choosing friends carefully, and obeying God. All of these will help us grow in wisdom.

We've talked about wisdom for a while now, so let's make sure we have a good definition. Knowledge, understanding, and wisdom may seem like they all mean the same thing, but the differences are important. **Knowledge** is having the facts about something. **Understanding** is taking the facts and being able to put them together to make a big picture. **Wisdom** is knowing how to apply knowledge and understanding in your everyday life as you follow God.

TODAY'S GOD SHOT

God cares for everyone, including those who are far away from Him. Proverbs 24:17 tells us not to be glad when our enemies fall. How can this be, when there are enemies who hurt God's kids? Every single person who has ever lived is someone God created in His image, and He wants all of us to repent from our sin and live His way. He welcomes *everyone* who wants to repent and be a part of His family! He's where the forgiveness is, and He's where the joy is!

SEVEN-DAY ROUNDUP

ZOOM OUT

We spent the last seven days in Proverbs, and hopefully we grew in the wisdom that God loves. We were reminded of some important truths: that God is sovereign, that He cares for everyone, and that He always hears the prayers of His kids.

WORDS TO REMEMBER

- Knowledge—having the facts about something
- Understanding—taking the facts and being able to put them together to make a big picture
- Wisdom—knowing how to apply knowledge and understanding in everyday life

APPLICATION

By ourselves, we can't become wise or keep all the advice in Proverbs. But God loves wisdom, and He loves helping His kids become wise. In chapter 7, Proverbs Dad told his son to be careful what his eyes see, what his hands do, and what his heart loves. God can help you with this! Draw eyes, hands, and a heart on a small piece of paper and put it where you'll see it every day. Each time you see it, ask God to help you guard your eyes, hands, and heart. Ask Him to let your eyes see Him, your hands do His work, and your heart love Him and others more!

1 KINGS 5–6; 2 CHRONICLES 2–3

ZOOM IN

I am planning to build a Temple to honor the name of the LORD my God, just as he had instructed my father, David. For the LORD told him, "Your son, whom I will place on your throne, will build the Temple to honor my name."

1 Kings 5:5

It's been about five hundred years since the Israelites left Egypt, and the time has finally come: They're building God's glorious dwelling place, where He'll live among His people. There are massive stones—one that weighs *over one million pounds!*—shaped into perfect cubes and boxes. There are cypress tree trunks from Lebanon and pure gold and precious stones. And there is a thick curtain separating the Holy Place from the Most Holy Place, where the ark of the covenant and God's earthly throne will be.

The structure of the temple is breathtaking, but God reminds Solomon that it's not the impressive building that guarantees that God will stay with or bless His people. Rather, it's God's covenant with them, and the people can show their love for Him through their obedience.

TODAY'S GOD SHOT

God works out the big picture, and He works out the details. The temple is built on Mount Moriah. Do you remember what else happened there? In Genesis 22, Abraham obediently offered his son Isaac as a sacrifice, but God stopped him and provided a ram instead. In the New Testament, we'll read that on the highest point of this same mountain, Golgotha, God provided the sacrifice for all of us: His Son, Jesus. God has been writing this beautiful story of redemption all along, down to every small detail. He's where the joy is!

ZOOM IN

Huram set the pillars at the entrance of the Temple, one toward the south and one toward the north. He named the one on the south Jakin, and the one on the north Boaz.

1 Kings 7:21

There's a pause in temple news today while we learn about Solomon's house. Solomon does good works for God, prays beautiful prayers, and follows many of God's laws, but he also has a divided heart. He spends a lot of time and money having his palace, his wife's palace, a throne hall, *and* a hall of pillars built. Solomon loves fancy things, and this will eventually become a problem for him.

As we go back to learning about the temple construction, we're on to furniture today. Solomon hires artists and craftsmen to build gorgeous furnishings for the temple: a gold altar, a bronze basin the size of a swimming pool, ten lampstands, and many extravagant decorations. When the work is finished, Solomon brings his father David's offerings into the temple.

TODAY'S GOD SHOT

God establishes in strength. The names of the pillars at the temple entrance are Jakin, which means "He establishes," and Boaz, which means "in strength." Even though Solomon built this temple to be a permanent earthly home for God, it will eventually be destroyed. But don't worry. You know what won't be destroyed? God's presence with His people. He doesn't need buildings to live in anymore because now He lives in His people! He establishes His home, in strength, *in us*—His people. He's where the joy is!

DAY 164

1 KINGS 8; 2 CHRONICLES 5

ZOOM IN

But will God really live on earth? Why, even the highest heavens cannot contain you. How much less this Temple I have built!

1 Kings 8:27

With the temple finished, the Levites begin moving the furniture inside. Solomon doesn't want any consequences for not following God's rules about the temple, so he makes sure the Levites move the ark of the covenant on poles. Once they place the ark inside the Most Holy Place, the cloud of God's presence fills the temple.

Solomon praises God for fulfilling His promise to David, and he asks God to act with justice and mercy for all sins. Solomon prays a blessing for all the people of the earth to know God.

And seven years after they began building, the temple is complete. Solomon dedicates the temple, and God's people offer so many sacrifices that the altar is overflowing. They feast for a week and then return home full of joy, knowing how good God is to them.

TODAY'S GOD SHOT

God lives among His people. King Solomon knows that the temple—and "even the highest heavens" (8:27)—can't contain God. He's in awe that God would come to live among people on earth, and he has no idea what's coming. God will indeed come to live among us on earth, and He's going to heal the blind, feed the hungry, free the captives, and raise the dead. The Israelites left God's house full of joy, but they didn't know what we know: how much more joy is coming! He's where the joy is!

ZOOM IN

Hear their prayers and their petitions from heaven where you live, and uphold their cause. Forgive your people who have sinned against you.

2 Chronicles 6:39

Solomon asks God—who is in the temple and who is also everywhere—to hear in heaven the cries of His people on earth and forgive them. Solomon gives offerings to God, and God sends down fire to consume the food, meaning He accepts the offerings. The people praise God and celebrate!

God tells Solomon in a vision that when the Israelites rebel against Him, He'll send discipline through drought, grasshoppers, or plagues of disease. If the people repent and turn back to Him, then He'll keep His covenant with them.

In today's psalm, the writer can't stop celebrating God's never-ending love. He praises God for who He is and what He's done.

TODAY'S GOD SHOT

God comes down to live with us, even in the middle of our great sin. Solomon knows that everyone has sinned (2 Chronicles 6:36), and he says this at the dedication of the temple, where God comes to dwell. Every single one of us is born into fallen humanity and will sin. So it's even more amazing that God comes down to live with us. He's here, He's not leaving us, and He's where the joy is!

PSALMS 134, 146–150

Psalm 134, the final Song of Ascent, has been prayed by God's people for three thousand years, and they're still praying the blessing today: "May the LORD, who made heaven and earth, bless you from Jerusalem."

Psalm 146 reminds us that only God is worthy of our trust, and Psalm 147 teaches us how attentive God is. He created everything, and He pays attention to everything. He loves when we delight in Him and when we trust Him. Psalm 149 reminds us of God's justice.

Psalms 148 and 150 command all creation to praise God!

TODAY'S GOD SHOT

God shows His love to everyone: the oppressed, the hungry, the imprisoned, the blind, the sorrowful, the righteous, the displaced, the widow, the orphan, and even the wicked. No matter who you are, where you are, what you've done, or what's been done to you, God shows you His love. He's where the joy is!

1 KINGS 9; 2 CHRONICLES 8

ZOOM IN

The LORD said to him, "I have heard your prayer and your petition. I have set this Temple apart to be holy—this place you have built where my name will be honored forever. I will always watch over it, for it is dear to my heart."

1 Kings 9:3

After the temple is complete, Solomon stays busy. He oversees the building of his own house, his wife's house, twenty cities, and a whole fleet of ships. Solomon keeps the holy calendar of feasts and sacrifices, and tries to remain faithful to God's laws.

God tells Solomon that as long as His laws are kept, His eyes and heart will stay fixed on the temple. God also tells Solomon what will happen if Israel rebels against Him. This passage may be hard to understand, and may make it seem like God is unkind. But remember who God is, what He's done, and how much He loves His kids. He's always kind and always loving, and He's already told the Israelites what they need to do to keep their part of the covenant He's made with them.

But He wants more for and from them than just following a list of rules, so He keeps reminding them of how much He's done for them: He rescued them from slavery. He led them through the wilderness. He brought them into the promised land. He came to dwell among them. God doesn't want only their obedience—He wants their *hearts*.

TODAY'S GOD SHOT

God gives us rules because His way is the best way for us to live. He knows that we will sin and fail to follow His rules, but He's forgiving. We never have to wonder if we've sinned too badly for God, because He will forgive us. He is righteous, just, and loving. He's where the joy is!

PROVERBS 25–26

It is God's privilege to conceal things and the king's privilege to discover them.

Proverbs 25:2

As we read more wisdom today, remember that Proverbs isn't a book of God's laws. It's a book of good advice about life. That advice can be useful in a lot of situations we find ourselves in. Today we read about the importance of patience and self-control. Both are hard to live out, but both have great power.

We finish today's reading with Solomon reminding us again—after he already told us a few times today—how important our words are. Gossip, lies, and **flattery** are wicked.

TODAY'S GOD SHOT

God gets the glory, even in mystery. Sometimes He chooses to reveal His plan and thoughts to us, and sometimes He chooses not to. He may not tell us everything we *want* to know, but He always tells us everything we *need* to know. He gives us all the details we need, when we need them, and not a minute earlier. He knows the answer to every mystery, and He's where the joy is!

SEVEN-DAY ROUNDUP

ZOOM OUT

About five hundred years after God delivered them from slavery in Egypt, God's people finally saw the temple built! He made His presence known to them, and they celebrated for days. They were filled with joy because of who God is, what He's done, and how much He loves them.

WORD TO REMEMBER

- Flattery—an insincere compliment, often used to manipulate

APPLICATION

A few times this week, we read about the importance of our words. Proverbs reminds us many times of the power of what we say. Solomon asks God to have attentive ears to hear the prayers of His people. Psalm 150 says everything that breathes should praise the LORD! Pay attention to your words. Pray and **think** before you speak. Are your words **t**rue, **h**elpful, **i**nspiring, **n**ecessary, and **k**ind? Use your words to talk *to* God and *about* God.

PROVERBS 27–29

The wisdom from today's reading keeps pointing us back to trust in God. Instead of putting our trust in our own wisdom or plans for the future, we can put our trust in the one who holds our future. And instead of being afraid when hard times come, we can ask God for His strength and guidance. We need Him. He may give us more than *we* can handle, but He'll never give us more than *He* can handle.

Chapter 28 teaches us that trusting God shapes the way we view our sin. When we trust God and grow in wisdom, we confess our sins and turn away from them. The Holy Spirit will make us aware of our sins; our job is to confess and turn.

~TODAY'S GOD SHOT~

God is outside of time, and He knows the future; He's already there! It's wise to think about and make plans for your future, but don't get too caught up there. We don't know what will happen in our future, but God does. That truth can bring us joy, because He's where the joy is!

ZOOM IN

I know that whatever God does is final. Nothing can be added to it or taken from it.

Ecclesiastes 3:14

Ecclesiastes was probably written by either Solomon or someone writing as if he were Solomon. The author is rich and decides to find out what makes life meaningful. He starts his experiment with working way too much, but it leaves him feeling empty. So then he tries to run after pleasure and fun at every moment, but that also leaves him feeling empty. At last, he decides the best plan is to live and work for the Lord.

Life brings many different seasons: pain and joy, work and rest, war and peace. Through every season, God is working.

TODAY'S GOD SHOT

God and His works endure forever. We spend so much time and energy working for or worrying about things that don't matter and that won't last. The things of God are worth our time and energy because they're eternal. He's where the joy is!

ECCLESIASTES 7–12

ZOOM IN

But even though a person sins a hundred times and still lives a long time, I know that those who fear God will be better off.

Ecclesiastes 8:12

Life is shorter than we realize, but we should take it seriously. We have to wait for God's timing and realize that every moment He gives us is a gift. Whatever our work is, we should work well, like we're working for God.

There are also some short pieces of wisdom wrapped up in today's reading: Even a little foolishness leads to ruin; guarding our thoughts is as important as guarding our words; and God is the giver of life—even before a baby is born.

The writer wraps up his experiment with this conclusion: Our lives will have both pain and joy, and—in order for our lives to be meaningful—our job is to enjoy and obey God through all of it.

TODAY'S GOD SHOT

God can be trusted with our lives. There isn't a magic formula for a long, successful life. Our job is to delight in God, obey Him, and trust Him with whatever happens. When we do these things, we still may not get the things we think we want. But if the things we want aren't what God has planned for us, then they wouldn't bring us joy anyway. No matter what our lives turn out to look like, living His way brings us joy, because He's where the joy is!

1 KINGS 10–11; 2 CHRONICLES 9

ZOOM IN

Praise the LORD your God, who delights in you and has placed you on the throne as king to rule for him.

2 Chronicles 9:8

The queen of Sheba travels a long way to visit Solomon, bringing gifts and questions. She's heard that he's wise, and she wants to see for herself. When she meets Solomon, she understands that his wisdom and power come from God.

But sadly, Solomon doesn't follow the rules God gave for Israel's kings. He lets greed and pride build up in his heart and starts to collect horses and gold and even wives. He even builds places for worshipping idols. None of this is God's way, and Solomon's kingdom starts to fall apart.

Before Solomon dies, God raises up an enemy. One of Solomon's servants, Jeroboam (let's call him Jerry), has been suspicious of Solomon for a while. Jerry was told by the prophet Ahijah that he will lead ten of Israel's twelve tribes. Of course, Solomon sees Jerry as a threat, so Jerry has to hide in Egypt until Solomon dies. When Solomon dies, his son Rehoboam (let's call him Rey) inherits his throne.

~ TODAY'S GOD SHOT ~

God is in charge of everything, including leaders. The queen of Sheba tells Solomon that God put him on the throne of Israel so that Solomon can lead the people God's way: with justice and righteousness. It's easy to believe that God is in charge of leaders when the leader is good, but it's still true when leaders are bad. We may not understand what God is doing, but we can trust that His plans are good. No matter who leads on earth, God is still in charge of it all. And He's where the joy is!

PROVERBS 30–31

ZOOM IN

Charm is deceptive, and beauty does not last; but a woman who fears the LORD will be greatly praised.

Proverbs 31:30

A man named Agur wrote chapter 30, and he teaches us that God is wise and powerful and that we need to spend time in God's Word to know what's true. Agur asks God to keep him honest and to keep him from sin.

Proverbs opened with Proverbs Dad giving wisdom to his son, and it ends with Proverbs Mom giving wisdom to her son. She's telling him what kind of woman he should marry and what kinds of things to value.

If you're a girl reading this chapter, does the woman's example seem impossible to live up to? How does she find time to sleep or take a shower with everything else she does? But the chapter tells us about what she does *throughout her life*, not in one day. And remember, this is Proverbs, so it's wisdom, not the law. It's not meant for women to compare themselves to, but to look at her heart and her values. She's a hard worker, humble, and supportive, and most importantly, she trusts God.

TODAY'S GOD SHOT

God is the true Hero. When we read Bible passages like Proverbs 31, or Bible stories about David or Moses, it's easy to make a person into a hero. But when any of God's kids are strong or wise or praiseworthy, it's because they're depending on God for everything! The people in the Bible—even the great ones—aren't our heroes, but they point us to our Hero. God is the one who's strong and wise and praiseworthy. He's where the joy is!

ZOOM IN

Ahijah said to Jeroboam's wife, "Go on home, and when you enter the city, the child will die. All Israel will mourn for him and bury him. He is the only member of your family who will have a proper burial, for this child is the only good thing that the LORD, the God of Israel, sees in the entire family of Jeroboam."

1 Kings 14:12–13

After Solomon dies, his son Rey becomes king. But the prophet Ahijah had told Jerry that *he* would be the king, so Jerry returns from Egypt and hatches a plan. The plan works in dividing the people, and Israel is split into two kingdoms. King Jerry is in charge of the ten tribes in the north, or Northern Israel. King Rey is in charge of the two tribes in the south, or Southern Judah.

King Jerry is worried his people will want to go back to the temple in Jerusalem, so he builds his own temples, complete with golden idols and altars to false gods. He even makes his own religious calendar with new feast days, doing whatever he wants and completely ignoring God's ways. Because of his disobedience, there are great consequences for Jerry.

TODAY'S GOD SHOT

God can be trusted with life, and He can be trusted with death. Jerry's son is the only one in the family who God found good in, but he dies anyway. Death is really hard to understand, especially when the person who dies is young or good. But Jerry's son surely found comfort, since he left the wicked world ruled by his earthly father to go to the peaceful home of his heavenly Father. Jerry's son found joy with God because He's where the joy is!

2 CHRONICLES 10–12

ZOOM IN

This is what the LORD says: Do not fight against your relatives. Go back home, for what has happened is my doing!

2 Chronicles 11:4

The ten tribes in Northern Israel don't want the Levites to be their priests anymore, so without jobs or homes, the Levites make their way to Southern Judah. For a while, the Levites help Southern Judah live God's way, but eventually it falls apart.

King Jerry (of Northern Israel) had already led his kingdom away from God. And now, sadly, so does King Rey (of Southern Judah). The armies of Egypt come for Southern Judah. They take land and treasures, and the two tribes of Southern Judah are humbled. In their humility, they repent of their sins.

Meanwhile, King Jerry continues down his sinful path of worshipping and making sacrifices to idols, false gods, and even evil spirits.

TODAY'S GOD SHOT

God's plan isn't always easy. God told Rey not to fight back against Jerry, even though Jerry had taken away some of Rey's people. It wasn't easy, but Rey obeyed God and sent his soldiers home. Sometimes following God means we have to take the harder path, but it's always worth it. He can be trusted even when the path is hard and the plan isn't clear. He's where the joy is!

SEVEN-DAY ROUNDUP

ZOOM OUT

There was a lot of action the last seven days! Solomon died, and Israel was split into two kingdoms: Northern Israel (with ten tribes and King Jerry) and Southern Judah (with two tribes and King Rey). We also finished two more books of the Bible, which means we've read fifteen books together so far!

By the way, if you want a trick to help keep these names and places straight, remember that the kingdoms and their first kings are alphabetical from top to bottom: *Israel* in the north, *Judah* in the south (*I* comes before *J*); Jerry in the north, Rey in the south (*J* comes before *R*).

BIG PICTURE: PROVERBS

Proverbs is a collection of wisdom and advice. Even though man's advice isn't God's law, the wisdom of Proverbs helps God's kids make wise choices. And of course, the best advice in Proverbs points us to God and how much we need Him.

BIG PICTURE: ECCLESIASTES

Written by someone who calls himself "the Preacher," Ecclesiastes reminds us that the way to a meaningful life isn't through work or riches, but through enjoying God and obeying Him.

APPLICATION

God told Solomon to ask for anything he wanted, and he asked for wisdom. James 1:5 says, "If you need wisdom, ask our generous God, and he will give it to you. He will not rebuke you for asking." That means we can pray the same prayer Solomon prayed, and God will answer with a yes! God is wise, and He loves when His kids ask Him to make them wise like Him. Ask God for wisdom, and see how He answers with a yes.

1 KINGS 15; 2 CHRONICLES 13–16

ZOOM IN

The LORD will stay with you as long as you stay with him! Whenever you seek him, you will find him.

2 Chronicles 15:2

We covered a lot of time in today's readings, so let's review by kingdom. In Northern Israel, King Jerry's army attacks Southern Judah, and even though Jerry's army is twice as big, more than half of them die. They lose some land too. After Jerry dies, Northern Israel's next king is Nadab. He's an evil king who only lasts two years. Next, Baasha—who killed Nadab—rules over Northern Israel. He tries to close off one of Southern Judah's major routes of travel in an attempt to defeat them, but it backfires.

In Southern Judah, King Rey dies and is replaced by his son Abijah. Like his dad, Abijah doesn't follow God. Abijah dies and is replaced by his son Asa. Asa fears God and wants to make things right in Southern Judah, but he still sins. He doesn't ask God for direction and relies on his own plans instead. When a prophet tells Asa that he has sinned, Asa is furious. He throws the prophet in jail and continues to rely on himself instead of God. He lives a long time, and sadly spends the rest of his life arrogant and angry. When he dies, his son Jehoshaphat becomes Southern Judah's next king.

TODAY'S GOD SHOT

God is with you, and when you seek Him, you'll find Him! For 176 days, you've been seeking God. What do you know about Him now that you didn't before? You probably know Him better today than you did last week or last year. And if you keep seeking Him, you'll know Him even better next week and next year. He's where the joy is!

ZOOM IN

Then the fear of the LORD fell over all the surrounding kingdoms so that none of them wanted to declare war on Jehoshaphat.

2 Chronicles 17:10

After a few terrible but not really memorable kings in Northern Israel, Ahab takes the throne. You might be hoping that Israel finally got another good king. Sadly, they didn't. In fact, Ahab "did more to provoke the anger of the LORD, the God of Israel, than any of the other kings of Israel before him" (1 Kings 16:33). Yikes.

In Southern Judah, Jehoshaphat has taken over, and Jehoshaphat is a good king who seeks God and keeps His laws. Even Judah's enemies become their allies under Jehoshaphat. Under their king's leadership, Southern Judah honors God.

TODAY'S GOD SHOT

God is sovereign, even over the enemies of His kids. When surrounding kingdoms were struck by "the fear of the LORD" (17:10), it's not the good kind of fear. This kind of fear in Hebrew (the original language of the Old Testament) means that the other kings and armies were scared of God and of Jehoshaphat. Even when God doesn't turn the hearts of His enemies toward Him, He turns them away from hurting His kids. And this is good: God's kids are protected, and God's plan is accomplished. He's sovereign over hearts, and He's where the joy is!

1 KINGS 17–19

Elijah, a prophet who tells people the truth about God, confronts Northern Israel's king, Ahab, about his sinful ways. Elijah tells Ahab a drought is on the way. In the third year of the drought, God informs Elijah that it's time for rain. Elijah challenges Ahab and 450 prophets of Baal—a false god—to see whose god is best. He brings two bulls up to the top of a mountain to see whose god will burn up the sacrifice in acceptance of it.

The prophets of Baal cry for hours, and even cut themselves, but nothing happens to their bull. Then Elijah drenches the altar, the wood, and the ground around his bull with water. God sends fire from heaven, burning up the bull, the wet wood, the stones, and the dirt. Wow! The people of Northern Israel worship God and the drought is over.

When Ahab's wife Jezebel—a Baal worshipper—hears what happened, she is furious. She promises to kill Elijah, so he hides out in Southern Judah. He is lonely and scared, but God speaks to him, instructing Elijah to appoint two kings and a prophet. The prophet's name is Elisha.

～TODAY'S GOD SHOT～

God does big and powerful things, and He does small and beautiful things too. God brought a tornado, an earthquake, and a fire, but Elijah already knew how powerful God was. Elijah needed to see God in the whisper. God is powerful enough to send an earthquake, and He's close enough to whisper. He's where the joy is!

ZOOM IN

Do you see how Ahab has humbled himself before me? Because he has done this, I will not do what I promised during his lifetime.

1 Kings 21:29

Northern Israel is at war with Syria. A prophet tells King Ahab he'll win, even though his army is smaller. The prophet instructs Ahab on what to do after the war: Wipe out all of the enemy. But the Syrian king asks for mercy, and Ahab spares his life. This sounds like a good move, but it's the exact opposite of God's command.

Another prophet comes to call Ahab out on his sin, but Ahab doesn't repent. He decides what he needs isn't repentance, but more land. He demands land from his neighbor Naboth, who says no. And now Ahab's wife Jezebel is back. Like the deceiver she is, she writes a letter pretending to be her husband and invites Naboth over for dinner. Instead of honoring God at the feast like they said they would, they kill Naboth. Then, Ahab takes Naboth's land.

God sends Elijah to tell Ahab that because of Jezebel's sin, Ahab, Jezebel, and all their family members will die. Ahab repents, and God shows mercy.

TODAY'S GOD SHOT

God keeps His promises. The only time He modifies them is when He's giving mercy or grace. This is what happens with Ahab. Even though "no one else so completely sold himself to what was evil in the LORD's sight as Ahab did" (21:25), God showed Ahab mercy. God loves to show mercy and grace, even to those who do wicked things. He's eager to forgive, and He's where the joy is!

1 KINGS 22; 2 CHRONICLES 18

ZOOM IN

An Aramean soldier, however, randomly shot an arrow at the Israelite troops and hit the king of Israel between the joints of his armor.

2 Chronicles 18:33

Northern Israel's Ahab and Southern Judah's Jehoshaphat team up to recapture Ramoth-gilead, a city taken by Syria. Jehoshaphat is wise and asks that they seek God's counsel before they make their plan. So Ahab brings in four hundred prophets, but it's likely that they're false prophets. Jehoshaphat wants another opinion.

They ask the prophet Micaiah, who wicked King Ahab does not like one bit. That's because Ahab knows Micaiah won't lie to him and tell him what he wants to hear. So when Micaiah tells the kings the truth, Ahab has Micaiah thrown in jail.

When the battle begins, Ahab dresses in a disguise, but tells Jehoshaphat to wear his royal robes so the enemy will aim for Jehoshaphat! But of course, nothing can stop God's plan. Ahab is killed, and his son Ahaziah takes the throne.

TODAY'S GOD SHOT

God will always accomplish His plan. Even though the man who shot the arrow that killed Ahab probably didn't mean to hit him, God was in control of where everyone stood, how Ahab's disguise and armor were worn, when the man took his shot, and where the arrow went. Nothing happens outside of God's control, and He's always working to accomplish His plan. He's where the joy is!

ZOOM IN

O our God, won't you stop them? We are powerless against this mighty army that is about to attack us. We do not know what to do, but we are looking to you for help.

2 Chronicles 20:12

Jehoshaphat appoints judges and commands them to make righteous choices. When a group of armies comes to attack Southern Judah, Jehoshaphat tells the people to fast and pray. He worships God in the temple and prays a beautiful prayer full of faith. A worship leader prophesies that they don't even have to fight because the battle is God's. And as the people of Southern Judah are worshipping, the enemy armies fight *each other* instead of Judah. Wow!

Jehoshaphat dies, and there are three wicked rulers after him. A priest has been raising a boy born into the family of rulers in secret. Joash is only seven years old, but he's the **heir** to the throne. The priest who raised him brings back worship in the temple and destroys the altars to Baal. The people of Judah rejoice!

TODAY'S GOD SHOT

God is trustworthy, and His timing is always right. Jehoshaphat knows that no matter what happens to them—"war, plague, or famine" (20:9)—God is in control and He will ultimately rescue them. They look to God for help, which is always right. He's where the joy is!

OBADIAH 1; PSALMS 82–83

The events in the book of Obadiah likely take place between the time Egypt invaded Jerusalem (2 Chronicles 12) and the time Edom revolted against one of Judah's evil kings, Jehoram (2 Chronicles 21). Obadiah rebukes the Edomites for not helping God's people. They are Israel's and Judah's closest relatives and neighbors, all descending from Isaac. But when Jerusalem was invaded, Edom didn't help.

Obadiah speaks to the Edomites from God, telling them, "The day is near when I, the LORD, will judge all godless nations! As you have done to Israel, so it will be done to you. All your evil deeds will fall back on your own heads" (1:15). God will bring justice, both soon and at the end of the earth.

TODAY'S GOD SHOT

God takes it personally when His kids are treated badly. He isn't going to sit back and let Judah get bullied without doing something about it! But in these situations, God doesn't get revenge for Himself; He gets **vengeance** for His kids. His vengeance is perfect and just. He's powerful and protective, and He loves His kids. He's where the joy is!

SEVEN-DAY ROUNDUP

ZOOM OUT

We've now read seventeen books together, and tomorrow we cross the halfway point in this trip through Scripture! *Congratulations!* This week we followed the split kingdom through many kings. Most of them did not live God's way. But there were a few who knew and worshipped God. They found their strength in Him.

BIG PICTURE: 1 KINGS

God gave the law, which tells how people should live. In 1 Kings, Israel is unfaithful, and because of their sin, they suffer. But God keeps His promises, and He is always ready to forgive those who repent.

BIG PICTURE: OBADIAH

This short book shows us that nations that oppose God and His people will experience God's judgment. It also points ahead to the glorious promise that God will establish His eternal kingdom!

WORDS TO REMEMBER

- Heir—someone who gets money or property when someone else dies
- Vengeance—justice done on behalf of someone who was mistreated or wronged

APPLICATION

We've seen in the Old Testament how God called His kids to repentance. No matter how big their sin, when they confessed and asked for His mercy and grace, He granted their request. Today, God still calls His kids to repentance. Repentance reminds us of who we are (sinful) and who God is (perfect). Is there sin (whether an action, word, thought, or motive) you need to confess to Him today? Pray a prayer like this:

God, You are holy and perfect. I know I sinned when I _____. Thank You for forgiving me. Please help me to live Your way. I love You.

God's promise is true each time we sin: "If we confess our sins to him, he is faithful and just to forgive us our sins and to cleanse us from all wickedness" (1 John 1:9). Praise God!

2 KINGS 1–4

ZOOM IN

This is what the Lord says: This dry valley will be filled with pools of water! You will see neither wind nor rain, says the Lord, but this valley will be filled with water.

2 Kings 3:16–17

Remember Elisha, with an *s*? He's the prophet that God told Elijah, with a *j*, to appoint. (To remember which one came first, recall that *j* comes before *s* in the alphabet.) It's almost time for Elijah to die, and Elisha is heartbroken. Elisha asks his teacher Elijah for a double portion of the spirit of God. When Elijah asks God on Elisha's behalf, God gives it to him. And He also sends a chariot of fire down from heaven to take Elijah!

Through three miracles, Elisha confirms to Israel that he is Elijah's rightful replacement. Then, Northern Israel and Southern Judah team up against Moab. They go to war, but in their foolishness, they end up in the desert without water. They ask Elisha what to do, and his answer leads them to victory.

God uses Elisha in so many ways—from helping a poor widow provide food for her family to raising a rich family's only son from the dead.

TODAY'S GOD SHOT

God is always working, even when we can't see what He's up to. When Elisha tells the kings how they'll defeat Moab, he says they won't see the wind or the rain in process, only the effects of it. It's hard to trust that God is working when we can't see it, isn't it? The next time you wonder if God is really at work, remember today's story and pray for faith. He's always working, and He's where the joy is!

ZOOM IN

Naaman said, "Now I know that there is no God in all the world except in Israel. So please accept a gift from your servant."

2 Kings 5:15

Naaman is a military commander from Syria, and God has given him many victories in battle. But he also has a serious skin disease called leprosy. His servant girl says Elisha can heal him, but because Israel is an enemy territory, both kings have to give their permission for this meeting to happen. And they do! When Naaman goes to Elisha's house, a messenger tells him to go wash himself seven times in the Jordan River. Naaman is furious because Elisha didn't even see him and the river is dirty. But his servants convince him to try, and he does. Naaman is healed, and he confesses that YHWH is God!

God pays attention to the big things and the small things too. When a young prophet lost a borrowed axe-head in a river, Elisha miraculously found it. And God also kept Elisha safe and protected from his enemies. Elisha is God's prophet, and every prophecy he makes is fulfilled.

TODAY'S GOD SHOT

God seeks out His enemies to bless them. Naaman doubts God, but God turns his heart around using a servant girl, the permission of Syria's king, the doubt of Israel's king, and the encouragement of Naaman's servants. God has already blessed Naaman with so much, and then He blesses Naaman with the greatest gift of all: an eternal relationship with Himself. He's where the joy is!

2 KINGS 9–11

ZOOM IN

Nonetheless the LORD said to Jehu, "You have done well in following my instructions to destroy the family of Ahab. Therefore, your descendants will be kings of Israel down to the fourth generation."

2 Kings 10:30

In ancient Israel, God runs the nation, and He speaks through prophets. Prophets are powerful; they even get to anoint kings. Elisha sends a prophet to anoint Jehu as Israel's next king. But Jehu also has to fulfill God's prophecy by wiping out all of Ahab's descendants, including the current king of Northern Israel, Joram. Ahab's wickedness meant that even though he had already died, the rest of his family would die as well.

Jehu does his job, and all of Ahab's family members are killed. This plan seems extreme—and it is—but it's all part of God's covenant with His people. Jehu is a king who God blesses, but eventually his heart wanders. He reigns for twenty-eight years, and toward the end of that time, Israel begins to lose wars and land.

TODAY'S GOD SHOT

God is always working out His plan. Even when wicked or sad or confusing things are happening all around, God is still at work. Just because we can't see His hand doesn't mean it isn't there. His plans will come true, and they will bring Him glory and His kids good. He's where the joy is!

ZOOM IN

Once when some Israelites were burying a man, they spied a band of these raiders. So they hastily threw the corpse into the tomb of Elisha and fled. But as soon as the body touched Elisha's bones, the dead man revived and jumped to his feet!

2 Kings 13:21

Not long ago, we met Southern Judah's new king, Joash. (Your Bible might call him Jehoash; that's the same guy.) He's only seven years old when he becomes king. He's been raised by a wise priest who gives him good advice, but when the priest dies, Joash makes all kinds of terrible decisions. He gets his advice from the wrong people who lead him into worshipping idols. Things go from bad to worse with Joash, and he is killed by his own people.

Meanwhile in Northern Israel, Jehu has died and his son Jehoahaz is king. He is wicked but smart. He notices that Israel is under God's judgment, so he tries to get God's favor. He doesn't do this because he loves God; he does it so Israel won't get any more punishment. Even though God knows Jehoahaz's heart, He is merciful and sends help to Israel.

Elisha dies and is buried. Later on, some local men are burying someone else. They make a mistake and put the dead body in Elisha's grave. When the body touches Elisha's bones, the man comes back to life!

TODAY'S GOD SHOT

God is powerful! The accidental resurrection of the dead man shows us Elisha's powers never came from Elisha himself; they came directly from God. Remember Elisha's request before Elijah died? He asked for a double portion of God's Spirit. God chooses who He uses to accomplish His plans, but He doesn't need us because of our power or anything else. The power isn't ours anyway. It's His. He's powerful, and He's where the joy is!

2 KINGS 14; 2 CHRONICLES 25

Now that Joash is dead, his son Amaziah is Southern Judah's new king. Amaziah kills the people who killed his father, but he doesn't hurt their families. At the time, it was common to punish children for their father's sins. But God told His people not to do that, so Amaziah didn't.

Amaziah is a mostly good king, but after a big military victory against Edom, he worships the false gods of the people he defeated. God sends a prophet to tell him his sin is wrong, but Amaziah's pride keeps growing. He picks a fight against Northern Israel, and during that battle, Amaziah is killed. His son Uzziah (who is also called Azariah) becomes Judah's king.

TODAY'S GOD SHOT

God holds both victory and loss in His hands, so when He gives victory to one side, He gives loss to another. We see that with Judah and Edom. Sometimes we think God doesn't pick sides, but the Bible shows us that's not true. It's all part of God's good plan. He is always victorious, and He's where the joy is!

ZOOM IN

Those who worship false gods turn their backs on all God's mercies.

Jonah 2:8

God tells Jonah to go to Nineveh and rebuke the people there for their wickedness, but Jonah is proud and arrogant and hates the Ninevites. They don't look like him or talk like him, and he doesn't want them to be God's kids. So instead of following God's instructions, Jonah gets on a boat heading in the opposite direction.

God sends a huge storm; it's so big that even the sailors—who would've sailed through many storms—were terrified. Jonah tells the sailors the storm came because he's running from God. They throw Jonah overboard and the sea calms. The sailors offer a sacrifice to God.

God sends a big fish to swallow Jonah whole, and for three days and nights Jonah lives in its belly. Did you notice anything missing in Jonah's prayer? He gives thanks, but he doesn't re-pent of his sin. God tells the fish to vomit him up on the shore anyway, and Jonah goes to Nineveh to tell *them* to repent, even though he needs to as well.

God still uses Jonah, and the entire nation repents of their wicked ways. God is merciful to Jonah even in his sin.

~ TODAY'S GOD SHOT ~

God's love is the only thing that can leave us satisfied. When Jonah prayed inside the fish, he said, "Those who worship false gods turn their backs on all God's mercies" (2:8). When we chase things the world offers, we think getting them will make us happy. But it won't. But when we pursue God, we will always find love. He's where the joy is!

2 KINGS 15; 2 CHRONICLES 26

ZOOM IN

As long as the king sought guidance from the LORD, God gave him success.

2 Chronicles 26:5

Depending on what version of the Bible you're reading, you might have read today about Judah's King Uzziah or King Azariah. They're the same guy! We'll call him Uzziah here. He's mostly a good king, and when he follows God, he's successful. But after winning a lot of battles, he gets rich, famous, and prideful.

Uzziah decides to burn incense in the temple in Jerusalem. This might seem like a way to honor God, but only priests are allowed to do this! The priests are shocked when Uzziah tells them why he's there, and they try to stop him. When Uzziah gets angry with them, God strikes him with leprosy. Because of God's cleanliness rules, someone with leprosy can't be in the temple, so Uzziah has to leave immediately and separate himself from everyone. His son Jotham becomes king.

Meanwhile in Northern Israel, things aren't great. They move quickly through five kings, each with a short reign, most of whom killed the king before him to gain power.

TODAY'S GOD SHOT

God is both holy and merciful. When Uzziah rebels against God and enters the temple, God gives him leprosy. In His holiness, God won't let the king **defile** His temple. God takes Uzziah off the throne, but He doesn't kill him. In His mercy, God lets Uzziah live. He's holy and He's merciful and He's where the joy is!

SEVEN-DAY ROUNDUP

ZOOM OUT

We've finished eighteen books together! In the past seven days, Northern Israel and Southern Judah went through a lot of kings, and some were good but most were bad. We learned about the power God gave Elisha. And we also read about Jonah's trip to Nineveh, which happened during this time of the split kingdom.

BIG PICTURE: JONAH

Through a storm, a big fish, and a bitter missionary, the book of Jonah teaches us that God is in charge of everything, and that God is generous in giving mercy.

WORD TO REMEMBER

- Defile—to spoil or corrupt

APPLICATION

God does big, breathtaking things. He sent a storm and a fish to make sure Jonah told the people of Nineveh about Him. He brought a body back to life when it touched the bones of one of His prophets. And God also does small, beautiful things. He used Elisha to provide food for a widow and her family. He gave Jonah a vine for shade. He's in the big details and the small ones. Make a list of some of the big things God has done. Make another list of some of the small things you've seen Him do. Thank Him for both the big and small ways He shows His goodness and love!

ISAIAH 1–4

ZOOM IN

He will provide a canopy of cloud during the day and smoke and flaming fire at night, covering the glorious land. It will be a shelter from daytime heat and a hiding place from storms and rain.

Isaiah 4:5–6

Isaiah the prophet is writing to Southern Judah, mostly telling them about what's been happening in Northern Israel. God is dealing with their sins, and they've been attacked by the Assyrian army. Isaiah warns Southern Judah that they should repent of their own sins or the same thing will happen to them.

When Israel is being attacked by Assyria, God tells them that He doesn't want their offerings. God hasn't changed His mind about offerings; He knows that their hearts aren't honest even if they sacrifice an animal. He tells everyone what a changed heart should look like.

Because of Assyria's victory, Judah gets scared. They stop listening to God and start making themselves feel safe by making friends with the enemy nations around them. Isaiah tells them that their safety isn't real, because it can only be found in God.

TODAY'S GOD SHOT

God is our refuge. In today's reading, there were lots of pictures of Israel's time in the wilderness. He was with them there, in a fire and a cloud. And even though they're not in the wilderness anymore, He's with them still. He's our refuge, a safe place to live. No matter where we are, God is with us. He makes His home with His people. He's where the joy is!

In a love poem to God's people, Isaiah compares God to a vine keeper and the Israelites to wild grapes. But in Hebrew—the language of the Old Testament—the word for the grapes actually means "stinking things." Yikes. That's not what God wants in His garden, and the grapes are trampled.

Isaiah then paints a beautiful word picture of God's throne room. The people of Israel need God's mercy, and so does Isaiah. In his vision, he sees seraphim—fiery, flying creatures with six wings—covering their eyes and crying, "Holy, holy, holy." When he is reminded of God's holiness, Isaiah is humbled. Isaiah is called by God to point out the sins of Israel, but since he is God's messenger, he also understands his own sin.

God tells Isaiah that Judah is going to be destroyed but that Isaiah shouldn't be afraid.

TODAY'S GOD SHOT

God purifies us from sin. In Isaiah's vision in the throne room, Jesus is prophesied to be there! When the seraph takes a burning coal and touches it to Isaiah's lips to purify him, the coal is from the altar of sacrifice. What's on the altar of sacrifice that purifies all who believe from our sin? Jesus! Because God sent His Son as the sacrifice for us all, we are forgiven. He's where the joy is!

AMOS 1–5

ZOOM IN

When the ram's horn blows a warning, shouldn't the people be alarmed? Does disaster come to a city unless the LORD has planned it?

Amos 3:6

Amos is a prophet writing at about the same time as Isaiah. God gives Amos eight statements. Six of those statements are about the nations around Israel. They don't know YHWH as their God, but they are still held to His standards of morality, or what's right and wrong. They are guilty of cruelty, slavery, murder, and more.

The seventh statement is about Southern Judah. Even though they're in a covenant with God, they keep sinning. They think they'll get a free pass because He chose them, but really, they're held to a higher standard. And God says they've rejected Him.

The eighth statement is about Northern Israel. They've sold people into slavery, mistreated the poor, ignored the hurting, and worshipped false gods. They've broken their covenant, and God has tried to lead them to repentance with drought, famine, disease, and more. But even though He has been patient with them, they've ignored Him. So now He will bring judgment.

TODAY'S GOD SHOT

God doesn't cause the disaster mentioned in 3:6, but He does allow it. This can be hard to understand, and that's okay. It's important to remember that God is sovereign over everything, even the things we don't like or understand. It's also important to remember that God's judgment for sin is always righteous. And finally, it's important to remember that God's judgment on His people is for the purpose of restoring them into a right relationship with Him. He's faithful to us, even when we rebel against Him. He's where the joy is!

ZOOM IN

"In that day," says the Sovereign LORD, "I will make the sun go down at noon and darken the earth while it is still day. I will turn your celebrations into times of mourning and your singing into weeping. You will wear funeral clothes and shave your heads to show your sorrow—as if your only son had died. How very bitter that day will be!"

Amos 8:9–10

God gives Amos visions of destruction like locusts eating a field, a fire burning everything, and a construction tool used to show whether a wall is built straight. If the wall isn't straight, it'll collapse. Likewise, Northern Israel is so far away from God's standards that it will also collapse.

God will send His judgment, and while it may be hard to understand, it's righteous. The point of God's judgment isn't destruction—it's restoration. His people suffer because of the consequences of their own actions, but God still loves them. He promises to raise them back up, rebuild, and restore.

TODAY'S GOD SHOT

God went through everything Israel is about to go through. Amos describes the day of God's judgment: The earth will tremble, the sun will set during the day, a feast turns into mourning, and singing will turn into crying. Amos says it's as if an only son has died. Seven hundred years after this writing, during the celebration of the Passover feast, the earth trembled and the sky went black when God's only Son died on the cross. Sin requires severe punishment, which is why God sent Himself. Does that seem unfair? It is—we *don't* get the punishment we deserve. Jesus took it for us. He's where the joy is!

2 CHRONICLES 27; ISAIAH 9–12

ZOOM IN

His government and its peace will never end. He will rule with fairness and justice from the throne of his ancestor David for all eternity.

Isaiah 9:7

Jotham, Uzziah's son, has taken over as Southern Judah's king. He's a good king who follows God's rules. But when he dies, his son Ahaz takes over, and it's a different story. We'll get to that in a couple of days.

Isaiah 9 prophesies the birth of Jesus. The Israelites probably thought that their king would be a great military leader who'd win every battle, but Jesus is so much more than that. There are a few hints for the people about who the Messiah will be: 9:6 even calls Him "Mighty God."

We also read a lot about God's **wrath** (extreme anger) for the people whose hearts oppose God. God will wipe out the wicked but will save a group whose hearts still belong to Him. He knows who those people are, and He has a plan to save them and use them in His great plan of salvation for the world.

TODAY'S GOD SHOT

God's wrath is real, and sin has to be punished. Parts of Isaiah are hard to read because God's anger is so heavy. The only person who has never sinned and who doesn't deserve the Father's wrath is Jesus, who rules "with fairness and justice from the throne of his ancestor David for all eternity" (Isaiah 9:7). He took the punishment we deserve so that we don't ever have to face God's wrath. Instead of anger, we get love. He's where the joy is!

ZOOM IN

Then his people will live there undisturbed, for he will be highly honored around the world. And he will be the source of peace.

Micah 5:4–5

Micah writes to both Israel and Judah about their widespread sins: stealing land from the poor and oppressing the needy. Micah teaches that greed might start with just wanting more stuff, but if it's not dealt with, it grows and grows until you're willing to hurt others to get what you want.

The leaders of Israel and Judah think they're above the consequences of sin, but Micah tells them they're not. In fact, he gives them a specific prophecy: "Now you must leave this city to live in the open country. You will soon be sent in exile to distant Babylon" (4:10). And—spoiler—this *exact* thing happens about two hundred years later.

Whenever Micah gives a prophecy of warning, he also tells them that destruction isn't the end for them. Some of the people of Israel will be protected, and through their line of descendants, God will establish peace. Micah reminds the people that God is after their hearts, and he tells them to repent.

~TODAY'S GOD SHOT~

God is the source of peace and security. Micah says that—*because of Him*—His people will live peacefully. When God is most honored, we are most at peace. He's where the joy is!

2 CHRONICLES 28; 2 KINGS 16–17

ZOOM IN

But the Israelites would not listen. They were as stubborn as their ancestors who had refused to believe in the LORD their God.

2 Kings 17:14

Southern Judah's King Ahaz is wicked: He not only builds idols for worshipping but also tells his people to sacrifice children to the idols. *How terrible!* Most of the people follow him in his wicked ways. Judah is full of sin, and God allows them to be beaten in military battles. Ahaz sees that his kingdom is in trouble, but instead of going to the King of the universe for help, he goes to the king of Assyria. There are lies and tricks and more idols, and Judah ends up in a bigger mess than ever.

Up in Northern Israel, King Hoshea is also wicked. He's been paying Assyria money every year so that Assyria won't attack them. But one year he doesn't pay, so Assyria attacks. After three years, Assyria captures Israel's capital city and sends all the Israelites out of their homeland, exactly as the prophets said would happen.

～TODAY'S GOD SHOT～

God is patient with His people. God made His covenant with them and taught them how to live in a relationship with Him. He made them, delivered them, fed them, protected them, and lived with them. He also sent them warning after warning over hundreds of years when they continued to turn their hearts away from Him. Now they've been captured by their enemies, just like their hearts have been captured by false gods. Because of their suffering, they will understand their sin. And when they understand their sin, they will return to God. He's so patient, and He's where the joy is!

SEVEN-DAY ROUNDUP

ZOOM OUT

We've completed twenty books together, and we've seen some terrible events this week. Because of their great sin, Southern Judah is headed for a downfall. They've been warned by God through prophets, but their hearts are hard. And because of their sins, Northern Israel has already been captured by Assyria. They've been sent out of the land God gave them.

BIG PICTURE: AMOS

A shepherd named Amos is chosen by God to give a message of prophecy to Northern Israel. While Israel waits for God to judge their enemies, they ignore their own sin. Amos tells the people God will judge righteously, and the faithful will be protected and blessed.

BIG PICTURE: MICAH

Through the prophet Micah, God gives a message to Northern Israel and Southern Judah. He tells them that their sin will have great consequences, and that God is faithful to forgive, protect, and restore.

WORD TO REMEMBER

- Wrath—extreme anger

APPLICATION

Just like Israel, sometimes we're so focused on others' sins that we ignore our own. Think of the last time you faced a consequence for your own wrong choices. Which of these statements is closest to what you thought or said?

"Because I sinned, this consequence is fair. I want to pray to ask God to help me live His way next time."

"That's not fair! My brother did the same thing last week and didn't get in trouble for it."

If we're honest with ourselves, most of us probably think something similar to the second option.

The next time you experience a consequence for your sin, pray God will convict you and give you a heart that confesses, asks for forgiveness, and commits to living His way. He'll help you if you ask Him!

ISAIAH 13–17

ZOOM IN

So now I weep for Jazer and the vineyards of Sibmah; my tears will flow for Heshbon and Elealeh.

Isaiah 16:9

Isaiah uses most of his writing to warn God's people about their sin, but today he prophesies against pagan nations. God promises judgment on Babylon because—in about one hundred years—they'll take Judah into captivity. Babylon hasn't chosen to follow God, but He has chosen to use their sinful ways to work out His long-term plans. This will start with Judah's discipline, but it will turn into restoration.

Other pagan nations are addressed too. Assyria, who destroys Northern Israel, will be punished. The Philistines are reminded that God's promise is for His people, not them. And Damascus will be a pile of rubble, but God will preserve part of their nation who will turn their hearts toward Him.

The tone is different when Isaiah writes about God's message for Moab. He mourns over their coming destruction, but their sins require judgment just like everyone else's.

TODAY'S GOD SHOT

God doesn't change. He mourns Moab's destruction. His heart breaks for them, and 16:9 says He weeps. Moab is a pagan nation that has rejected God, but His heart is soft toward them anyway. A lot of people think of the Old Testament days as a time when God was angry and didn't show mercy, but He's always been the same, which means He's always been kind. In the Old Testament, New Testament, and today, He's where the joy is!

ZOOM IN

The Egyptians will lose heart, and I will confuse their plans.

Isaiah 19:3

There are more prophecies today for pagan nations, including a mystery nation that God will bring judgment to. For Egypt, who enslaved God's people for four hundred years, God will confuse their plans until they turn against each other.

But goodness is coming! Isaiah says that Egypt and Assyria—two of the most powerful enemies of God's people—will one day worship Him. God's heart is for all different kinds of people, and He brings them into His family.

Isaiah's final word today is for Jerusalem. God's people are held to a higher standard, and because of their sin, Jerusalem will be attacked and destroyed. Judah believes that their destruction is coming, but instead of repenting, they ramp up their sin.

TODAY'S GOD SHOT

God is sovereign, even over our thoughts. In 19:3, God says about Egypt that He'll "confuse their plans." It may seem strange that God works in our thoughts, but that's how God the Spirit guides us into truth (John 16:13) and reminds us of what Jesus said (John 14:26). Every thought we think is not God speaking to us, but He does give us His thoughts when we're seeking to live His way. He's where the joy is!

ISAIAH 23–27

ZOOM IN

LORD, you will grant us peace; all we have accomplished is really from you.

Isaiah 26:12

Today we read the last batch of judgment for foreign nations. Tyre and Sidon are centers for trade, so they are rich and powerful cities. Tyre is destroyed but then rebuilt. And even though it seems like they don't turn fully to God, He still uses their businesses to bless His people.

The judgment of the whole earth is a hard passage to read. Creation will be undone, and since God promised He'd never flood the whole earth again, the destruction will probably be caused by something like an earthquake or fire. When will this happen? On the coming day of the LORD.

But there is hope. For God's people who trust that He's sovereign and good, this passage is serious, but not scary. God can be trusted with our futures. He restored the earth after the flood, and He'll restore it again! His people will live and feast with Him in the new earth.

TODAY'S GOD SHOT

God accomplishes everything we need. God the Father created us. God the Son paid the price for our sins. And God the Spirit makes us able to fulfill God's specific plans for our lives. Philippians 1:6 says that "God, who began the good work within you, will continue his work until it is finally finished on the day when Christ Jesus returns." God began the good work, He's continuing it, and He will fulfill it. Like Isaiah wrote, "All we have accomplished is really from you" (26:12). He's where the joy is!

ZOOM IN

For the LORD your God is gracious and merciful. If you return to him, he will not continue to turn his face from you.

2 Chronicles 30:9

Southern Judah's King Ahaz was terrible, but his son Hezekiah is one of Judah's best kings. The Bible compares him to King David! When he becomes king, he restores the temple and brings back God's system for sacrifices. He also has the people celebrate Passover again, which they haven't done for a very long time. The people sing and praise God, and their hearts are finally turning back to Him.

Later on, the Assyrians attack Judah and take all the valuables from the temple. The Assyrians tell the people of Judah not to trust God, but God's people don't listen. They continue all the God-given practices they'd ignored for so long, teaching the next generation God's ways.

TODAY'S GOD SHOT

God is quick to forgive. Hezekiah knows God's heart for mercy, so he reminds the people that God won't turn away from them if they return to Him. Because His people's hearts had finally turned back to Him, "There was great joy in the city, for Jerusalem had not seen a celebration like this one since the days of Solomon, King David's son" (30:26). He's where the joy is!

HOSEA 1–7

ZOOM IN

Yet the time will come when Israel's people will be like the sands of the seashore—too many to count! Then, at the place where they were told, "You are not my people," it will be said, "You are children of the living God."

Hosea 1:10

God sends a message to both Israel and Judah in a unique way. He tells the prophet Hosea to marry Gomer, a woman who's been with many men, pretending like they were her husband. Even though Gomer hasn't lived her life by God's rules, God tells Hosea to commit to her anyway. Does this remind you of anything? Even though the Israelites haven't lived their lives by God's rules, God is committed to them.

Even after Hosea marries Gomer, she goes back to her old ways. She rejects him and leaves to live with another man, acting like *he's* her husband. But God tells Hosea to find his wife and bring her home. Israel has rejected God for so long. Because the elders and leaders didn't tell the next generation about Him, almost no one knows Him anymore. God knows the only thing that will bring Israel back to Him is a heart change. Forcing them to obey Him won't change their hearts; they have to love Him. So God keeps pursuing their hearts to bring them home.

TODAY'S GOD SHOT

God makes us His people! Did you catch Gomer's kids' names in today's reading? They might seem unkind, but they tell us the story of Jesus redeeming us. First, sin exists and must be punished. Second, we were people without mercy. Third, we weren't His children. But because of Jesus, God forgives our sin, gives us great mercy, and even makes us His children. He's where the joy is!

ZOOM IN

For my people are determined to desert me. They call me the Most High, but they don't truly honor me. Oh, how can I give you up, Israel? How can I let you go? How can I destroy you like Admah or demolish you like Zeboiim? My heart is torn within me, and my compassion overflows.

Hosea 11:7–8

Hosea reminds God's people that there are consequences for their sins. Their hearts have wandered far away from God, and it shows up in every area of their lives. When people are close to God, it shows up in what they say and do. And when people are far away from God, that shows up too.

Hosea begs the people to return to God and promises that if they do, God will meet them in love. God started the relationship with His people many years before they were born, and even though they've broken their part of the covenant again and again, He still goes after them. God's heart is to heal and save, meeting us in our sin with His arms wide open.

TODAY'S GOD SHOT

God's anger toward sin landed on Jesus, so it doesn't land on us. In 11:7, God is rightly furious, but in the next verse, His heart is broken at the idea of letting His people go: "My heart is torn within me, and my compassion overflows." Jesus took God's wrath so that we can get His mercy. He's where the joy is!

ISAIAH 28–30

ZOOM IN

Your own ears will hear him. Right behind you a voice will say, "This is the way you should go," whether to the right or to the left.

Isaiah 30:21

Today we read about three of the six **woes**, or troubles, coming for Israel. The first woe talks about how the people have spent too much time drinking wine and not nearly enough time with God. Instead of repenting, the leaders mock Isaiah.

The second woe speaks to Jerusalem about acting like they love God by doing a bunch of religious acts but not really loving Him. But instead of bringing discipline, He says that He'll do wonderful things to reveal Himself to them (29:14).

The third woe addresses fear. When people are taken over by their own fear, they rush to solutions that won't work. But when they take their fear to God, they can be still and wait for His solution.

TODAY'S GOD SHOT

God promises to teach and guide us. He warns us about the consequences of *not* following Him, and because He's kind, of course He'll show us *how* to follow Him! He wants us to learn to hear His voice. How do we do that? By spending time with Him, in prayer and in His Word. You're doing that now, so you already know that He's where the joy is!

SEVEN-DAY ROUNDUP

ZOOM OUT

We've finished twenty-one books together so far! There were a lot of hard things to read in the past seven days. We read about the consequences of sin, both for pagan nations and for God's people. Passages like these can be hard to read, but you're doing it! And God will teach you through it. Remember to look for who God is, what He's doing, and how much He loves His kids.

BIG PICTURE: HOSEA

Hosea's marriage is a picture of how Israel has turned away from God, and how God continues to love Israel. The story of Hosea and Gomer—and the larger story of God and Israel—teaches us that God's love is bigger than our sin.

WORD TO REMEMBER

- Woe—a great trouble or problem

APPLICATION

A few times this week, we read about hearing God's voice. Today, that usually means hearing His voice in our minds, like a thought. You are probably wondering, *How do I know if a thought comes from God?* God the Spirit can—and does—put His thoughts in our minds (John 14:26, 16:13–15). But not every single thought we have is from Him.

Here are two good questions to ask yourself if you think God might have spoken to you through a thought in your mind:

Does this thought match what I know to be true about God from His Word?

Does this thought match what I know to be true about me from God's Word?

If you can answer both of those questions with yes, then God might be speaking to you. But if you're not sure, talk to a trusted grown-up who loves Jesus. They'll help you figure it out!

ISAIAH 31–34

And this righteousness will bring peace. Yes, it will bring quietness and confidence forever.

Isaiah 32:17

Today we finish reading about the six woes that are coming to Israel. In the fourth woe, Isaiah reminds the stubborn people of Judah that relying on Egypt won't save them. Only God can save them, and His salvation is better than a simple military victory!

In the fifth woe, Isaiah specifically warns women who rely on their wealth and status. Because of what they have, they think they're safe and secure, but within a year, trouble is coming. But Isaiah doesn't give a warning without hope. He tells them God's Spirit will be poured out all over the land, and people's hearts will return to Him.

The sixth woe is for the destroyer, the one who hurts God's people. They will be judged. God promises to bring judgment to all nations of the earth.

TODAY'S GOD SHOT

God gives us righteousness, and His righteousness gives us peace. We don't have to become righteous on our own. In fact, we couldn't, even if we tried our hardest! But because Jesus paid for our sins, the Holy Spirit is poured out on us, making us righteous. He makes our hearts peaceful and helps us trust God forever. He's where the joy is!

ZOOM IN

Say to those with fearful hearts, "Be strong, and do not fear, for your God is coming to destroy your enemies. He is coming to save you."

Isaiah 35:4

Because of the people's sin and God's judgment over all the nations, Edom was turned into a smelly wasteland covered in weeds. Today, we read about how the captives are brought back into the land.

We read Isaiah's beautiful prophecy about the restoration of that wasteland. And it points to two times: the return of the Israelites to the promised land (which already happened in history) and the eventual return of all God's adopted kids (including us!) to the fully restored new earth. Today, the desert is a place that grows beautiful fruits and flowers and trees because of the streams that flow through it. But that's just the beginning! One day, the earth will be completely restored to the way God intended it to be. And there will be no more tears, no more evil, and no more fear. Just joy, forever!

The new earth isn't here yet, though—for the people of Israel or us. So back in our story, the Assyrians try to convince King Hezekiah's workers to mistrust him and doubt God. But King Hezekiah is wise and leads his people away from their enemies' lies.

TODAY'S GOD SHOT

God is a promise maker and a promise keeper. The rejoicing wilderness and blossoming desert Isaiah wrote about in chapter 35 thousands of years ago exists today! There are streams and flowers *already*, and the new earth isn't even here yet. *Everything* God promises will come true. He's where the joy is!

ISAIAH 37–39; PSALM 76

ZOOM IN

But have you not heard? I decided this long ago. Long ago I planned it, and now I am making it happen. I planned for you to crush fortified cities into heaps of rubble.

Isaiah 37:26

King Sennacherib of Assyria is threatening God's people, but Judah's King Hezekiah trusts God to rebuke the Assyrians for their threatening words. Isaiah tells Hezekiah's staff that God is in the process of taking King Sennacherib off the throne. In fact, Isaiah tells Hezekiah's men Sennacherib will die by a sword.

Even when the Assyrian army is surrounding Jerusalem, Hezekiah continues to trust in God. God sends the Angel of the LORD—who is likely Jesus—to wipe out the Assyrian army in one night. And King Sennacherib is killed by his own sons, by a sword, of course.

Hezekiah becomes sick and cries out to God for mercy. God gives him fifteen more years, keeping His covenant with King David. Psalm 76 praises God for saving Judah!

Hezekiah's heart starts to wander away from God, and when the king of Babylon comes to visit, Hezekiah shows off the places that hold all his expensive treasures. *Not wise, Hezekiah.* Isaiah knows this won't end well and warns that the Babylonians will steal everything.

~TODAY'S GOD SHOT~

God is sovereign over everything, including what happens with King Sennacherib: "Long ago I planned it, and now I am making it happen" (37:26). For a pagan king who is an enemy of God, God's sovereignty is bad news. For God's kids who are deeply loved and cherished, His sovereignty is a comfort! God's plans are to bring glory to Him and good to us. No matter what we do, we can't mess that up. He's sovereign, and He's where the joy is!

ZOOM IN

But as for you, Israel my servant, Jacob my chosen one, descended from Abraham my friend . . . I have chosen you and will not throw you away.

Isaiah 41:8–9

Today we read Isaiah's prophecy for the Israelites' return from exile. Israel returns to their land, and God comforts them. But Israel doesn't trust God like they should. They fall into worshipping the idols and false gods of Babylon, just like their ancestors in the wilderness worshipped the gods of Egypt. They're missing the entire point: YHWH rescued them!

Isaiah tells Israel to trust God and what He's doing; He's capable of more than they can possibly imagine. He also tells them to wait *with* God while they wait *on* God; learning to trust Him will give them strength.

Isaiah also points ahead to Jesus. In chapter 42, God provides a true servant to fulfill His mission and restore Israel to Himself. And in chapter 43, God tells His people not to be afraid. This doesn't mean things will be easy, but it does mean He'll be with them.

TODAY'S GOD SHOT

God chooses His people to fulfill His purposes. Even after all their sin and rebellion, God calls Israel His "servant," Jacob His "chosen one," and Abraham His "friend" (41:8). There are no perfect people for God to use. We're all full of sin from the start. But He still chooses us, makes us His, writes us into His story, and forgives our sins. He's where the joy is!

ISAIAH 44–48

I would not have told the people of Israel to seek me if I could not be found. I, the LORD, speak only what is true and declare only what is right.

Isaiah 45:19

God can make even His enemies bend to His will. King Cyrus of Persia doesn't follow God, but God will use him to set His people free from Babylon.

In chapter 48, God tells Israel that it was only and always Him who had rescued them. Then, He tells them about some new things He's going to do, teaching them about the Messiah long before the Messiah came!

God seeks out opportunities for forgiveness and mercy. This shows us who He is: a God who forgives sinners. God keeps His anger toward sin away from His kids, pays for our sins, and adopts us into His family!

TODAY'S GOD SHOT

God will be found when we seek Him! He says in 45:19, "I would not have told the people of Israel to seek me if I could not be found." Even on the days when we don't feel close to God, He's there. And if we continue learning about Him and looking for Him, we will find Him. He loves when we seek Him, and He loves to be known by His kids. He's where the joy is!

ZOOM IN

I know the greatness of the LORD—that our Lord is greater than any other god.

Psalm 135:5

Today's story might seem familiar, and it is! It's a different account of how Hezekiah responds to King Sennacherib's threats. We get some new information today: that God Himself didn't mislead Sennacherib, and that God is in charge of evil spirits. This may seem strange or scary at first, but it's actually comforting. If evil can go only as far as God allows it, then we know He's still in charge and holds the ultimate power. *What a relief!* God allows Sennacherib to be misled by others, using their rumors for His good purposes.

Just like Isaiah told Hezekiah, God wins the war for His people. His people didn't even do anything; the Angel of the LORD did it all! That's why Psalm 46:5 says, "God dwells in that city; it cannot be destroyed. From the very break of day, God will protect it."

TODAY'S GOD SHOT

God is pleased to adopt sinners into His family and call them sons and daughters. No other god does that! Our God's heart is for forgiveness and redemption. He created us, He protects us, He forgives us, and He redeems us. He's where the joy is!

ISAIAH 49–53

ZOOM IN

But it was the LORD's good plan to crush him and cause him grief. Yet when his life is made an offering for sin, he will have many descendants. He will enjoy a long life, and the LORD's good plan will prosper in his hands.

Isaiah 53:10

God chose Israel to be His special people, and through their line, He would send the Messiah. Through the Messiah, all nations on earth will be blessed. Through Jesus, God's love will reach those who hate Him, and He will turn enemies into family. But that's *someday*. And right now in our story, Israel feels forgotten. God reminds them that He hasn't forgotten His people; He's written their name on the palm of His hand.

We read some beautiful prophecies about Jesus today. He will help those who are hurting, speak kindly to those who are ignored, and suffer greatly for our sins.

TODAY'S GOD SHOT

God the Father, God the Son, and God the Spirit are three persons of equal value in the Trinity. In 53:10, we see that it was the Father's plan to crush the Son, so what does that mean? God the Father is the authority, and the Son and Spirit complete His plans. But because the Trinity works in unity, God the Son and God the Spirit were all on board with the Father's plan—they *share* a unified plan. This is a really hard idea to understand, and that's good! We wouldn't want God to be as easy to understand as we are. God's ways are so much bigger than our ways, and God's thoughts are so much bigger than our thoughts. He gave us Jesus, and He's where the joy is!

SEVEN-DAY ROUNDUP

ZOOM OUT

We spent most of the last seven days in Isaiah's prophecy. We learned about the coming troubles for Israel, but also the coming redemption. And we saw some beautiful pictures of our Messiah, written thousands of years before He was born.

APPLICATION

Some of the promises in the Bible were written for very specific people at a very specific time. So even though these promises teach us about who God is, they may not all apply to us. But did you know there are promises in the Bible that *do* apply to us today?

Read the following verses in your Bible and thank God for being a promise maker and a promise keeper!

Hebrews 13:5

Philippians 1:6

Luke 12:40

ISAIAH 54–58

ZOOM IN

I have seen what they do, but I will heal them anyway!

Isaiah 57:18

God promises a special blessing to the people of Israel: He'll enlarge His family through them, and the family will include people from all over the world! This may have seemed like a strange blessing at the time, because other nations were actually Israel's enemies. But God promises them that this is nothing to fear.

God has good plans for His people, ideas that our human brains couldn't even dream up! Every single one of His plans will come true. It will take time, but He'll eventually restore all of creation.

Isaiah reminds the Israelites that they still have a job to do: put away their idols and worship God alone.

TODAY'S GOD SHOT

God doesn't run away from sinners; He draws near to help them. God sees all our wickedness, but He helps us anyway. When you sin, you don't have to run and hide from God! (You couldn't hide from Him anyway, even if you tried.) He sees you, He knows you, and He loves you. He's where the joy is!

ZOOM IN

I will tell of the LORD's unfailing love. I will praise the LORD for all he has done. I will rejoice in his great goodness to Israel, which he has granted according to his mercy and love.

Isaiah 63:7

Isaiah writes down the people's confession of sin. They know they can't fix what's broken in themselves, but God does for them what they can't do for themselves. God gives them everything He requires of them, just like He does for us.

In the future glory of Israel, people from all nations will come to bless **Zion**—the Hebrew name for Jerusalem—and to bless God. This points forward to Jesus's first coming and the day when He'll come again.

As a part of God's plan of redemption, He's given Israel beauty and majesty greater than their own. God Himself will be the light, and it will all happen in His perfect timing.

~TODAY'S GOD SHOT~

God's goodness is so much bigger than His wrath. Remember, He should be—and is—angry with our sin. In today's reading, however, we read that there's a *day* of His wrath but a *year* of His favor. What a difference! Yes, sin has to be punished, but He's such a good and loving God. He's made a way for forgiveness so that we can be close to Him. He's where the joy is!

ISAIAH 64–66

I will perform a sign among them. And I will send those who survive to be messengers to the nations.

Isaiah 66:19

Isaiah compares Israel's false worship to dirty underwear. The Israelites worship God but also idols. They **fast**—or keep themselves from eating food—but only to show off how religious they are. Righteous things done for the wrong reasons aren't righteous at all.

When we sin, we might feel like God is hiding His face from us because we've hurt our relationship with Him. But we should always remember that He is infinitely loving and forgiving and wants us to come back to Him!

Isaiah finishes his writings with reminders of both God's judgment and salvation. Those who don't know Him will be punished, and those who do will be blessed. When God restores all of creation, we'll get to live with Him forever!

TODAY'S GOD SHOT

God extends His blessing to all nations. He sent His Son, and He'll send messengers all throughout the world to tell people about Him. And when they follow God, He doesn't make them feel like outsiders. He welcomes them right in as family. He's where the joy is!

ZOOM IN

Go back to Hezekiah, the leader of my people. Tell him, "This is what the LORD, the God of your ancestor David, says: I have heard your prayer and seen your tears. I will heal you."

2 Kings 20:5

Remember that everything we've read so far about the Israelites in Southern Judah being taken captive by Babylon has been prophecy—meaning it hasn't happened yet. There are a few kings still to go before we get there.

When we left off in Hezekiah's story, he had started wandering away from God. When he was sick, he begged God for more time. God gave him the time he asked for—fifteen more years, in fact—but he wastes it. In the final years of Hezekiah's life, he's foolish, prideful, and selfish. His son Manasseh becomes king, and he builds back the places for idol worship his father had gotten rid of. He does many evil things, and his people follow along. (But that's not his whole story. We'll find out more soon!) When Manasseh dies, Amon becomes king. He's awful, and his servants kill him. Amon's son Josiah is the next king.

~TODAY'S GOD SHOT~

God is the one who blesses us. The more God blessed Hezekiah with treasures and riches, the less Hezekiah thought He needed God. But God is the Giver of all the blessings! No matter what God has given us, and no matter whether we think we have a little or a lot, God has blessed us. And whether we have a little or a lot, God wants us to know that we always need Him the most. He's where the joy is!

2 CHRONICLES 32–33

Today we get another perspective of the final days of King Hezekiah. When Assyria attacks Judah, Hezekiah is still a wise and faithful king, serving God and the people of Judah. So—like you probably remember—God sent the Angel of the Lord to take out the Assyrian army for His people. Even though the world's advice is to believe in the power of *ourselves*, God's true wisdom has always been to believe in *His* power.

We also get more information about Manasseh today. He does a lot of evil things, reversing some of his father Hezekiah's best work. But God gets his attention by allowing him to be taken as a prisoner. When that happens, Manasseh pays attention, and God changes Manasseh's heart.

～ TODAY'S GOD SHOT ～

God gets Manasseh's attention, using some pretty extreme measures, because God wants to bless him! Manasseh's story with God is the opposite of his dad Hezekiah's. Hezekiah began following God early but wandered away from Him. Manasseh began by doing evil things but repented and turned to God. At the point in his life when Hezekiah turned his eyes on himself, Manasseh turned his eyes on God, finding out that He's where the joy is!

ZOOM IN

The LORD is good, a strong refuge when trouble comes. He is close to those who trust in him.

Nahum 1:7

Nahum is a prophet who writes to Nineveh, the capital of Assyria. The Assyrian army planned an attack on Jerusalem, which we read about yesterday, and Nineveh is where God sent Jonah to rebuke them. At the time, Nineveh repented of their sin and turned to God. But a hundred years later, they've fallen back into wickedness.

God judges Assyria for the way they've treated His people. He reminds everyone who He is: slow to anger and great in power. He also reminds them He will punish sin. Nahum explains that God's eyes aren't only on the wicked who will receive judgment, but also on the faithful who will receive blessing.

TODAY'S GOD SHOT

God is the defender of His people. God sees what wicked people do to His kids, and He takes care of it. He may not take care of injustice as quickly as we would like Him to, but He *will* take care of it—in the right time and the right way. God created righteousness and justice, and in His perfect timing, He'll make everything right. He's where the joy is!

2 KINGS 22–23; 2 CHRONICLES 34–35

ZOOM IN

But Josiah refused to listen to Neco, to whom God had indeed spoken, and he would not turn back. Instead, he disguised himself and led his army into battle on the plain of Megiddo.

2 Chronicles 35:22

Josiah becomes the king of Judah when he's only eight years old. He's a good king, and under his leadership, the temple is cleaned and repaired. During that process, his servant Hilkiah finds the book of the law, which is probably the book that we call Deuteronomy today.

God's people had been so far away from Him that they didn't even realize it was missing! Josiah reads the book and is heartbroken. He understands how far off track God's people have gone and how the leaders made it worse. Josiah spends the rest of his life leading the people back to God.

Josiah is the last good king Judah will have. After he dies, his son Jehoahaz takes his place, and he's wicked. When Jehoahaz dies, the Egyptian pharaoh appoints Eliakim (also called Jehoiakim—we'll get to that soon). He does whatever Egypt wants, which means he sends them a lot of money.

TODAY'S GOD SHOT

God can speak through anyone, including people who don't know or love Him. Josiah was killed when he didn't listen to Egypt's Pharaoh Neco. Josiah probably thought that because Neco didn't love God, everything he said would be a lie. But that's not always true. God can speak through anyone—or anything—He chooses. It's so important to ask God for wisdom so that we learn to listen for His voice, which always brings truth. He's where the truth is, and He's where the joy is!

SEVEN-DAY ROUNDUP

ZOOM OUT

We finished two more books this week, bringing our total so far to twenty-three! We followed the split kingdoms through a few more kings—some good and some bad. Some kings started strong but wandered away, and others were changed by God at the end of their lives. Did you notice what the people did during all these different reigns? They followed the lead of whoever was in charge. This is why God gave so many specific laws for kings and priests; people who have the power to influence others need to be held to higher expectations. So much depends on their example!

BIG PICTURE: ISAIAH

Isaiah's ministry of prophecy takes place over forty years. Through poems and vivid images, Isaiah teaches that God does all things for His own glory and that His people can find strength, hope, and joy only when they rest in His promises.

BIG PICTURE: NAHUM

Nahum the prophet speaks to Nineveh, but also future wicked nations. It's a short book with a heavy message: God will always judge evil.

WORDS TO REMEMBER

- Fast—not eating food in order to focus on God, get closer to Him, repent, or hear from Him
- Zion—the Hebrew name for Jerusalem

APPLICATION

Since the beginning, God has had a plan to reach all nations. And it's working! The good news of who God is, what He's doing, and how much He loves His kids made it all the way to *you*. On a world map or globe, find Bethlehem, where Jesus was born. Then find your city. Pray a prayer to thank God that—all the way from Bethlehem to you—the gospel made a way.

ZEPHANIAH 1–3

ZOOM IN

The remnant of the tribe of Judah will pasture there. . . . For the LORD their God will visit his people in kindness and restore their prosperity again.

Zephaniah 2:7

Zephaniah is the great-great-grandson of Judah's King Hezekiah. He opens his letter of prophecy with destruction: God will judge sin, both now and in the future. God will punish those who do outright wicked deeds and those who don't care about God's commands, who are too lazy to live His way.

But if the people repent, there's hope for forgiveness. He points to the small **remnant**—remaining group—of people who God will protect and preserve during and after His coming judgment.

There are two promises that Zephaniah, like most of the other prophets in the Bible, reminds the people of. First, God will save people from all the nations. And second, God is *with* His kids. He gets rid of their fears simply by being with them!

TODAY'S GOD SHOT

God makes a peaceful home for His kids, despite their sin and rebellion. In chapter 2, God promises the destruction of the enemy nations. He told the Israelites when they moved into the promised land to destroy those nations, but they didn't obey Him. And through the generations, they became wicked people who did evil and mocked God. So God will now clear those enemies out of the land for His own glory, and also for the good of His kids. They'll have a peaceful home. God's patience and goodness can be seen everywhere. He's where the joy is!

ZOOM IN

I knew you before I formed you in your mother's womb. Before you were born I set you apart and appointed you as my prophet to the nations.

Jeremiah 1:5

Jeremiah's ancestors were priests, but God calls him to be a prophet. God gives Jeremiah three assignments: pluck up and break down, destroy and overthrow, and build and plant. There will be destruction, but also restoration.

God tells Jeremiah to walk through Jerusalem and tell the story of His relationship with Israel out loud. God has loved them all along. And they used to love Him, but over time they've forgotten what He's done for them. They're thirsty, and He's the living water. But instead of turning to Him to drink, they try to solve their thirst themselves, and they fail miserably.

God begs the people to confess their sin and repent. He tells them His Spirit will live with them, not in the ark of the covenant in a room most of them can't get to. (By the way, at some point when their hearts were away from him, they lost the ark.) He wants to build them a home in Jerusalem where He dwells with them.

TODAY'S GOD SHOT

God not only created Jeremiah, but He *knew* him and set him apart before he was even born. Though these verses are specific to Jeremiah, the same beautiful truth applies to all of us. We see this idea throughout Scripture: God created each of us with a plan. He wants to use us for His glory and our joy. He's where the joy is!

JEREMIAH 4–6

ZOOM IN

Your wickedness has deprived you of these wonderful blessings. Your sin has robbed you of all these good things.

Jeremiah 5:25

Jeremiah pleads with Judah and Israel to repent. God doesn't want their fake apologies or their showy religious talk; He wants their hearts.

God gives Jeremiah some troubling visions and messages: the destruction of Jerusalem, the undoing of creation, and the hard-heartedness of God's people. All this is heartbreaking to Jeremiah, and God reminds him that it's because of their sin. Sin is a thief that steals everything good.

TODAY'S GOD SHOT

God is patient and persistent. He chose Jeremiah to beg His people to repent, knowing that they wouldn't. And He also sent other prophets before and after Jeremiah with the same message. God knew the whole time that His people wouldn't repent and that they'd be sent into exile. And He also knew the day was coming when Jesus would take the punishment for all the sins of His people: past, present, and future. He's where the joy is!

ZOOM IN

But those who wish to boast should boast in this alone: that they truly know me and understand that I am the LORD who demonstrates unfailing love and who brings justice and righteousness to the earth, and that I delight in these things.

Jeremiah 9:24

Jeremiah stands outside the temple entrance and prophesies to the people of Judah. They've come to worship God inside the temple, but *outside* they make sacrifices to idols and false gods. *Can you imagine?* They pretend He can't see them there, and it seems like they're not really worshipping God anyway; they're worshipping the temple building. God rebukes them.

The people are breaking nearly every commandment: stealing, murdering, committing adultery, lying, and worshipping other gods. God calls them to change the way they treat others and to change the way they treat Him. He promises that if they do, He'll bless them. But if they don't, He'll cast them out.

Like you have probably guessed, they don't change their hearts. Jeremiah probably knew, and of course God knew. Jeremiah is heartbroken over Israel's sins and his own.

TODAY'S GOD SHOT

God leads with love. Even when we read Bible passages like today's three chapters—where there is a lot of judgment—His love is still there. In 9:24, God says He "demonstrates unfailing love" and "brings justice and righteousness to the earth." Not only does He bring these things, He says He *delights* in these things! Love, justice, and righteousness bring joy, so of course He's where the joy is!

JEREMIAH 10–13

ZOOM IN

I know, LORD, that our lives are not our own. We are not able to plan our own course.

Jeremiah 10:23

Jeremiah tells the people that everything they've made idols from—trees, gold, silver—is material God made. Jeremiah tries one last time to pray on behalf of Jerusalem. He prays as if he's speaking for the whole city and their leaders, but God knows the whole city isn't turning toward Him.

Jeremiah tells God he's suffering; his neighbors are threatening his life because they don't like his prophecies. He says it seems like the wicked are just getting richer and more powerful. God reminds Jeremiah that He never promised life would be easy; He promised something better: He promised to *be with* Jeremiah.

TODAY'S GOD SHOT

God is with you every day, in every moment. He's with you at the destination, and He's with you on the way there. And if you listen to Him, He'll help you and guide you. He'll give you directions and tell you which way to go. He's with you. Always. And He's where the joy is!

ZOOM IN

Do not do your work on the Sabbath, but make it a holy day.

Jeremiah 17:22

As part of the judgment for their sin, Judah is in the middle of a drought. They cry to God for help, but they don't repent. They're not sorry; they just want water. (They might not have even prayed the prayer for help themselves; Jeremiah probably did it *for* them again.)

When God answers the prayer with no, it may seem like He's being mean. But zoom out for a moment. Since God brought His people out of slavery in Egypt, He has provided for them, stayed with them, given them a home, and loved them. In return, they've disobeyed Him, forgotten Him, worshipped other gods, and done evil things—even sacrificing their own children to idols. God may be harsh with them, but His harshness is always just and righteous.

Jeremiah tells God he feels all alone again, and God reminds Jeremiah that He's with him. God will protect and preserve a remnant of people who will know and love God.

TODAY'S GOD SHOT

God calls His people to rest, which means obeying this call by resting is one way to worship Him! God doesn't demand we always work harder; He commands we *rest*. When we make ourselves quiet and still, we can focus our attention on Him. He wants us to remember that He's where the joy is!

JEREMIAH 18–22

ZOOM IN

This is what the LORD says: Be fair-minded and just. Do what is right! Help those who have been robbed; rescue them from their oppressors. Quit your evil deeds! Do not mistreat foreigners, orphans, and widows. Stop murdering the innocent!

Jeremiah 22:3

God sends Jeremiah to see a potter making jars out of clay. When one jar starts to fall apart, the potter shapes it into something new. It's the same clay, but with a different outcome. God tells Jeremiah that He is the potter and His people are the clay. He is heartbroken that His people have forgotten Him.

Even though Jeremiah has begged God for mercy on their behalf, the people have been cruel to Jeremiah. He understands why God has promised hunger, war, and disease.

God calls the people of Israel His people, but being a descendant of Abraham's doesn't make a person God's kid. God's family is made up of people who follow Him from every nation. God will preserve the few in Judah who love Him—the remnant—and judge those who don't.

TODAY'S GOD SHOT

God says to know Him is to do what He says. Like the people of Israel, if we choose to steal, lie, cheat, and kill, it looks like we don't know God at all. When we really know and love God, He changes the way we live. When we obey Him, we remember that He's where the joy is!

SEVEN-DAY ROUNDUP

ZOOM OUT

This week we wrapped up our twenty-fourth book! In the short book of Zephaniah and the first twenty-two chapters of Jeremiah, we read the prophecy of God's judgment of Judah. These are hard passages to read, but remember that God has been patient with His people for generations and has sent so many warnings about their sin. And even though most of Judah is disobeying God, we also saw the beautiful promise that He'll preserve a remnant of them to keep His covenant and bless the whole world.

BIG PICTURE: ZEPHANIAH

The people of Southern Judah continue to break their covenant with God. Zephaniah urges them to repent because the day of the LORD is coming. There will be judgment for those who rebel against God and blessing for those who follow Him.

WORD TO REMEMBER

- Remnant—remaining group, leftover

APPLICATION

It's easy to get frustrated or even angry with the Israelites for their sin and refusal to repent. But what about our own? When it comes to sin, we should be angry at our own sins and heartbroken over others' sins. Take some time to pray to God today, confessing your sin to Him. Ask Him to show you when you sin and to always keep your heart soft toward Him.

JEREMIAH 23–25

ZOOM IN

This will be his name: "The LORD Is Our Righteousness." In that day Judah will be saved, and Israel will live in safety.

Jeremiah 23:6

God promises to raise up a King from the line of David. When that King reigns on earth, His people will have so many new things to praise Him for. This is a prophecy that points to Jesus!

In the meantime, God is judging Judah. The people of Judah are pretending to speak for God, but they worship false gods and oppress the poor. The people of Southern Judah and Jerusalem are held to an even higher standard than the people of Northern Israel. Jerusalem has the temple, all of the scrolls of God's Word so far, and the Levites to guide them. But they still disobey.

Jeremiah reminds the people that God has sent many messengers warning them of the coming judgment. He tells them that if they don't repent, Babylon's King Nebuchadnezzar (let's call him King Nebby) is going to make their lives miserable for seventy years. Jeremiah begs the people to turn back to God.

TODAY'S GOD SHOT

God promised to raise up a new king named "The LORD Is Our Righteousness" (23:6). This is a giant, glorious promise. The people of Judah weren't righteous on their own, and neither are we. We need someone else to be righteous for us. This prophecy points to Jesus! Jesus is the LORD, and He gives us His righteousness. Before He was born, God told His people about Jesus, our perfect King. He gives us His righteousness, and He's where the joy is!

ZOOM IN

These men have done terrible things among my people. . . . I am a witness to this.

Jeremiah 29:23

God sends Jeremiah to prophesy over people going into the temple. Later, Jeremiah meets with the kings of five other nations and prophesies to them. And he also goes to speak to the false prophet Hananiah. In some of his encounters, Jeremiah is accused of things that aren't true. Ugh!

Jeremiah tells God's people they'll be in exile for seventy years, so they should make the most of their time. They should build houses, plant gardens, raise families, and bless the people who took them captive. He reminds them that God has a good plan to bring them back and restore everything they'd lost. The exiles are the remnant, the people God will preserve. The ones who don't listen to God's warnings won't even make it that far.

~TODAY'S GOD SHOT~

God sees and God knows. Every time Jeremiah was the target of a false accusation, God protected him. All Jeremiah had to do was stand firm and trust in the place God put Him. God sees everything and knows the truth, and He's where the joy is!

JEREMIAH 30–31

ZOOM IN

They will come home and sing songs of joy on the heights of Jerusalem. They will be radiant because of the Lord's good gifts.

Jeremiah 31:12

God reminds His people of His plan for Israel and Judah. After His judgment, He will heal and restore them, bring them back into the land, and bless them. It may sound cruel that He's going to bring judgment first, but without it, He knows that they won't turn to Him. He wounds them so that He can heal them. The hard times to come will shape them into people who are more like God.

God promises to be with them in their exile, to bring them back to their land, and to raise up a new King—Jesus—who will bring a new covenant.

TODAY'S GOD SHOT

God gives His kids every good gift, and they are radiant because of Him! He is the best gift, and everything else reminds us of how good He is. We can always know that we have everything we need because we have Him. And we can be radiant because of Him. He's where the joy is!

ZOOM IN

In that day Judah will be saved, and Jerusalem will live in safety. And this will be its name: "The LORD Is Our Righteousness."

Jeremiah 33:16

Jeremiah is in prison because Judah's King Zedekiah didn't like his prophecies. While he's in prison, even though he has doubts and questions, he listens to God and shows his faith. He buys some land that he knows he won't get to use until the exile is over. This is a huge act of faith, because it means he believes God's promise that the exile will end. The Babylonian army is already beginning to take over parts of Judah—including this land—but God reminds him who He is.

God says He'll gather the faithful back in the land and restore their fortunes. He's sovereign over land and wars, and He's also sovereign over hearts. God reminds Jeremiah that someday Jerusalem will have a righteous King and priests. The King is Jesus, and according to 1 Peter 2:5–9, *all* believers are priests (priests are people who can go directly to God without someone else mediating). If you follow Jesus, that's *you* too! You've been made righteous and you've been made a priest because of what Jesus did on your behalf.

TODAY'S GOD SHOT

God does all the work of making us righteous. There's nothing we can do or give that will make us more holy in God's eyes. And that's good news. We don't have to live up to righteousness; we couldn't anyway. God does it for us. He's where the joy is!

JEREMIAH 35–37

ZOOM IN

Get another scroll, and write everything again just as you did on the scroll King Jehoiakim burned.

Jeremiah 36:28

God tells Jeremiah to write down everything He's said. That's twenty-two years' worth of prophecy so far! Jeremiah sends his scribe Baruch on a mission to read the scroll to the people. The officials want to hear it themselves, so they tell Baruch to come read to them. They believe the prophecies and tell Baruch and Jeremiah to hide because they know the king will be angry.

They are right. When Judah's King Jehoiakim hears the scroll's words, he tears it into pieces and burns it. He wrongly thinks that by destroying the words, he can stop the prophecy. God protects Baruch and Jeremiah and tells Jeremiah to start writing all over again.

The Babylonian army is continuing their attack on Judah, and Jeremiah gets mixed up in the mess. He goes to jail again, where he continues to obey God and deliver messages to the king.

TODAY'S GOD SHOT

God wants to be known, so He gives us His Word. He repeated the same words to His people again and again, and He had Jeremiah write it all down so they could hear it again. And after the scroll was destroyed, God even told Jeremiah to write it all down again. In Mark 13:31, Jesus says, "Heaven and earth will disappear, but my words will never disappear." Almost everything you see will one day be gone, but God and His Word will last forever. He's eternal, and He's where the joy is!

ZOOM IN

Help us, O God of our salvation! Help us for the glory of your name. Save us and forgive our sins for the honor of your name.

Psalm 79:9

Jeremiah tells the people of Judah to surrender to Babylon and submit to God's judgment. So the people think Jeremiah's message means he's on Babylon's side. The leaders want Jeremiah to stop spreading his message, so they throw him in a deep, empty well. But God promises to deliver Jeremiah.

Ebed-melech, a man from Ethiopia who lives in the king's house, asks for permission to save Jeremiah. After he rescues him, the king meets with Jeremiah. The king is scared of Jeremiah's prophecy coming true. Even after all Jeremiah has endured, his message does not change; he tells the king to surrender to Babylon.

Just like God said it would happen, one and a half years after Babylon began their attack on Judah, Jerusalem falls to Babylon. The Babylonians kill many of the people and take the remainder of them into exile.

Psalms 74 and 79 remind us of the consequences of sin. The psalmist begs God to help them because He is merciful and good.

TODAY'S GOD SHOT

God is our Deliverer. When the psalmist prays in Psalm 79, "Save us and forgive our sins for the honor of your name," the answer is yes! God sent Jesus to atone for the sins of God's people—past, present, and future. Jesus's death covers the sins of Asaph the psalmist and the sins of the remnant of Judah. And His death covers our sins too. He is our Deliverer, and He's where the joy is!

2 KINGS 24–25; 2 CHRONICLES 36

ZOOM IN

He supplied Jehoiachin with new clothes to replace his prison garb and allowed him to dine in the king's presence for the rest of his life.

2 Kings 25:29

Today we read about the final five kings of Judah. It's been a little while since we read about this, so here's a refresher: After Josiah died, his wicked son Jehoahaz took his place. When he is killed, the Egyptian pharaoh appoints Eliakim and renames him Jehoiakim. The pharaoh demands that Judah pays Egypt money in exchange for protection. Then Babylon defeats both Judah and Egypt, and they take Jehoiakim captive.

After Jehoia*kim*, his son takes the throne—Jehoia*chin*. King Chin is only on the throne for three months before Babylon surrounds Jerusalem. He surrenders himself to Babylon and they take him prisoner. Babylon appoints a new king for Judah: Mattaniah, who the Babylonians rename Zedekiah. King Zed doesn't listen to Jeremiah's final warnings, and he dies a long, painful death. Jerusalem falls to Babylon and is destroyed, but God already has a plan for restoration.

TODAY'S GOD SHOT

God frees us. After King Nebby died, King Evil-merodach treated King Chin in a way that shows us a beautiful picture of who God is and what He does for His kids. He brings us out of captivity, speaks kindly to us, gives us new clothes, and saves us a special seat at His table. Our sin makes us prisoners, and God sets us free. He's where the joy is!

SEVEN-DAY ROUNDUP

ZOOM OUT

We're twenty-six books deep into this trip through Scripture! This week we saw the sad event that God warned His people about come true: Jerusalem was destroyed, and the people were taken captive. The consequences of sin are heartbreaking, but even before the people were captured, God already had a plan to restore them.

BIG PICTURE: 2 KINGS

Only God is to be worshipped, but Israel disobeys this command repeatedly. Despite Israel's sin, there is hope for the nation because God keeps His promises. He's chosen David's family line to be a royal line that will bless the whole world.

BIG PICTURE: 2 CHRONICLES

In the second book of the Chronicles highlight reel of God's covenant with Israel, we see the covenant fulfilled through the building of the temple. We see that even when God's people were unfaithful to Him, He blessed them.

APPLICATION

Did you notice the name changing that happened with two of Judah's final kings? The Egyptians gave Eliakim the name Jehoiakim. And the Babylonians changed Mattaniah's name to Zedekiah. This was the conquering armies' way of letting the kings know who was in charge.

When God saves us, He has new names for us too. And His names for us don't just remind us who's in charge; they remind us how much He loves us. Read these verses to learn some of the names that God calls His kids.

John 1:12
Romans 8:17
Ephesians 1:4

HABAKKUK 1–3

ZOOM IN

Even though the fig trees have no blossoms, and there are no grapes on the vines; even though the olive crop fails, and the fields lie empty and barren; even though the flocks die in the fields, and the cattle barns are empty, yet I will rejoice in the LORD! I will be joyful in the God of my salvation! The Sovereign LORD is my strength!

Habakkuk 3:17–19

Before the fall of Jerusalem and the exile to Babylon, Habakkuk was a prophet to Southern Judah. Usually, we think of prophets as talking to people with messages from God, but Habakkuk has the reverse role: He talks to *God* for the *people*. Habakkuk tells God that the people of Southern Judah aren't being treated fairly.

God doesn't give Habakkuk everything he asks for, so Habakkuk thinks God isn't listening to him. Of course, that isn't true. God is listening, and His answer is no. God corrects Habakkuk.

God wants His people to live by faith, remembering Him and His promises even when Babylon takes over. Habakkuk commits to trusting God and His timing, even when times are hard.

TODAY'S GOD SHOT

God gives strength and joy. Habakkuk 3:17–19 is a beautiful example of faith when nothing is working out. Even if the crops flourished and the livestock multiplied, those things alone wouldn't build faith. Wealth isn't the source of our strength, and abundance isn't the source of our joy. God is. He's with us even when nothing goes the way we want it to. He's where the joy is!

JEREMIAH 41–45

ZOOM IN

The people refused to obey the voice of the LORD and went to Egypt, going as far as the city of Tahpanhes.

Jeremiah 43:7

The people of Southern Judah are terrified. Everything around them is chaos and destruction. They ask Jeremiah if they can flee to Egypt in hopes of finding protection there. They promise to do whatever God says, so Jeremiah spends ten days in prayer. He then tells the people, "Don't go to Egypt. If you trust in God and do what He says, He'll protect you and provide for you right here." But they don't believe him. And in fact, they accuse him of trying to trick them. They kidnap Jeremiah and take him with them . . . to Egypt. Can you imagine how devastating this is for him?

Jeremiah tells them that because of their sin, they will be destroyed. The people don't believe him, and Jeremiah tells them the scariest thing he's ever said: *Go ahead and keep sinning. God is done with you.* Wow.

~TODAY'S GOD SHOT~

God is slow to anger, merciful, and gracious. And He also must punish sin. God had been so patient with His people, and the time had come for His punishment of their sin. In His wrath, God allowed the people of Judah to become wrapped up in their sin. Today, because we have the blessing of the Holy Spirit in our lives, God's kids don't have to fear His wrath. And we don't have to fear Him leaving us. He promises that the Spirit will dwell in us forever, convict us of our sin, and lead us to repentance. What a gift! The next time the Spirit convicts you of your sin, *give thanks to God*, because it brings you back to the heart of our Father. He's where the joy is!

JEREMIAH 46–48

ZOOM-IN

"As surely as I live," says the King, whose name is the LORD of Heaven's Armies, "one is coming against Egypt who is as tall as Mount Tabor, or as Mount Carmel by the sea!"

Jeremiah 46:18

Jeremiah has given Israel and Judah messages from God, and he also gives the surrounding nations messages from God, including the Egyptians, the Philistines, and the Moabites. Jeremiah warns each of them that trouble is coming, but he has a special note for the Moabites. Remember Ruth? She was a Moabite who trusted God, so that means King David and Jesus both come from a Moabite line. God says He'll show them mercy and grace when He restores their fortunes.

God also talks again to the Israelites who disobeyed Him and are hiding in Egypt. He's gentle with them and reminds them not to be afraid, because He's with them.

TODAY'S GOD SHOT

God is sovereign over all people and all nations. We've seen God send His prophets to talk to enemy nations, and it's because He's a different kind of God from all the others. He created everything and everyone, and everyone will one day answer to Him, whether they worship Him now or not. He's the God over all gods, and He's your Father who loves you. He's where the joy is!

ZOOM IN

"In those days," says the LORD, "no sin will be found in Israel or in Judah, for I will forgive the remnant I preserve."

Jeremiah 50:20

God judges the nations around Israel and Judah for how they've treated His people. But He'll also bring restoration, and He will personally take care of their orphans and widows.

You might be wondering—like those who heard the prophecy at the time did (49:12)—whether those who didn't treat God's people badly deserve His destruction. God says that if the remnant of His people who have always loved Him are suffering in exile, then His enemies are definitely not off the hook. This seems harsh, but sin is harsh, and its consequences impact far more people than just the sinner. It also points us forward to Jesus. Jesus, the only one who never sinned at all, suffered because of our sin.

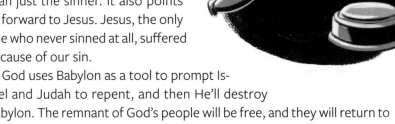

God uses Babylon as a tool to prompt Israel and Judah to repent, and then He'll destroy Babylon. The remnant of God's people will be free, and they will return to Zion—Jerusalem—with hearts that love God and remember and rejoice in His covenant!

TODAY'S GOD SHOT

God forgives our sin. In 50:20, God says, "No sin will be found in Israel or in Judah," but that doesn't mean that the people *won't* sin. It means that God will have forgiven them! When God looks at His kids, He doesn't point to our sin. He points to our righteousness—which is Jesus's righteousness. Jesus's death paid for our sins, so we get His righteousness. He's where the forgiveness is, and He's where the joy is!

JEREMIAH 51–52

ZOOM IN

But the God of Israel is no idol! He is the Creator of everything that exists, including his people, his own special possession. The LORD of Heaven's Armies is his name!

Jeremiah 51:19

While they're in Babylon, God reminds His remnant that He is with them and that He will bring them back to their land. Babylon will already be defeated, and all God's people will have to do is pack up and leave!

In chapter 52, we zoom out and get a big-picture view of the story we've been reading, starting with Jerusalem being overthrown. The temple is robbed of its valuable items, then destroyed. Judah's kings and leaders are killed, and the people are exiled. But in the middle of all of this, there are stories of redemption, freedom, and hope. God provides and protects.

TODAY'S GOD SHOT

God gives Himself to His people. What an amazing gift! Not only did He create everything, but He calls His people His "own special possession" (51:19). And to His own special people, He gives Himself. It's the best gift we will ever receive, because nothing is better than Him. He's where the joy is!

LAMENTATIONS 1–2

ZOOM IN

Rise during the night and cry out. Pour out your hearts like water to the Lord.

Lamentations 2:19

The poems in Lamentations *lament* (remember that word?) everything that's happened since the people refused to listen to Jeremiah's warnings to repent.

Jerusalem has been emptied, and her enemies rule over the people who used to live there. God told them all along to remember their covenant with Him. But they forgot what God did for them in the past, and they forgot what He's promised He'll do for them in the future. They've chosen sin instead. When they mourn, they're not mourning their sin. They're mourning days that were easier for them, even though those days were full of sin. Those two types of mourning are *very* different. One focuses on our relationship with God, and one focuses on our circumstances.

But then the people of Judah begin to understand their role in the destruction: "My heart is broken and my soul despairs, for I have rebelled against you" (1:20). The consequences of sin are heartbreaking. Even the prophets don't get visions or messages from God. But they remember that God has a plan and know that He won't stay silent forever.

TODAY'S GOD SHOT

God can handle our feelings, even when they're uncomfortable. When we are frustrated or angry or scared or lonely, God invites us to share our feelings with Him: "Pour out your hearts like water to the Lord" (2:19). He wants us to be honest with Him about how we're feeling; He already knows, anyway! He will meet you in your uncomfortable feelings and bring you comfort. He's where the peace is, and He's where the joy is!

LAMENTATIONS 3–5

Though he brings grief, he also shows compassion because of the greatness of his unfailing love.

Lamentations 3:32

Even in the midst of all the destruction and evil, God is faithful. The people's trials are a result of their sins, and God warned them for years that the trials would come if they didn't repent. The author reminds the people that any punishment for sin is justified: "Then why should we, mere humans, complain when we are punished for our sins?" (3:39). He is humble and leads the people back toward God.

God's people finally repent. His discipline brought them back to Him, like He knew it would. They beg God for forgiveness and praise Him in the middle of their trials.

TODAY'S GOD SHOT

God doesn't prefer grief for His kids, but there are times when He does bring it. He knows that grief is sometimes the only tool that will bring us to obedience, and obeying Him is the best way to live. Even when He disciplines us, it's because He loves us. Even when it's hard to see, He's where the joy is!

SEVEN-DAY ROUNDUP

ZOOM OUT

In the past seven days, we finished three books, bringing our total to twenty-nine! We saw God's discipline in full effect, but His people were never without hope, because He stood ready to offer His forgiveness.

BIG PICTURE: HABAKKUK

Habakkuk is a prophet who speaks to God on behalf of the people of Southern Judah. Through their conversations, we see first that God is in control. Second, God will punish all sin: both His people's *and* His enemies'. And third, God's plan for His people is that we live by faith.

BIG PICTURE: JEREMIAH

Over forty years and the reigns of five different kings, Jeremiah speaks a powerful message from God to His people. Through his prophecies, he reminds the people, who have rebelled against God, that sin must be punished. But God will restore a remnant through which He'll bless the entire world.

BIG PICTURE: LAMENTATIONS

Lamentations is a book of poetry grieving Jerusalem's destruction and the Babylonian exile. It teaches us that God's mercy and forgiveness give hope.

APPLICATION

Judgment and discipline are the consequences of people's sin, not the wishes of a harsh God. At the end of Lamentations, God's people finally understood, and they repented. And still, God gave them reminders of His great love for them throughout their trials. If you need help remembering some from this week, go back and read Jeremiah 50:20 and Lamentations 3:21–23.

Sometimes our trials are the consequences of our own sin, and sometimes they're the result of living in a sinful world. What doesn't change is God's great love for us. The next time you go through a trial, reread these verses. Ask God to remind you of His great love for you.

EZEKIEL 1–4

ZOOM IN

I have made your forehead as hard as the hardest rock! So don't be afraid of them or fear their angry looks, even though they are rebels.

Ezekiel 3:9

We went back in time a little bit today to seven years before Jerusalem fell. Ezekiel is a prophet from the line of priests, but he's exiled to Babylon. God gives him visions, including one of a windstorm, creatures with four wings and four faces, and a man on a throne.

God made Ezekiel and gave him everything he needs to speak to the people of Israel. God has Ezekiel do strange things like eat a scroll. God even temporarily takes his voice away, making him mute. For over four hundred days (which is longer than our reading plan), God has Ezekiel lie down and look at a model of Jerusalem being surrounded by the enemy. Every day, he's allowed to drink just enough water to survive, and eats only a small amount of food that was cooked over animal poop. Sounds pretty humbling, right? It is. It's a physical picture of the spiritual thirst and starvation the exiles go through. More than that, it's a picture of what Jesus did for all of us, humbling Himself to come to save us.

TODAY'S GOD SHOT

God is intentional about how He makes every single person. In 3:9, He tells Ezekiel that He made him stubborn on purpose. God knew Ezekiel wouldn't get scared or discouraged delivering God's message to stubborn people, because he was just as stubborn. Whatever personality traits God gave you, it was on purpose. And if you ask Him, He'll show you how to use those traits for His glory! He's where the joy is!

ZOOM IN

Then when they are exiled among the nations, they will remember me. They will recognize how hurt I am by their unfaithful hearts and lustful eyes that long for their idols.

Ezekiel 6:9

In the timeline of our story, the destruction of Jerusalem is still a few years away. There's been one round of exile, but there are still two more rounds to go. God tells Ezekiel to shave his head and divide his hair into three parts. Each part represents the three ways God will respond to the people's rebellion against Him: violence, disease, and hunger. The punishments relate to their sins.

The remnant will be punished as well, but some will remember God. You see, they weren't innocent; they were sinners too. God doesn't preserve them as a remnant because they're perfect. Instead, God in His mercy redirects their sinful hearts toward Him. And He saves them and uses them to fulfill His covenant and bless the whole world.

God plans to remove His presence from the temple, and Ezekiel has a vision of Jerusalem's leaders worshipping idols outside and inside of the temple.

TODAY'S GOD SHOT

God's heart is broken by sin. In 6:9, He says the people will recognize how hurt He is by their unfaithful hearts. Because of our sin, which breaks God's heart, we deserve God's wrath. But Romans 6:23 says, "For the wages of sin is death, but the free gift of God is eternal life through Christ Jesus our Lord." Because God the Son came to take God's wrath for us, we get eternal life! He's where the joy is!

EZEKIEL 9–12

ZOOM IN

As I watched, the cherubim flew with their wheels to the east gate of the LORD's Temple. And the glory of the God of Israel hovered above them.

Ezekiel 10:19

Ezekiel's vision of Jerusalem continues with God calling for death. Like we've seen before, even when it's hard for us to read, it's right for sin to be punished. And like we've seen before, God is still merciful. He tells one of seven angels to mark with a symbol those who are grieved by the evil of Jerusalem. God will spare them. Does this remind you of anything? In Exodus, God's people marked the doorways of their homes with lamb's blood, and the Angel of the LORD passed over, leaving those inside unharmed.

God's presence leaves the temple, rests on a throne carried by cherubim (heavenly guardians of holy places), and moves east to Babylon. God tells His remnant that the temple itself isn't their **sanctuary**. *He* is their sanctuary.

～TODAY'S GOD SHOT～

God is with His people, even in exile. In 10:19, the glory of the Lord leaves the temple and goes with His people *into* exile. This is a moment full of pain over the way God's people have broken His heart, and grief over the loss of the land He gave them. But even in all this sadness, He doesn't remove Himself from His people. Even in exile, He's there. And He's where the joy is!

ZOOM IN

You have discouraged the righteous with your lies, but I didn't want them to be sad. And you have encouraged the wicked by promising them life, even though they continue in their sins. Because of all this, you will no longer talk of seeing visions that you never saw, nor will you make predictions. For I will rescue my people from your grasp. Then you will know that I am the LORD.

Ezekiel 13:22–23

God gives Ezekiel a special message for false prophets. These people make up stories and say God gave them a vision. They lie and say they have a message from God. God says these messages aren't from Him, and that they'll be punished for their lies.

Some of the leaders—who haven't been worshipping God—come to Ezekiel for advice from God. God knows the sin in their hearts, but He welcomes them to ask for His guidance. God lets them know that if they turn to Him, He'll show them the way.

God is sending judgment, and things are going to get really bad. But He will preserve the remnant He has chosen to be merciful to, and they will be a testament to God's goodness. God will make them righteous.

~TODAY'S GOD SHOT~

God wants His people to be at peace and to walk in the truth. In 13:22, He promises punishment for the false prophets who lied and led His people astray. God cares deeply about peace and truth, so He'll punish those who lead His people away from them. He wants us to walk in peace every day as His kids, who know and love the truth of who their Father is. He's where the joy is!

EZEKIEL 16–17

ZOOM IN

Then another message came to me from the LORD: "Son of man, confront Jerusalem with her detestable sins."

Ezekiel 16:1–2

God compares Israel to an abandoned orphan who is unloved and about to die. But then someone—*the King of the universe*—rescues her and takes care of her and nurses her back to health. Eventually, she loves the King's gifts more than the King Himself. She trusts in her own beauty to get whatever she wants, and she even cheats on the King. The more she forgets who she is and who the King is, the more of a mess her life becomes. God will judge her sins, which come from her pride and arrogance.

After the metaphor of Israel as an ungrateful and unfaithful woman, God shares another image with Ezekiel. God will take a branch and plant it on Israel's tallest mountain. It will grow into a magnificent cedar tree that will give fruit and shade and be a home for birds of every kind. This points forward to Jesus and His coming kingdom!

TODAY'S GOD SHOT

God expanded His covenant even after His people had turned away from Him. The people broke the covenant that depended on their participation in it, so God made a covenant that would last *forever*. All along, He had a plan to atone for their sins, and all along, He's been giving them hints about it. He will bring His people back to Himself. God's love is so big that it's breathtaking. He's where the joy is!

ZOOM IN

You will know that I am the LORD, O people of Israel, when I have honored my name by treating you mercifully in spite of your wickedness.

Ezekiel 20:44

God tells His people that they are responsible for their own sin, not someone else's. At that time, they believed children were punished for their parents' sins, but God tells them that's not true. While our sin always impacts more than just ourselves, and while other people's sins often impact us, we're each responsible for only our own sinful choices.

God reminds the people that it's never too late to turn to Him and have their sins forgiven. But if they don't repent, their sin requires punishment. The people refuse to repent, and they even think God is being unfair.

Ezekiel laments over Judah's demise. Then God reminds the leaders of Israel about everything He's done for them, and what the people have done in return. But He reminds them that in the end, He'll restore everything.

TODAY'S GOD SHOT

God the Son kept every law perfectly, and He paid the debt that we owe for our sin. As Ezekiel 20:44 says, when we're treated with mercy in spite of our sin, God honors His own name! Because of God the Father's great mercy and God the Son's ultimate sacrifice, we're adopted into their eternal family. He's where the joy is!

EZEKIEL 21–22

ZOOM IN

I will heap on their heads the full penalty for all their sins. I, the Sovereign LORD, have spoken!

Ezekiel 22:31

God gives Ezekiel a harsh message today: He'll take out His sword against the people, both righteous and wicked. Did this make you stop and ask why? Why would God punish the righteous? He answers this question at the end of today's reading.

God has given His people time to repent, but instead of turning toward Him, they sin even more. They've murdered, worshipped idols, hated their parents, taken advantage of foreigners and the vulnerable, thrown out the Sabbath, lied, and cheated. They've broken all the commandments. Even the pagan nations around Israel and Judah think the people are wicked.

So why will God punish the wicked *and* the righteous? Because there aren't any truly righteous people. There's not even one.

TODAY'S GOD SHOT

God hates sin. He loves His kids, and sin hurts His kids, so He must hate sin. Because Jesus took the full wrath of God's hatred of sin, we can be righteous in God's eyes. If we are God's kids, sin still hurts us, but it doesn't stop us from being God's kids. God made a way for us to be His forever. He's where the joy is!

SEVEN-DAY ROUNDUP

ZOOM OUT

We spent seven days in the book of Ezekiel, and we'll spend nine more there before we finish it. It's a long book, and it can be difficult to read and understand. One of the themes that comes up a lot is knowing who the Lord is. If you get stuck or frustrated in Ezekiel, pray that God will use these hard passages to show you who He is. Keep going; you're learning more about Him every day!

WORD TO REMEMBER

- Sanctuary—a place of safety

APPLICATION

God wants us to know the truth about who He is and how much He loves us. Write down at least three adjectives—descriptive words—that tell a little bit about who God is. If you need help, go back and reread some of our daily God Shots. Keep adding to your list as you learn more about who God is, what He's doing, and how much He loves His kids. Remember that even in the dark and challenging places, He's where the joy is!

EZEKIEL 23–24

ZOOM IN

The time has come, and I won't hold back. I will not change my mind, and I will have no pity on you. You will be judged on the basis of all your wicked actions, says the Sovereign LORD.

Ezekiel 24:14

The people of Samaria (Northern Israel's capital) and Jerusalem (Southern Judah's capital) are compared to cheating wives. They start their sin by wanting something that's not theirs, and pretty soon, their sin grows until they use their bodies in sinful ways that God hates. God begs them to repent, but—even though their sin is hurting them—they don't.

God tells Ezekiel that his wife will die, and he's only allowed to mourn her in private. The other exiles notice, and Ezekiel lets them know about Jerusalem's tragedy. The people shouldn't be allowed to mourn because their sin is what caused this.

God tells Ezekiel that when Jerusalem finally falls, a messenger will confirm it, and Ezekiel will get his voice back. Did you catch that? If Ezekiel hasn't been able to talk this whole time, how did he prophesy to the people? We'll come back to this in a few days, so stay tuned!

TODAY'S GOD SHOT

God gave Judah a prophet who understood her pain. Ezekiel lost his wife right before the people of Judah lost everything. Ezekiel knew that his loss served a greater purpose, but what he might not have known was just how big. When he became a prophet who understood the people's pain, he pointed forward 2,500 years to Jesus—our Prophet who understands our pain. He perfectly understands our mourning and our grief, and He's where the joy is!

ZOOM IN

This is what the Sovereign LORD says: Because you clapped and danced and cheered with glee at the destruction of my people, I will raise my fist of judgment against you.

Ezekiel 25:6–7

God's enemies are the pagan nations who have been acting wickedly. They loved watching Judah get destroyed and the people be exiled. They think Judah's destruction will lead to their own gain, and they celebrate death. But God says His enemies will be destroyed.

TODAY'S GOD SHOT

God is our Defender. Throughout Israel's history, we've seen that God is against the people who are against *His* people. Even though Israel's great sin has broken God's heart, He still promises justice for their enemies. As God's kids, we can always trust God to take care of justice. We don't have to use our words or our hands or even weapons to defend ourselves. Let Him be your Defender. He's where the joy is!

EZEKIEL 28–30

ZOOM IN

This is what the Sovereign LORD says: The people of Israel will again live in their own land, the land I gave my servant Jacob. For I will gather them from the distant lands where I have scattered them.

Ezekiel 28:25

Tyre is an enemy nation close to Israel and Judah. God says that He made Tyre beautiful and full of wise people. But they give themselves credit for their beauty and wisdom. In the same way, Egypt is full of pride because they're powerful. They take credit for what God gave them.

God promises that He will bring His people back to the land He gave them, where they will live in peace.

TODAY'S GOD SHOT

God hates pride. It's built on the lie that we're better than we really are. The truth is, if we're strong, it's because God made us strong. If we're smart, it's because God made us smart. If we're beautiful, it's because God made us beautiful. Every single good thing about us is a gift from God. We should praise Him for it! Pride points to ourselves, but praise points to God. And pointing to God reminds us all that He's where the joy is!

ZOOM IN

As surely as I live, says the Sovereign LORD, I take no pleasure in the death of wicked people. I only want them to turn from their wicked ways so they can live.

Ezekiel 33:11

Ezekiel is responsible for only his own obedience to God. He isn't responsible for how the people respond to him or to God. He knows that—no matter how much he begs them—he can't change people's hearts; only God can do that.

The people finally admit they've sinned, and Ezekiel reminds them it's never too late to repent. They can't save themselves—only God can save them.

When Jerusalem falls to Babylon, a messenger comes to tell Ezekiel, just like God said would happen. And just like God promised, Ezekiel can speak again! So how was he giving the people messages from God all this time if he was mute? Most Bible teachers believe Ezekiel was able to speak *only* about prophecy, but nothing else. The only words he spoke warned others about God's coming judgment.

∼ TODAY'S GOD SHOT ∼

God delights in the salvation of sinful people. In 33:11, He says He wants them "to turn from their wicked ways so they can live." When sinners repent and turn to Him, He is glad! He loves to save and to sanctify people. He delights in us, so we can delight in Him. He's where the joy is!

EZEKIEL 34–36

ZOOM IN

I will increase not only the people, but also your animals. O mountains of Israel, I will bring people to live on you once again. I will make you even more prosperous than you were before. Then you will know that I am the LORD.

Ezekiel 36:11

God says that the wicked kings are like shepherds who've ignored their sheep. They're selfish, using the sheep for meat and wool without taking care of them. God gave Israel more than enough for its kings to care well for their people, but they didn't. God will hold these wicked kings accountable, punishing the shepherds and rescuing the sheep.

God uses eighteen verbs to tell us about His good plan for His kids: He'll gather, bring, cleanse, give, and so much more! He'll change stubborn hearts to tender hearts. He'll put His Spirit in His kids. Then and today, He's at work on His plan for restoration and redemption. He already began it. He's **sustaining** it. And He'll fulfill it!

TODAY'S GOD SHOT

God is good to His people, even when they sin. In 36:11, He sees His people, who have sinned against Him for generations, and tells them, "I will make you even more prosperous than you were before." He's always been good to them, and He promises them He's going to be even better to them in the future. What a generous God! He's where the joy is!

ZOOM IN

I will never again turn my face from them, for I will pour out my Spirit upon the people of Israel. I, the Sovereign LORD, have spoken!

Ezekiel 39:29

Ezekiel has a vision of a valley filled with bones. God commands the bones to live, and they do! The bones represent the twelve tribes—people from both Israel and Judah. God is going to give them new life and bring them back to their land.

God has Ezekiel tie two sticks—representing Northern Israel and Southern Judah—together. God has preserved a remnant from both kingdoms, and He'll bring them back to their land. He'll give them a Good Shepherd from David's family line, and He will sanctify them.

God will protect them from their enemies using an earthquake, fire, hail, and confusion. His people won't even have to fight because God will make the enemies kill each other. Wow!

~ **TODAY'S GOD SHOT** ~

God is better than fair: He's merciful and gracious. Nothing God's people have done has earned them closeness with Him. They've sinned, and the only thing they've earned is separation from Him. But when they turn back to Him, God doesn't just forgive them. He gives them a new heart and teaches them how to follow Him. And He promises an eternal kingdom! No one gives as much mercy and grace as our God. He's where the joy is!

EZEKIEL 40–42

ZOOM IN

So the area was 875 feet on each side with a wall all around it to separate what was holy from what was common.

Ezekiel 42:20

The rest of Ezekiel is one of the most confusing sections in the Bible. Bible teachers who have studied these passages for years disagree on what the text means, so we'll focus on the most important pieces. God gives Ezekiel a vision while the people are in exile in a foreign land. And for nine chapters, God talks about the temple. It's like He's showing up to say, "I know you've lost everything. I know the First Temple (the one Solomon built 350 years ago) was destroyed. I know you're living in the land of our enemies, but I haven't forgotten you! I'm with you, and I have a plan for your restoration."

God gives Ezekiel a tour guide at the temple; we'll call him Bronze Man. Bronze Man brings some measuring tools, and they go on a tour of the temple together.

TODAY'S GOD SHOT

God separates the holy from the common. The outer wall around the temple is long, but not very tall. So its purpose isn't to keep people out. In 42:20, we find out that its purpose is to "separate what was holy from what was common." God's salvation separates holiness from unholiness, but He invites *everyone*. He opens up His family to include anyone who believes that the Son is the way to the Father. God's wall doesn't keep people out; it shows people how to come in. He makes a way to holiness, and He's where the joy is!

SEVEN-DAY ROUNDUP

ZOOM OUT

For seven more days of reading, God gave His people messages through Ezekiel. We were reminded that even after all their sin, God was with His people, and promised them He had a plan to redeem and restore them. He is so good to His kids!

WORD TO REMEMBER

- Sustain—to keep going, to uphold

APPLICATION

Many of the sins of the people of Israel and Judah started as pride. Because the strong kings were proud, they acted like they couldn't be beaten. Because the rich men were proud, they acted like they deserved more wealth. Because the beautiful women were proud, they cheated on their husbands. Strength, wealth, and beauty are all gifts from God, and they're meant to be used for His glory, not our own. When we really believe this, these gifts from God make us grateful, not prideful. They point our hearts toward *Him*, not toward ourselves.

Pride steals joy. It makes us believe we've earned things that we haven't, or that we deserve things that we don't. Pride also leads to other sins. Have you seen this in your own heart? Maybe the pride in your heart led you to boast or make fun of others or gossip or lie. Pray and ask God to show you the ways in which you are proud. Ask Him to remind you that everything good about you is a gift from Him. Ask Him to turn your pride into praise and gratitude!

EZEKIEL 43–45

ZOOM IN

I looked and saw that the glory of the LORD filled the Temple of the LORD, and I fell face down on the ground.

Ezekiel 44:4

In Ezekiel's vision of the new temple, he sees the glory of God! He falls down in awe, and the Spirit lifts him back up. The Most Holy Place—where God dwells—is the smallest space in the temple, but of course God isn't only in that space. He's everywhere!

God tells Ezekiel to write down all the dimensions of the temple and to write down all the laws God gives. Ezekiel is supposed to tell the people about both of these things. God hasn't changed His laws, even though His people have shown over time that they'll never be able to keep them all. God's standards stay the same, and our failures point us to our need for a Savior.

TODAY'S GOD SHOT

God is perfectly and powerfully holy. When Ezekiel sees the glory of God in his vision, he falls flat on his face in worship. In Exodus, God told Moses that no one can see Him and live. Today, we read that the priests have to change clothes after being in God's presence because it's so powerful. God gets as close to us as we can handle, and we get to draw near. Every step toward Him gives us more love and more delight because He's where the joy is!

ZOOM IN

From that day the name of the city will be "The LORD Is There."

Ezekiel 48:35

God instructs His people to leave the temple through a different gate from the one they entered through. This represents the change God makes in people when we come before Him to worship Him. Ezekiel also sees water flowing from the temple, through land that's currently a desert, and into the Dead Sea. The fresh water brings new life to the desert and the salty sea.

The plans for this temple are magnificent, but it hasn't been built. When the Second Temple was built, it didn't match these measurements or descriptions. Bible **scholars** say this could mean one of three things. First, it could mean that God will still build this temple in the future. Second, it could mean that the vision of this temple wasn't meant to show an actual temple, but a symbol pointing to God's great glory. Or third, the vision is a mix of both literal—actual—elements and symbolic elements. It's not absolutely necessary to decide which of these you agree with; prophecy doesn't always give us clear answers, even when we want them. What's important is that God is—and will be—present with His people!

TODAY'S GOD SHOT

God promises that whenever Ezekiel's vision comes true—literally or symbolically—God will be there! No more time in the wilderness, no more captivity, and no more exile. He promises to be there, and stay there forever. That's where we want to be, because He's there, and He's where the joy is!

JOEL 1–3

ZOOM IN

I will pardon my people's crimes, which I have not yet pardoned; and I, the LORD, will make my home in Jerusalem with my people.

Joel 3:21

Joel is another prophet, who most likely wrote after Judah's exile to Babylon. God sends a plague of locusts that destroy everything. The people don't have food for themselves, and they don't have grain or oil or wine for offerings at the temple. Joel tells the people to lament and fast in repentance.

He says the day of the LORD is coming. God will send an army for judgment, but the people can avoid disaster if they repent and obey. For those who repent, God promises to give them more than what they need. He'll give them grain, oil, and wine to make offerings. He'll get rid of the invading army. And everything will bloom again.

But what's better than all of that is that God promises His people He'll give them His Spirit! In the Old Testament, God's Spirit didn't yet dwell *in* all believers. He's mentioned as being with only a select few to empower them with what they need to complete a specific assignment. The promise of His Spirit is a *magnificent* promise!

TODAY'S GOD SHOT

God's Word fills us with hope. In just three chapters, Joel used Scripture from seven other prophets, plus Exodus. He'd been studying! Knowing God's Word helped Joel understand Israel's current state, and it also helped him have hope for the future. When we study God's Word, we see that God always keeps His promises. The more we know God and His Word, the more hopeful we'll be. He's where the joy is!

ZOOM IN

Praise the name of God forever and ever, for he has all wisdom and power.

Daniel 2:20

Daniel and his three friends—Shadrach, Meshach, and Abednego—are teenagers in Jerusalem when Babylon attacks and takes the people captive. These four teens are smart and strong, so King Nebby puts them in the best Babylonian schools. Nebby's not being kind here; he's trying to convince the captives that the Babylonian way is the right way. He wants them to forget God's way, but they don't.

God is with Daniel and his friends, and while they're in Babylon, they make choices that please God. One day, Nebby has a dream that scares him. When none of his people can tell him what it means, Daniel asks God for help. Daniel tells King Nebby what his dream was *and* what it means. Nebby is impressed and gives Daniel a special position in his court.

But then Nebby sets up a giant gold statue and makes everyone bow down to worship it. Shadrach, Meshach, and Abednego, however, refuse. Furious at this news, Nebby throws them into a furnace to kill them, but they don't even get burned. While the three friends are in the furnace, Nebby notices that someone else is in the fire with them; Bible teachers believe this fourth person was God the Son! The king is amazed, and he worships YHWH.

TODAY'S GOD SHOT

God has all wisdom and all power. When God reveals the meaning of King Nebby's dream to Daniel, he praises God. Daniel says God is sovereign over wisdom, power, kings, knowledge, and mysteries. We read just three chapters of the Bible today, and we saw that all these things are true. As Daniel says, "Praise the name of God forever and ever." He's where the joy is!

DANIEL 4-6

ZOOM IN

He rescues and saves his people; he performs miraculous signs and wonders in the heavens and on earth. He has rescued Daniel from the power of the lions.

Daniel 6:27

King Nebby has another weird dream, and Daniel is again the only one who can explain it. Though Daniel warns him that the dream isn't good, Nebby doesn't listen. About a year later, while Nebby's busy writing a praise song about himself, the dream becomes reality. For seven years, he lives in a field like a cow, eating grass. At the end of the seven years, his mind clears, he's finally humbled—for real this time—and he returns to the throne. He writes another praise song, but this time it's to YHWH!

Then we meet King Belshazzar, who is probably Nebby's grandson, while he's throwing a wild party to worship pagan gods. He decides he's going to serve wine out of the vessels that Babylon stole from Jerusalem's temple. But then God shows up and scares everyone half to death when a hand without a body writes a message on a wall! Daniel is called to explain what it says. Daniel explains that God is not pleased with Belshazzar, and the king dies that night!

King Darius takes over and makes a new rule that everyone must pray only to him. Daniel continues to pray to God, so Darius's men throw him into a lions' den to kill him. But God sends an angel to close the lions' mouths, and Daniel lives! Wow!

TODAY'S GOD SHOT

God is the hero of Daniel's story. Daniel is faithful to live God's way, but on his own, he couldn't have known Nebby's dreams or closed lions' mouths. God did those things! God is the hero of every story, and He's where the joy is!

ZOOM IN

The moment you began praying, a command was given. And now I am here to tell you what it was, for you are very precious to God.

Daniel 9:23

You might have noticed a change in the way Daniel is written today. That's because we made a shift from the storytelling part of Daniel to a part that's full of prophecies about the end of the world. If some of today's reading was confusing, that's okay! Parts were confusing for Daniel too. He has two dreams that he doesn't understand, so an angel helps him, explaining that the dreams point to things that will happen in the future.

Daniel reads Jeremiah and realizes that their exile is almost over. He fasts, prays, and begs God for mercy. He knows that God's people have sinned and broken their covenant with God. He asks God to bring an end to their judgment, not because they've earned it, but because God is merciful. God sends the angel Gabriel to Daniel, who helps him understand the timeline for the end of the exile and the restoration.

TODAY'S GOD SHOT

God is sovereign over all things, and He still makes time to care for His kids. In today's reading, we saw that God is sovereign over the timeline of the entire earth. But even with everything that He's in charge of, He hears Daniel's prayer and sends Gabriel to remind Daniel that he's "very precious to God" (9:23). What kindness! God is in charge of everything, and He still takes time to whisper to His kids. He's where the joy is!

DANIEL 10–12

"Don't be afraid," he said, "for you are very precious to God. Peace! Be encouraged! Be strong!"

Daniel 10:19

Daniel mourns for three weeks, and God gives him a vision of a man dressed in linen and gold—probably an angel. The angel tells Daniel how much God loves him. He also tells Daniel about a time in the future when Israel will go through a terrible war. But all of God's people will survive.

For the first time in the Bible, God talks specifically about the afterlife. The angel tells Daniel that those who die will wake up to face one of two realities: everlasting life, or everlasting shame and disgrace. The angel tells Daniel to keep being faithful until his death. Then he will receive the inheritance God has for him!

TODAY'S GOD SHOT

God is outside of time, so He not only *knows* the future, He's already *in* the future. Most of us really want to know exactly what will happen and when, but God doesn't tell us. He wants us to trust Him, and if we knew the future, we might not trust Him. Some of the prophecies in Daniel are confusing, but they don't have to scare us. We can pray and ask God to help us trust Him with the present and the future. He's already there, and He's where the joy is!

SEVEN-DAY ROUNDUP

ZOOM OUT

We finished three more books of the Bible, which brings our total to thirty-two books so far! During the time of Jerusalem's fall and the people's exile, we heard from three prophets who all had messages for the people from God.

BIG PICTURE: EZEKIEL

While in exile in Babylon, Ezekiel gives the people strong warnings to repent from their sin and return to their merciful God. The prophet reminds the people that God wants to be known.

BIG PICTURE: JOEL

During a time of national disaster, Joel tells the people of Judah to repent and return to the Lord. He reminds them that the day of the LORD will bring judgment for some and blessing for others.

BIG PICTURE: DANIEL

When Jerusalem is destroyed, Daniel is taken to Babylon and given a position of importance. God uses him as a prophet to minister to pagan kings and nations. And God shows him that while other kingdoms will pass away, the kingdom of God will last forever.

WORD TO REMEMBER

- Scholar—someone who studies something

APPLICATION

Daniel gave all the credit for every good thing in his life to God. In chapter 2, Daniel wrote a beautiful prayer of praise to God for who He is and what He does. Go back and read Daniel 2:19–23. Then write your own prayer of praise to God!

EZRA 1–3

ZOOM IN

With praise and thanks, they sang this song to the LORD: "He is so good! His faithful love for Israel endures forever!"

Ezra 3:11

Ezra is a short book that covers a long period of time—almost one hundred years, in fact. The book opens with King Cyrus of Persia, who has just defeated Babylon, Israel's captors. Cyrus is a pagan, but God puts a desire in his heart to rebuild the temple in Jerusalem.

So not only does he send fifty thousand exiles back home, but he also sends them food and supplies for the journey *and* the vessels that were stolen from the temple! The remnant from Northern Israel and Southern Judah, called **Jews** or Jewish people, return to Jerusalem.

The people give generous offerings to God, and they use that money—plus some of the money Cyrus gave them—to buy supplies. After about two years, they appoint priests and begin laying a foundation for the temple. Some of the people are so overwhelmed—maybe because they are homesick for the First Temple, or maybe because they can't stop thinking about their difficult exile—that they cry. But most of the people are excited, and they have a worship service.

TODAY'S GOD SHOT

God keeps His promises. The Israelites are back in their land! The people make offerings; the priests are given back their jobs; the foundation of the temple is being built. God said He'd bring back a remnant of His people to their land to restore them, so of course He does! He keeps His promises, and He's where the joy is!

Moreover, I hereby decree that you are to help these elders of the Jews as they rebuild this Temple of God. You must pay the full construction costs, without delay, from my taxes collected in the province west of the Euphrates River so that the work will not be interrupted.

Ezra 6:8

Not long after the former exiles started rebuilding the temple, their work stops. A few local enemies do everything they can to make sure the Jews don't get to rebuild the temple. And for about fifteen years, they don't build. Then, the new governor sends Persia's new king, Darius, a letter asking about the Jews and their temple. They've told the governor what Cyrus did for them, and he wants to find out if it's true.

King Darius finds all the old records and even discovers that the royal treasury is supposed to pay for the rebuilding costs! God's people finish the temple and dedicate it to God. Seventy years after their exile, they celebrate the Passover. And this time, it's not just Jewish people. **Gentiles** (anyone who isn't Jewish) who worship YHWH are included too!

∼ TODAY'S GOD SHOT ∼

God can take people's worst intentions and use them as tools to accomplish His plans. When their enemies tried to stop the Jews from rebuilding the temple, God took their bad intentions and made things even better for His people. Not only do they get to rebuild the temple, but their enemies have to pay for it! Incredible! He thwarts His enemies, blesses His people, and accomplishes His plans. He's where the joy is!

HAGGAI 1–2

ZOOM IN

The future glory of this Temple will be greater than its past glory, says the Lord of Heaven's Armies. And in this place I will bring peace. I, the Lord of Heaven's Armies, have spoken!

Haggai 2:9

Haggai is a prophet who we just met in the book of Ezra. Today we go back in time a little while, and the people are rebuilding the temple. Haggai tells Jeshua (the high priest) and Zerubbabel (the governor of Judah) that the people's priorities are all mixed up. They're focused on themselves and their own homes, and not on God's home. Haggai reminds them that God is with them, and God moves the people to want to obey Him. They start building again.

God tells Haggai that the people's hearts aren't clean. And because their hearts aren't clean, their hands aren't clean. So they're building God's temple with unclean hands. God doesn't want them to finish building before their hearts and hands are clean because He wants to live with them in the temple. God tells Haggai that He is going to work in the people's hearts and that He has big plans for Zerubbabel, a direct descendant of King David.

TODAY'S GOD SHOT

God rebuilds, no matter what is destroyed. And when God rebuilds, He makes it even better. After everything His people have done to break God's heart, most people would agree that they don't deserve another temple. It seems like they never learn their lesson. But God still promises them that He'll live among them again and that it'll be even better than it was before! He's where the joy is!

---ZOOM IN---

Jeshua's clothing was filthy as he stood there before the angel.
So the angel said to the others standing there, "Take off his filthy
clothes." And turning to Jeshua he said, "See, I have taken away
your sins, and now I am giving you these fine new clothes."

Zechariah 3:3–4

Zechariah is a priest and a prophet. Through him, God tells His people how much their ancestors' sins hurt Him and them. He begs them not to walk the same path.

Today we read about five visions God gives Zechariah. These visions are prophecies about things that will happen in the future. In the fourth vision, the high priest Jeshua stands in front of the Angel of the LORD; like we've seen before, the Angel of the LORD (not just *an* angel of the LORD) is likely Jesus. Jeshua has on filthy clothes, and Satan accuses him. But God rebukes Satan for his accusations and gives Jeshua clean clothes.

~~TODAY'S GOD SHOT~~

God is the one who takes our sins away. God is the one who makes us righteous. When Jeshua's filthy clothing needs to come off, the Angel of the LORD takes care of it. And when Jeshua gets fine new clothes, they are given to him by God. We can't clean ourselves up or forgive our own sins or make ourselves righteous. God does all of it. He's where the joy is!

ZECHARIAH 5–9

ZOOM IN

Rejoice, O people of Zion! Shout in triumph, O people of Jerusalem! Look, your king is coming to you. He is righteous and victorious, yet he is humble, riding on a donkey—riding on a donkey's colt.

Zechariah 9:9

Today we read four more of Zechariah's visions. Not all of the promises God has made to His people have happened yet, and not all of the things that their ancestors lost have been restored yet. Where the people are hurting, God speaks truth and gives them hope, even saying that one day their city will be filled with children playing in the streets (8:5). And today in Jerusalem, this prophecy has already been fulfilled!

God gives Zechariah hints about the coming Messiah. A priest wears a crown and sits on a throne, because Jesus is the ultimate Priest and King.

TODAY'S GOD SHOT

Jesus was in today's reading. Did you see Him? In Matthew 21, Jesus rides through Jerusalem "righteous and victorious," yet He's humble, "riding on a donkey's colt" (Zechariah 9:9). What's more, He speaks peace; He sets prisoners free; He saves people and they shine. Everything about Him is wonderful and beautiful, and it's *almost* time for Him to come. He's where the joy is!

ZOOM IN

My anger burns against your shepherds, and I will punish these leaders. For the Lord of Heaven's Armies has arrived to look after Judah, his flock. He will make them strong and glorious, like a proud warhorse in battle.

Zechariah 10:3

God promises to punish Judah's wicked leaders. Because they didn't lead the people, the people went to wicked places instead—like fortune tellers and false gods. But when God Himself is their Shepherd, He will bring them back from all the nations where they've been scattered. He'll multiply them in the promised land again.

Zechariah prophesies about Jesus, the fountain who washes His people clean from sin. And he prophesies about the kingdom of heaven. When it arrives, God will stand on the Mount of Olives, which will be split open, and a river will flow out of Jerusalem. God will reign on the earth and over everything in it!

TODAY'S GOD SHOT

God looks after His people. Zechariah's prophecy points to Jesus, our Good Shepherd. Though His sheep rejected Him, He became the sacrifice for them. He's the Shepherd *and* He's the sacrificial Lamb, because when it comes to His kids, God provides everything He requires. He's where the joy is!

ESTHER 1–5

ZOOM IN

If you keep quiet at a time like this, deliverance and relief for the Jews will arise from some other place, but you and your relatives will die. Who knows if perhaps you were made queen for just such a time as this?

Esther 4:14

Esther is the only book in the Bible that doesn't mention God's name, but He's still in every moment, keeping His promises and working things out according to His plan.

The king of Persia is Xerxes. (Your Bible might call him Ahasuerus; it's the same guy.) Xerxes isn't a good man; he gets mad at his wife and decides that he wants a new one. So his men go out into all the surrounding towns and kidnap a lot of young, beautiful women. One of those women is a Jew named Esther. She has been raised by her cousin, Mordecai, who has a good position in the kingdom. He tells Esther not to tell anyone that she's a Jew. Xerxes chooses Esther—who acts in wisdom and humility—to be the new queen.

Haman, a royal official, gets angry when Mordecai won't bow down to him, so he decides that all the Jews in Persia need to be killed. *How wicked.* Esther knows she could be killed for going to the king without an invitation, but Mordecai reminds her that Haman's proclamation puts her life in danger too, and she comes up with a plan.

~TODAY'S GOD SHOT~

God always does what He says. Mordecai tells Esther, "If you keep quiet at a time like this, deliverance and relief for the Jews will arise from some other place" (4:14). He knows that God has promised to protect His people, and he trusts that God will do it. Trusting God is our best plan and our only hope. He's where the joy is!

SEVEN-DAY ROUNDUP

ZOOM OUT

You finished two more books this week, so you've read thirty-four books since we began! And you only have *one* more week in the Old Testament. Are you learning who God is? Are you learning how much He loves His kids? Are you seeing how He is revealing His plan of making a way for us to be with Him forever? Keep reading. Keep learning. Keep believing that He's where the joy is!

BIG PICTURE: HAGGAI

Haggai ministers to the Jews who had returned to Jerusalem after their exile in Babylon. He reminds them that God is with them and wants to renew His covenant with them.

BIG PICTURE: ZECHARIAH

A prophet and a priest, Zechariah encourages the people of Jerusalem to turn toward God, because He cares for them. Zechariah points to Jesus's birth and death and to the day when God will reign over everything.

WORDS TO REMEMBER

- Gentiles—all people who aren't Jewish
- Jews (or Jewish people)—descendants of God's people from the kingdom of Southern Judah that split from the kingdom of Northern Israel

APPLICATION

A number of times in the Bible, God is described as our Shepherd. That makes us His sheep. Sheep aren't known for being the smartest animals, and they usually do whatever the other sheep around them are doing. That's why they need good shepherds, and that's why it's such a joy that we have *the* Good Shepherd. Draw a picture of a sheep and place it somewhere that you'll see every day. When you see your sheep, thank God for being your Shepherd. Ask Him to show you which way to go and how to live.

ESTHER 6–10

ZOOM IN

In every province and city, wherever the king's decree arrived, the Jews rejoiced and had a great celebration and declared a public festival and holiday.

Esther 8:17

On our last day of reading, we read that Mordecai stopped King Xerxes from being killed by telling his cousin, Queen Esther, about a plot he'd overheard. Today, Xerxes realizes that he never thanked Mordecai and wants to honor him. So Xerxes tells Haman—who hates Mordecai and who got Xerxes to send a royal decree saying all of the Jews will be killed—to lead a parade in Mordecai's honor. Haman is *not* happy.

At a banquet, Xerxes offers to give Esther anything she wants. She tells him about Haman's evil plan. The king is furious. He sentences Haman to death and makes Mordecai a royal official in Haman's place.

Since royal decrees can't be reversed, Esther and Mordecai come up with a plan to save their people. They send another royal decree that gives Jews permission to fight against—and take the possessions of—anyone who tries to attack them. And when the day comes that the Jews are attacked, they fight back and they win. They celebrate their victory and decide to remember this day—called Purim—every year.

TODAY'S GOD SHOT

God is at work on every page of a book that doesn't even mention His name. Esther isn't the hero of this story, and neither is Mordecai. God is the Hero. He is sovereign over every detail and He rescues His people. Even if you feel like you can't see God, He's there. He's sovereign and He's at work in your life. He's where the joy is!

ZOOM IN

While Ezra prayed and made this confession, weeping and lying face down on the ground in front of the Temple of God, a very large crowd of people from Israel—men, women, and children—gathered and wept bitterly with him.

Ezra 10:1

Today, we return to Ezra and meet . . . Ezra! About sixty years have passed since the Jews and Gentiles first celebrated Passover together in the re-built temple. Ezra lives in Babylon, but when Persia conquers it, King Arta-xerxes sends him and some other Jews back to Jerusalem. The king sends them with provisions and promises to give them anything they need. He tells Ezra to appoint leaders to teach God's laws.

Ezra fasts and prays and asks God to deliver them safely to Jerusalem, a journey that takes months. They arrive safely and make their offerings to God. Then they learn how bad things are in Jerusalem.

The exiles have only been back in Jerusalem a few decades, but they've disobeyed God already. They married people who worship false gods, which led to them worshipping false gods too. Ezra is heartbroken. He mourns, and the people confess their sin.

～TODAY'S GOD SHOT～

God is hope. When Ezra and the large crowd weep for their sins, Shecaniah says, "We have been unfaithful to our God. . . . But in spite of this there is hope for Israel" (10:2). And he's right! Their hope isn't that they'll do better next time. Their hope is that God has entered into a covenant with them, that God has protected them, and that God offers forgiveness. God Himself is their hope, and He's where the joy is!

NEHEMIAH 1–5

ZOOM IN

The God of heaven will help us succeed. We, his servants, will start rebuilding this wall.

Nehemiah 2:20

Nehemiah is an Israelite official who works as a personal assistant to the king of Persia, so he has an important job! A family member who lives in Jerusalem comes to visit Nehemiah, and he learns that things aren't going well there. Even though the exiles have been back in Jerusalem for almost a hundred years, they haven't rebuilt the city or the walls.

Nehemiah is upset; he fasts and prays. God puts a plan in his heart, and with the king's help, he goes to Jerusalem. At first he's quiet about his plans, sneaking out at night to inspect the city's roads and walls. Then he steps up to lead the people as their governor and explains his plan. Everyone is on board, except some other local governors. But Nehemiah isn't afraid of them; he keeps working and trusting God with every problem that comes up.

TODAY'S GOD SHOT

God works in so many different ways, big and small. Sometimes He does the work *for* His people, and sometimes He does the work *through* them. It's important to pay attention to God and always ask Him for direction, like Nehemiah does. God always has a plan; our job is to ask Him what our part in the plan is. His plan is good, and He's where the joy is!

ZOOM IN

But I prayed, "Now strengthen my hands."

Nehemiah 6:9 NIV

Two bullies, Sanballat and Geshem, try to trick Nehemiah into meeting up with them. When that doesn't work, they send him a threatening letter, accusing him of trying to be king and saying that he's making the prophets lie. Nehemiah knows this is completely made up, and he asks God to give him strength.

God answers Nehemiah with a yes, and gives him the strength to finish rebuilding the city wall in fifty-two days! Nehemiah starts to prepare for the grand opening, making his brother the castle governor. He gives rules about when to open and close the city gates.

God tells Nehemiah to take a record of all the families who have returned from exile. All together, there are fifty thousand people and eight thousand animals. To restore the city and the temple, the people gave about eight hundred pounds of gold and six hundred pounds of silver.

TODAY'S GOD SHOT

God gives strength, direction, and wisdom. Nehemiah asks God for these things because he knows they're all gifts from God. Nehemiah is strong, confident, and wise, not because of himself, but because of God. Nehemiah knows about God what we also know—that He's where the joy is!

NEHEMIAH 8–10

ZOOM IN

Our God, you are the great God. You are mighty and wonderful. You keep the covenant you made with us. You show us your love.

Nehemiah 9:32 NIrV

The remnant has been restored, the temple has been rebuilt, and the walls have been replaced. But God isn't done with His people. He cares about way more than where they live and worship; He cares about their hearts. Nehemiah teams up with Ezra, and they gather the people together. Ezra reads aloud from God's Word, probably the Torah (the first five books of the Bible). Whenever they get to a confusing place, the Levites help them understand.

They realize they've forgotten about the Feast of Booths, a seven-day festival where the people thank God for providing for the Israelites in the wilderness. They celebrate the festival together. Ezra prays, thanking God for the many, many ways He's been faithful to the people. He admits to God that the people have ignored and forgotten Him, but God has always shown them His steady love. Ezra humbly asks for God's continued mercy.

TODAY'S GOD SHOT

God makes Himself known to His people, even when they've ignored or forgotten Him. He's so patient and persistent with His people, and after all this time, they're finally seeing how awesome He is. They're learning that He's where the joy is!

ZOOM IN

When the LORD brought back his exiles to Jerusalem, it was like a dream! We were filled with laughter, and we sang for joy. And the other nations said, "What amazing things the LORD has done for them." Yes, the LORD has done amazing things for us! What joy!

Psalm 126:1–3

Once people have moved into Jerusalem, Nehemiah holds a grand opening celebration. The people offer sacrifices and sing praises to God and march along the wall. Their shouts of praise are so loud that people in nearby towns hear them. People in the city are assigned to different jobs, like storehouse manager and gatekeeper. They keep reading from the Torah to learn more about God's laws. They learn and obey.

But it doesn't take long until God's people go their own way. They break God's laws, and Nehemiah is furious. He beats people up, pulls out their hair, curses at them, and makes them promise to stop. He knows how badly this has gone for God's people in the past, and he doesn't want to see Israel fall again.

Even though the peace and joy didn't last long, it was a beautiful time, and even though sin still exists, there is so much to praise God for. Psalm 126 is a song of praise to God for all the great things He has done. The people's mouths are filled with shouts of joy.

～ TODAY'S GOD SHOT ～

God gives His people joy. Nehemiah 12:43 says that when the people celebrated in the rebuilt city, "the joy of the people of Jerusalem could be heard far away." God gave them every reason to be joyful. Even when they break His laws, their hearts know deep down that He's where the joy is!

MALACHI 1–4

God tells Israel how much He loves them, but they don't believe Him. Even the priests, who know all that He's done for them and their ancestors, have rejected God. They're making a mockery of Him and leading the people into sin.

Malachi reminds the people that they belong to God and asks why they aren't living like it. He prays that God will cut off anyone who loves their own ways more than His ways. The people keep lying to themselves and justifying their sin. God begs His people to return to Him and tells them that if there's any cost to following Him, it will be repaid in ways they can't even imagine. A day is coming when God will judge people who do evil. But for those who love Him, the sun will rise, and it will shine healing on them.

Malachi also gives a final Old Testament prophecy about the Messiah: A messenger will prepare the way for the one who *is* the way. Do you know who the messenger is? Do you know who the Messiah is? Stay tuned. You'll find out on our next day of reading.

TODAY'S GOD SHOT

God gives justice and mercy. For evil people, there is justice in God's judgment. But for those who love Him, there is such great mercy. We don't deserve it, but He shines on us like the sun as it rises. He provides healing, and He's where the joy is!

SEVEN-DAY ROUNDUP

ZOOM OUT

You finished all thirty-nine books of the Old Testament! From creation to the flood, to slavery, to the exodus, to the wilderness, to the promised land, to the judges, to the kings, to the split kingdom, to the exile, to the prophets, to the temple's rebuilding, God has been working and faithful.

BIG PICTURE: ESTHER

Through Esther, a Jew who becomes queen of Persia, God protects the Jewish people. And through the Jewish people, God will offer salvation to the whole world.

BIG PICTURE: EZRA

Covering about one hundred years, the book of Ezra reminds us that God is full of mercy and faithful to keep His promises.

BIG PICTURE: NEHEMIAH

God appoints Nehemiah to lead His people back to Him. Nehemiah reminds the people of everything God has done for them and leads them to rebuild Jerusalem. He encourages the people to find their joy in living God's way.

BIG PICTURE: PSALMS

The book of Psalms teaches us to pray. Written at times throughout the Old Testament, this is the songbook of God's people. Psalms teaches us that no matter our circumstances, God wants us to come to Him and He is worthy of our praise.

BIG PICTURE: MALACHI

Malachi is the last Old Testament prophet. He calls the deeply discouraged people of Israel to keep their part of the covenant with God.

APPLICATION

Ask a grown-up who loves Jesus for the "zoomed out" version of how God has worked in their life. There are likely a few things that didn't make sense at the time they happened. But now it's clear how God was working all along.

The next time something happens in your life that doesn't make sense, ask God to show you, in His time, how He is working through it. And until He does, ask Him to help you remember that every word He said is true and every promise He made He'll keep.

FOUR HUNDRED YEARS

OF SILENCE

After the Old Testament ends, four hundred years pass before the New Testament begins. During that time, God doesn't send prophets, and we don't have written records of how He interacts with people. But we know He's there. And we know He's working out His plan.

Because of other historical records, we do know some of what was happening in Israel at the time. The Babylonians were defeated by the Persians, who were defeated by the Romans. So now Rome is in charge of Israel, and even though they're back in their homeland, the Jews are once again ruled by an enemy. The Roman Empire is cruel, and as you'll soon see, they treat the Jews terribly.

So now it's about 7 BC, a year before Jesus is born. (Did you know He wasn't born in year 0? Our global calendar is off by a few years.) The people of Israel are oppressed and exhausted, wondering where the Messiah is. And that's where our story continues. . . .

LUKE 1; JOHN 1

ZOOM IN

Mary responded, "Oh, how my soul praises the Lord. How my spirit rejoices in God my Savior!"

Luke 1:46–47

The first four books of the New Testament are called the **Gospels**, a word that comes from a Greek word meaning "to bring good news." These books tell the story of Jesus's life. Some of the events are repeated among the books, but each gospel has a unique perspective, so even the repeated stories often include different details from one book to another. Since we're reading the Bible in chronological order, we'll skip around to events in the order that they happen.

Luke writes about Zechariah and Elizabeth, who haven't been able to have a child. The angel Gabriel meets Zechariah and tells him he'll have a son named John. God has a special assignment for John. (Remember Malachi's prophecy?) He'll be filled with the Spirit of God and will be a messenger who prepares the way for the Messiah. He'll grow up to be known as John the Baptist, so we'll call him JTB.

A few months later, Gabriel meets a young woman named Mary. He tells her that even though she's not married, she is going to have a baby named Jesus. Jesus's Father is God, and He will bring an eternal kingdom to earth.

Fast-forward thirty years. One day, JTB is baptizing people in the wilderness when his cousin Jesus shows up. JTB knows the truth about who Jesus is, so he tells everyone, "Here He is!" The Messiah has come!

～TODAY'S GOD SHOT～

Jesus's birth is the yes to all our prayers. Mary and Zechariah rejoice and sing when they hear the news from God. The one all of humanity has been waiting for is *here*. He has come to rescue the world from sin and darkness. He's where the light is, and He's where the joy is!

ZOOM IN

I have seen your salvation, which you have prepared for all people. He is a light to reveal God to the nations, and he is the glory of your people Israel!

Luke 2:30–32

Matthew starts his gospel with a genealogy of Jesus. Did you notice anything special about it? It includes women and Gentiles—an uncommon thing in Jesus's day. In God's perfect plan, He used unlikely people to bring hope and salvation to the whole world.

We go back in time a little bit today and read that God sent an angel to Joseph, who is engaged to be married to Mary. The angel tells Joseph not to be afraid.

In Luke 2, we read the story of Jesus's birth. Because everyone is in town for the census, there's nowhere for Mary and Joseph to stay in Bethlehem. Now here's where the real story is different from what you've probably seen in drawings or nativity sets. Mary and Joseph don't stay in a barn; it was probably more like a cave, which is where animals were kept. And it isn't winter, since the census would usually happen sometime in the summer. So on the floor of a cave on a hot night, Mary gave birth to the Savior of the world.

Jesus's parents take Him to the temple eight days later to dedicate Him. They give a small offering, which is all they can afford. A widow named Anna and an elderly man named Simeon are both prophets who have waited for the Messiah; they praise God when they see Jesus.

TODAY'S GOD SHOT

God keeps His promises. At some point during the four hundred years of silence, God the Spirit promised Simeon that he'd see the Messiah before he died. When Simeon holds Jesus, he knows the promise has come true. Jesus the Messiah is here! He's where the joy is!

MATTHEW 2

Now when they had departed, behold, an angel of the Lord appeared to Joseph in a dream and said, "Rise, take the child and his mother, and flee to Egypt, and remain there until I tell you, for Herod is about to search for the child, to destroy him."

Matthew 2:13 ESV

Today we read Matthew's account of the birth of Jesus. He's born in the city of Bethlehem in the kingdom of Judea, and Judea is under Roman occupation, which means there are Roman soldiers all over the kingdom. So even though the people of Judea don't want the Romans there, they still have to pay taxes to support the army.

Herod the Great is in charge of Judea. Under his leadership, Judea grows. But then Herod turns jealous and afraid. So when wise men—who probably study the stars—show up from far away asking about the new King, Herod starts to make an evil plan. He tells the wise men to report back to him after they find the child.

The wise men find Jesus thanks to the star God sent, and they worship Him and give Him gifts. Then God warns them in a dream not to go back to Herod, and they take a different route home. God also warns Joseph to take his family to Egypt, and he does. Then Herod orders all boys aged two and under to be killed.

TODAY'S GOD SHOT

God protects His people. In just three days in the New Testament, we've seen Him send angels, dreams, and angels *in* dreams. God protects the wise men on their way home, and He protects Joseph's family from Herod's evil plan. God doesn't say that nothing bad will happen to His kids. But because of who He is, we know that no matter what happens, God can be trusted. He protects us. He's always working. And He's where the joy is!

ZOOM IN

When Jesus was baptized, immediately he went up from the water, and behold, the heavens were opened to him, and he saw the Spirit of God descending like a dove and coming to rest on him; and behold, a voice from heaven said, "This is my beloved Son, with whom I am well pleased."

Matthew 3:16–17 ESV

John the Baptist—JTB—lives in the desert, wearing clothes made from animal skins and eating locusts and honey. As God's messenger, he isn't concerned with where he lives, what he wears, or what he eats. He's focused on the message and preparing the way for Jesus. He tells people to repent, and he baptizes those who do.

Jesus asks JTB to baptize him. JTB knows that Jesus has never—and will never—sin, so He doesn't need to repent. But JTB also knows Jesus is the Messiah, so he obeys and baptizes him.

After His baptism, Jesus spends forty days in the wilderness being tempted by Satan, but He doesn't sin. And then, Jesus begins His ministry.

~ TODAY'S GOD SHOT ~

God the Father, God the Son, and God the Spirit—the three persons of the Trinity—are all present at Jesus's baptism. God the Son is in the water. God the Spirit descends like a dove. God the Father speaks from heaven, identifying and approving of Jesus. They all have different jobs to do, and they're all God. The Trinity is hard to understand because there's nothing to compare it to. It's completely unique to who God is. He's awesome, and He's where the joy is!

MATTHEW 4; LUKE 4–5

ZOOM IN

"The Spirit of the Lord is upon me, because he has anointed me to proclaim good news to the poor. He has sent me to proclaim liberty to the captives and recovering of sight to the blind, to set at liberty those who are oppressed."

Luke 4:18 ESV

While Jesus is in the desert for forty days, He fasts and He prays. Satan tempts him, but Jesus—who has to be hot, tired, thirsty, and hungry—doesn't sin. During this time, JTB is arrested.

When Jesus teaches in Nazareth, He says God has sent Him to share good news for the poor and the prisoners. He says that He is *Himself* the good news, and at first the people are excited. But when He teaches about loving foreigners and enemies, the people get angry.

In Capernaum, Jesus calls His first **disciples**. He helps four fishermen, who weren't catching any fish, fill their nets. Then He tells them to come fishing with Him, for people. Then He tells a tax collector—who is considered a traitor and is hated by his own people—to join them. Jesus's unlikely bunch of disciples sees Him heal people and cast out **demons**.

TODAY'S GOD SHOT

Jesus looks for the people who've been rejected. This was good news for the poor, oppressed, and imprisoned, but bad news for the people who took advantage of them. Jesus knew all along that people would reject Him and kill Him, but He came anyway. He came to be rejected by people He loved, to lead them out of sin and into joy. Joy is found in Him, because He's where the joy is!

ZOOM IN

And as Moses lifted up the serpent in the wilderness, so must the Son of Man be lifted up, that whoever believes in him may have eternal life.

John 3:14–15 ESV

When His mother asks Him to, Jesus performs His first public miracle. At a wedding feast where the wine is running out, He turns water into wine. He kept the feast going!

The **Pharisees** are a group of Jewish scholars and leaders who concern themselves with making sure Jews keep God's law. (But they often exaggerate God's laws to include some that they made up. More on that later.) Nicodemus is a Pharisee who believes there is something special about Jesus and His understanding of God's law. He comes to Jesus at night to talk to Him, and Jesus teaches him about God's Spirit. He tells Nicodemus that everyone who wants to see the kingdom of heaven must be *born again*.

On Jesus's way back to Galilee from Jerusalem, he passes through Samaria. For hundreds of years, the Samaritans have been the Jews' enemies, but Jesus talks to a Samaritan woman at a well. He tells her "all that [she] ever did" (4:39), and changes her life. He takes her sadness and shame and gives her joy and hope. She becomes a **missionary**, telling everyone she knows about Jesus.

TODAY'S GOD SHOT

Jesus's first public miracle is turning water into wine. Moses's first public miracle was turning water into blood. Blood symbolizes death. Wine symbolizes life. Moses was the lawgiver, and Jesus is the law *fulfiller* and the *life* giver. Jesus is the greater Moses. He gives *life*. And He's where the joy is!

MATTHEW 8; MARK 2

ZOOM IN

Those who are well have no need of a physician, but those who are sick. I came not to call the righteous, but sinners.

Mark 2:17 ESV

A man with a serious and very contagious skin disease called leprosy has heard about Jesus. He kneels at Jesus's feet and asks for healing. Jesus heals him but tells him to keep it quiet. Did you think that was strange? Jesus knows that people will eventually turn against Him, and He has a lot of work left to do before the time for Him to die is right. So He tells some people—usually Jews—to keep His miracles and healings a secret, while He lets others—usually Gentiles—tell everyone.

A centurion, an official in the Roman army, comes to Jesus and asks Him to heal his sick servant. The Jews don't want Jesus to help their enemy, but Jesus points out how much faith the centurion has and heals the servant. Jesus can heal people from a distance!

Jesus calms a storm, casts demons out of people, and heals many more people. He has authority over everything!

TODAY'S GOD SHOT

Jesus is the Healer. You might have heard people say things that suggest that God only heals people whose faith is "strong enough." This isn't true! God heals who He chooses to heal, and we don't have to do anything to earn it. Jesus heals the centurion's servant, and the servant didn't even ask Him to! Jesus blesses people who have nothing to offer Him, not even a "strong enough" faith. He's so generous, He's the Healer, and He's where the joy is!

SEVEN-DAY ROUNDUP

ZOOM OUT

He came! The Chosen One, the Messiah, the King of the Universe, the Savior came! In the past seven days of reading, we saw the miraculous birth, holy baptism, and early ministry of Jesus.

WORDS TO REMEMBER

- Demon—an evil spirit that can tempt, mislead, or take over a person's body. When that happens, that person is described as *demonized*.
- Disciple—a follower or student of a teacher
- Gospel—to bring good news; one of the first four books of the New Testament, which tell about the life of Jesus
- Missionary—someone on a mission to tell others about Jesus
- Pharisees—a group of Jewish scholars and leaders who concerned themselves with making sure Jews kept God's law, and often, some extra made-up laws too

APPLICATION

When Jesus changed the life of the Samaritan woman, she couldn't help but tell everyone she knew about Him. And after they met Him themselves, many more believed in Him! John 4:42 says, "They said to the woman, 'It is no longer because of what you said that we believe, for we have heard for ourselves, and we know that this is indeed the Savior of the world'" (ESV).

When we hear the word *missionary* today, most of us think about someone who travels to another country to tell people about Jesus. A missionary does tell people about Jesus so they can meet Him themselves, but they don't have to travel anywhere to do it. Who in your life could you be a missionary to? Ask God to show you who you should tell about Jesus, and how. You can be a missionary too!

JOHN 5

Jesus said to him, "Get up, take up your bed, and walk." And at once the man was healed, and he took up his bed and walked. Now that day was the Sabbath.

John 5:8–9 ESV

In John 5, Jesus heals a paralyzed man. The man goes straight to the temple, but the Pharisees don't welcome him there. They're angry with him for bringing his sleeping mat. It's the Sabbath, so they believe he shouldn't be carrying anything. The Pharisees are very strict in the ways they read and understand God's law. They take it upon themselves to make sure that Jews follow not only God's laws, but also the laws they made up themselves. So when God said, "Do not carry a burden out of your houses on the Sabbath or do any work" (Jeremiah 17:22 ESV), the Pharisees now say it means you can't carry *anything* on the Sabbath.

This man—for the first time in thirty-eight years—*walks* into the temple after being healed. He wants to be in God's house. But then the Pharisees lecture him on carrying his mat. And when he explains *why* he's carrying his mat, the Pharisees tell him that no one should've healed him on the Sabbath. How embarrassing and heartbreaking that must have been for the man!

So just when the man needs Him again, Jesus finds him and encourages him. He tells the man to go and sin no more.

TODAY'S GOD SHOT

Jesus calls us to life. When Jesus heals the paralyzed man, the man goes to the temple so that he can be close to God. God the Son changes this man's life, not just by healing his legs but by calling him to a better life. The man who met the Life Giver face-to-face knows for sure that He's where the joy is!

ZOOM IN

They watched Jesus, to see whether he would heal him on the Sabbath, so that they might accuse him.

Mark 3:2 ESV

When the Pharisees accuse Jesus and the disciples of breaking Sabbath laws, Jesus teaches them that God made the Sabbath laws to serve people and give them the gift of rest and health. So people's needs—and health—are greater than the Sabbath law. All of God's laws point to who He is and how much He loves His kids, but the Pharisees have twisted and added onto His laws until they no longer point to God. As you can imagine, the Pharisees are not happy with Jesus. So they set a trap for Him using a man with a shriveled hand.

Jesus chooses twelve of His disciples as His students and closest followers. But His own family thinks He's lost His mind. Maybe they're mad at Him for making the Pharisees angry, or maybe they don't believe He's the Messiah, but whatever the reason, Jesus calls His closest twelve disciples His family. These twelve disciples have a special name, **apostles**, and Jesus gives them authority to preach and cast out demons in His name.

TODAY'S GOD SHOT

Jesus is falsely accused by the Pharisees, and even by His friends and family members. He knows what it's like to be misunderstood and mistreated, and He's so kind toward others who are treated the same way. The Pharisees use the man with the shriveled hand to try to trap Jesus, but Jesus saw their mistreatment of him and treated him with gentleness, mercy, and healing. He's so kind, and He's where the joy is!

MATTHEW 5–7

ZOOM IN

In the same way, let your light shine before others, so that they may see your good works and give glory to your Father who is in heaven.

Matthew 5:16 ESV

Today we read one of Jesus's most famous sermons, which we call the Sermon on the Mount. To start off, He says people who are aware of their own spiritual needs or who are mourning or even hated are blessed (happy)! Seems mixed up, right? That's because Jesus is describing the *upside-down kingdom* of God, which is the best kingdom ever.

To live in God's kingdom, we have to recognize how great our sin is and how much we need a Savior—that's Jesus!—and say yes to His offer of salvation.

Jesus warns against trying to impress others with how holy we are, because that would just be a show anyway. He says that while people can tell if actions are right or wrong, only God can know someone's heart. And He reminds everyone that God's kids don't have to worry, because God will provide for us.

TODAY'S GOD SHOT

God gets the glory when our light shines. He gave us His light, and God the Spirit is the one who leads us to do good works. We wouldn't have light and we couldn't do good works without God, so *of course* He gets the glory! That doesn't leave us with nothing, though. When God gets the glory, we get the joy. He's where the joy is!

─ **ZOOM IN** ─

Jesus turned, and seeing her he said, "Take heart, daughter; your faith has made you well." And instantly the woman was made well.

Matthew 9:22 ESV

The Pharisees are shocked that Jesus eats with sinners and tax collectors, but Jesus tells them He came for the sinners.

Jairus, a synagogue ruler, has a daughter who is dying. Jesus agrees to help the girl, but on the way there, He is stopped by a woman. This woman has a medical issue that's made her bleed for twelve years. According to the law, she's unclean, and unclean people are outcasts. She's lonely and exhausted and desperate, and when Jesus walks by, she touches His prayer tassel, believing that will heal her. And she is healed—by Jesus, not by something He's wearing.

By the time they get to Jairus's house, after Jesus stops to talk to the woman He healed, there are mourners crying that the girl is dead. Jesus tells them she's not dead, just sleeping, and He brings her back to life. Then He heals two blind men and raises a widow's only son from the dead.

Later, a broken and sinful woman washes Jesus's feet with her tears and anoints them with expensive oil. Again, the Pharisees are disgusted, but Jesus tells her that her sins are forgiven.

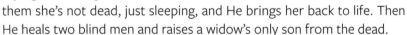

TODAY'S GOD SHOT

A few times today, Jesus told people that their faith healed them. But how can this be true? After all, He heals a girl on the brink of death and brings a dead boy back to life today. Dead people don't have faith. Faith itself cannot heal us. But if the object of our faith is God, *He* can heal us. Whether He heals someone's sickness or not, He's worth putting our faith in. He's where the joy is!

MATTHEW 11

Come to me, all who labor and are heavy laden, and I will give you rest.

Matthew 11:28 ESV

John the Baptist (JTB) is still in prison. He seems to be wondering, *If Jesus is the Son of God, why won't He get me out of prison?* At that time, prisoners weren't given food, water, clothes, or blankets unless their family or friends brought them, and prisoners were often abused. So JTB might not be doubting Jesus; he may just be worn down and desperate. But he sends some of his friends to ask Jesus directly whether He's the Messiah. Jesus sends back a message using Old Testament Scriptures that JTB will understand. The message basically means, "Yes, I'm the Messiah. But you will die in prison." Jesus knows that this news will be so hard to hear, and He praises JTB to His disciples.

Jesus does 90 percent of His miracles in His home base of Capernaum. They see the most evidence that He is God, but they believe Him the least. Jesus thanks His Father for giving soft hearts to the people who do believe in Him.

A **yoke** is a wooden beam put over the necks of two animals in order to help them pull something heavy. The "yoke" the Pharisees expected Jews to carry was the entire weight of God's laws *and* the laws they made up. It's impossibly heavy! Jesus says His yoke is easy and His burden is light. He invites people to rest.

TODAY'S GOD SHOT

Jesus gives rest. To sinful, broken, tired, sick, poor, worried, burdened people. He invites us to Himself—the giver and the source of rest. He's where the rest is, and He's where the joy is!

ZOOM IN

And so I tell you, keep on asking, and you will receive what you ask for. Keep on seeking, and you will find. Keep on knocking, and the door will be opened to you.

Luke 11:9

Jesus's apostles ask Him how to pray. Prayer is something we can all learn more about and get better at. Jesus teaches His followers to pray to the Father. Even though God the Father, God the Son, and God the Spirit are all God, they each have different roles. And since God the Father is the authority within the Trinity, Jesus teaches His followers to pray to the Father. Isn't it awesome that we can take our prayers directly to the supreme authority of the entire universe?

Jesus also teaches the apostles that His Father's will is good and right. We can tell God what we want, and even what we *think* we need, but He is ultimately the one who knows best and decides how to respond to us.

Later, as Jesus eats in a Pharisee's home, He rebukes the Pharisees for crushing people with the law. He says the experts in the law won't enter the kingdom of heaven, and that they're blocking other people from entering too.

~TODAY'S GOD SHOT

God loves to hear from His kids. Jesus uses little examples like bread, fish, and eggs to explain prayer; He wants us to know that *nothing* is too small or silly to talk to God about! Every time His kids pray, God answers. Sometimes the answer is yes, sometimes the answer is no, sometimes the answer is wait. No prayer is left unanswered. He's a good Father, and He's where the joy is!

DAY 287

MATTHEW 13; LUKE 8

ZOOM IN

The seeds that fell on the good soil represent honest, good-hearted people who hear God's word, cling to it, and patiently produce a huge harvest.

Luke 8:15

Jesus often taught using **parables**, or stories. Here, He compares the gospel to a seed. A farmer plants seeds on four different types of soil. The last type of soil is good soil, representing a person who hears the gospel, understands it, and grows in their faith.

Jesus's disciples are worried that the crowd doesn't understand Him, but Jesus says some people won't understand Him—their hearts are hard. He explains His parable to the disciples, but not to the whole crowd.

TODAY'S GOD SHOT

Jesus traveled with poor fishermen, wealthy tax collectors, family members of the king's officials, and a formerly demonized woman. Jesus didn't come for one group or type of people; He came for all types of people! His disciples may have looked like all different types of "soil," but the gospel grew in each of their hearts. God can take even the rockiest or driest soil and grow a garden. He's where the joy is!

SEVEN-DAY ROUNDUP

ZOOM OUT

As Jesus's ministry continued, He drew great crowds. Some of the people sought Him out for healing and miracles, while others were curious about His teaching. And the more people talked about Jesus, the angrier the Pharisees became. But Jesus continued doing the work He was sent for, teaching people about God and showing signs that He *is* God.

WORDS TO REMEMBER

- Apostle—a disciple who is given authority to preach and perform miracles in Jesus's name; twelve of Jesus's disciples during His ministry were apostles
- Parable—a short story, usually without named people or places, used to teach one main lesson
- Yoke—a wooden beam put over the necks of two animals so they can pull a cart or plow

APPLICATION

The Lord's Prayer is the name we use for the prayer Jesus taught His disciples. You can find it in your Bible in Matthew 6:9–13 and Luke 11:1–4. Go back and read Jesus's prayer again. Write it down and pray it every day. Pray that God will change your heart when you fill it with the words Jesus prayed!

MARK 4–5

ZOOM IN

When Jesus woke up, he rebuked the wind and said to the waves, "Silence! Be still!" Suddenly the wind stopped, and there was a great calm.

Mark 4:39

We read Mark's version of the parable of the four soils today. (Remember why we'll read some stories more than once? It's written by a different author, so it's a different perspective of the same story.) Then there's a question about the purpose of a lamp. The seed and the light both go everywhere. The seed has to fall on the right soil to grow, but the light shines no matter what!

When we read the story of the storm on the Sea of Galilee this time, we learn that the boat starts to fill with water. The disciples are scared, and that tells us a lot about this storm, because many of them were fishermen who were used to all kinds of stormy weather.

While they're panicking about what to do, Jesus is sleeping. The disciples wake Jesus up, and He rebukes the storm, calming and encouraging His disciples.

TODAY'S GOD SHOT

Jesus teaches the disciples something about Himself in every situation. They needed the storm because they needed to learn that He's sovereign over everything—even nature. They needed to learn that they can trust Him to take care of them. Soon they're all going to go through much harder things than a storm, and little by little, Jesus is preparing them. Their faith is growing, and they're learning that their relationship with God is the most important thing in their lives. And as we read God's Word, we're learning that too. He's where the joy is!

Don't carry a traveler's bag with a change of clothes and sandals or even a walking stick. Don't hesitate to accept hospitality, because those who work deserve to be fed.

Matthew 10:10

Jesus sends the twelve apostles out with a mission: Proclaim the kingdom of God, heal the sick, and raise the dead. He gives them authority to do all these things in His name. And more than that, He tells them what to pack (or really, what *not* to pack) and what to say. He's teaching them to rely on Him to take care of all their needs, even when He's not physically with them.

Jesus warns them that they'll be **persecuted** by people who don't understand their message, who might even be their own families. They'll be questioned, mistreated, and even brought to trial. But He also tells them that God the Spirit will tell them exactly what to say when that time comes. And He reminds them that nothing their enemies can do to them is eternal.

TODAY'S GOD SHOT

Jesus gives His disciples everything they need, down to every detail. Of course, He's watching over the most important detail: their souls. And He's watching over the medium-sized details: what they'll eat and where they'll sleep. He's even watching over the small details: He tells them what words to speak. God cares about all the details in our lives—big, medium, and small. He makes sure you have everything you need too! He's where the joy is!

MATTHEW 14; MARK 6; LUKE 9

ZOOM IN

They were all terrified when they saw him. But Jesus spoke to them at once. "Don't be afraid," he said. "Take courage! I am here!"

Mark 6:50

John the Baptist (JTB) has been in prison since the first days of Jesus's ministry. And now, because of the evil, twisted actions of Herod and his family, JTB is killed.

When Jesus is told about JTB's death, He and the disciples go off in a boat. He probably wants to grieve and talk to His Father, but some local people spot Him and form a large crowd to wait for the boat to dock. There were five thousand men, which means there would've been even more women and children. Jesus is heartbroken. He knows that the same government that killed JTB, His cousin and forerunner, will soon kill Him. He probably wants to be alone, and now a massive crowd wants something from Him. So He feeds them. After the miracle of feeding the crowd, there are twelve baskets of food left over—one for each of the apostles. He takes care of the crowd, and He takes care of them.

Later, another storm comes up while the disciples are in the boat. Jesus sees them from His place of prayer and goes out to calm them, walking on the water to get there.

TODAY'S GOD SHOT

God is with us, even in the worst storms. For the disciples, the storm would've been bad enough on its own. But they've been mourning the death of JTB, serving people, and traveling, and they're exhausted. They think things couldn't possibly get worse, and then they see a ghost! But what they think is scary is actually God moving in their lives, showing them He's with them. He's powerful, He's with us, and He's where the joy is!

ZOOM IN

Jesus said, "I chose the twelve of you, but one is a devil." He was speaking of Judas, son of Simon Iscariot, one of the Twelve, who would later betray him.

John 6:70–71

The crowd Jesus just fed wakes up and looks for Jesus. When they find Him, He tells them they're only following Him because He fed them. He knows they're more interested in His miracles than His teaching. And Jesus won't spend all His time on temporary things; He came to change *eternal* outcomes.

So when they ask Him what doing the work of God means, He tells them, "This is the only work God wants from you: Believe in the one he has sent." Surrendering yourself to the Truth is a sign you're a follower of Jesus. The crowd misses the point entirely, and they demand a sign. He just gave them one the day before, and they've already forgotten! Jesus tells them He is the bread of life, which means He's the source of every-thing we need. The people don't understand, and argue with each other.

TODAY'S GOD SHOT

Jesus tells the truth, even when it's hard to hear. He has twelve apostles, but one of them will betray Him and one of them will deny Him. Jesus knows that, but He keeps them close anyway. Jesus tells the truth about who we are, and He loves us perfectly. He's where the joy is!

MATTHEW 15; MARK 7

ZOOM IN

A vast crowd brought to him people who were lame, blind, crippled, those who couldn't speak, and many others. They laid them before Jesus, and he healed them all.

Matthew 15:30

The Pharisees are complaining about Jesus again. This time they're upset that His disciples don't wash their hands before they eat. God's law about this type of formal hand washing isn't for every Jew; it's for priests. So Jesus tells the Pharisees they can't make people follow rules they made up.

The Pharisees love being "right," but they have no idea how to be righteous. They love their rules more than they love God. Jesus tells His disciples that the Pharisees are blind, meaning they can't see the truth. Jesus also tells them that what matters is what comes out of your mouth, because that shows what's in your heart.

Later, Jesus heals a Gentile woman's demonized daughter. The woman shows great knowledge *and* great faith in the way she speaks to Jesus. Then, for three days Jesus stays on a mountain in a Gentile region, healing people.

TODAY'S GOD SHOT

Jesus is compassionate. So many people bring Him their sick family members and friends that He stays where He is for three days to heal them all. And while they're waiting, He tells His disciples to feed them. He provides for all their needs. He's where the joy is!

ZOOM IN

Simon Peter answered, "You are the Messiah, the Son of the living God."

Matthew 16:16

Jesus compares the Pharisees' and **Sadducees'** teachings to yeast: Even a little bit of bad teaching can have a huge impact. Both groups thought the goal of faith was to control your own actions, which means they'd never understand why Jesus came.

Jesus takes His disciples to Caesarea Philippi, a place with horrific pagan worship rituals. Terrible things happen there, including child sacrifices. He asks His disciples who people say the Son of Man—or the Messiah—is. Then He asks them who *they* think He is. Simon Peter answers, "You are the **Christ**, the Son of the living God" (Matthew 16:16 ESV).

Jesus tells Peter that he's right! Jesus is the *Christ*—which comes from a Greek word meaning the same thing as Messiah—and the Son of God. He's the Savior, He's the Chosen One, and He's God. Jesus says that this vital truth is the very foundation on which His **church** will be built. And it will outlast everything else on earth!

TODAY'S GOD SHOT

Jesus knows He'll die soon, so He prepares the apostles. He knows they'll be tempted to think all this work was for nothing, and He doesn't want them to turn away when they're persecuted. So He takes them to the worst place they know of to tell them that even the most evil, wicked things they can think of won't stop the kingdom of God. They can be bold, because God has already won. We can be bold, because He's our King. He's where the joy is!

MATTHEW 17; MARK 9

There are three major events in the New Testament that show God's power
and His kingdom in awesome and unique ways. Today, we read about the
first one, called the **transfiguration**.

Jesus has already warned the disciples that He's going to suffer and die,
which was hard for them to accept. Today He takes Peter, James, and John
up on a mountain and gives them a glimpse into the spiritual world, letting
them see things human eyes can't see. Jesus transfigures—or changes
forms—right in front of them. His face shines
like the sun and His clothes turn white.
Moses and Elijah show up, representing
the law and the prophets, which Jesus
came to fulfill! And then, God speaks
from heaven. He tells the disciples to
listen to His Son.

Later, Jesus heals a demonized boy.
Then He pays His and Peter's taxes
by sending Peter fishing. When Peter
opens the fish's mouth, the money is
inside!

∼ TODAY'S GOD SHOT ∼

God gives us faith. We don't have to rely on ourselves to make our faith
stronger. The demonized boy's dad confesses to Jesus that he has faith
and he also has doubts. He asks Jesus to help him believe more. God
wants us to come to Him for everything, including faith. He is the source
of everything, and He's where the joy is!

SEVEN-DAY ROUNDUP

ZOOM OUT

We are following Jesus's ministry, and we've seen Him tell parables, stop storms, cast out demons, heal the sick, challenge the Pharisees, and feed the crowds. He knew He was about six months away from His death, so He began preparing His disciples.

WORDS TO REMEMBER

- Christ—savior; from a Greek word meaning "chosen or anointed one"
- Church—a group of believers who practice their faith in Jesus together; it can also refer to all believers around the whole world
- Persecute—to oppress or abuse someone, usually because of their religious beliefs
- Sadducees—a group of religious leaders in Israel who believed that only the Torah (the first five books of the Bible) was God's Word
- Transfiguration—the event where Jesus changed form in front of three of His apostles, showing God's power in an awesome way

APPLICATION

Take a walk outside and look for some plants that are growing tall and strong. (If it's too cold where you live for plants to grow right now, think about a place where plants usually grow tall and strong.) Bend down and touch the soil under the plants. What is the soil like? Dry, wet, hard, soft? Pray and ask God to make the "soil" of your heart a place where the gospel will grow.

MATTHEW 18

> If a man has a hundred sheep and one of them wanders away, what will he do? Won't he leave the ninety-nine others on the hills and go out to search for the one that is lost?
>
> Matthew 18:12

The disciples ask Jesus which one of them is the greatest, but Jesus puts them in their place pretty quickly. He says that in His kingdom, greatness comes from humility. He points out that kids show humility in their faith—they're teachable and trusting—and to be great in the kingdom of heaven, you have to think like a kid. Back then, kids weren't seen as very important, but Jesus loves kids! They're made in God's image!

He also tells them what to do when they're tempted to sin. He gives them extreme examples, like this one: If your eye causes you to sin, pluck it out. Of course, Jesus overstates it here (don't *actually* do that), but it's to make this point: Sin is serious, and people who love God take their own sin seriously. He also teaches the disciples what to do when someone has sinned against them and hurt them.

Then He teaches them about forgiveness and tells a parable about a man who owes a great debt. All of us are that man. When we understand how much we've been forgiven, we forgive others in return.

TODAY'S GOD SHOT

God pays individual attention to His kids. When we run away, He sees and He acts. He finds us and He carries us back. And then He rejoices over us! He's always working, even when we run away. He's where the joy is!

---ZOOM IN---

Jesus spoke to the people once more and said, "I am the light of the world. If you follow me, you won't have to walk in darkness, because you will have the light that leads to life."

John 8:12

Three times a year, Jews travel to Jerusalem for a feast. Before one of these feasts, Jesus's brothers mock Him and say He should publicly display His power while He's there. They don't believe He's God's Son.

While Jesus is in Jerusalem, He teaches in the temple, and people are amazed by what He knows. He says He speaks with God's authority, and they're confused. Some wonder if He's the Messiah, but others want to arrest Him.

Then the Pharisees bring a woman to Jesus because they're trying to shame her for her sin. But Jesus doesn't fall into their trap. He treats her with mercy and kindness, and He tells her to leave her sin behind.

When Jesus says He's the Light of the World, the Pharisees question Him. Jesus tells them that if they recognized Him for who He really is, then they'd also know God the Father. But instead, they don't know God at all.

~~TODAY'S GOD SHOT~~

Jesus is the Light of the World, which means that we see everything because of Him! In Genesis 1:3, God looks out over the dark world that He knows will soon be broken by sin, and He says, "Let there be light." And light came immediately. But the better and eternal Light came when Jesus was born. Jesus is the Light, and He's where the joy is!

JOHN 9–10

ZOOM IN

I give them eternal life, and they will never perish. No one can snatch them away from me, for my Father has given them to me, and he is more powerful than anyone else. No one can snatch them from the Father's hand. The Father and I are one.

John 10:28–30

People in Jesus's time believe that if someone is sick or disabled, it's the result of sin. When Jesus's disciples meet a blind man, they ask Jesus if the man is the one who sinned or if it was his parents. This belief isn't in the Bible, and Jesus sets them straight. He says the man's blindness will actually be used to glorify God.

Jesus heals the man by spitting on the dirt to make mud, which He puts on the blind man's eyes. The Pharisees had decided that spitting on the dirt was illegal on the Sabbath, so they accuse Jesus of breaking God's law. But of course, Jesus didn't break God's law; He broke the Pharisees' law. They want Jesus to tell them once and for all: Is He the Messiah or not? Jesus says they don't believe in Him because they're not His sheep. Jesus calls Himself the Good Shepherd. He takes care of His sheep and keeps them safe.

TODAY'S GOD SHOT

God holds His kids in His hand, and no one can snatch us away. If you're God's kid, no one can separate you from God, not even yourself. *How great is that?!* For all of eternity, He holds you. He's where the joy is!

ZOOM IN

"Now which of these three would you say was a neighbor to the man who was attacked by bandits?" Jesus asked. The man replied, "The one who showed him mercy." Then Jesus said, "Yes, now go and do the same."

Luke 10:36–37

A lawyer asks Jesus how to get eternal life, but he doesn't really want to know. He's either testing Jesus or trying to prove that he's earning eternal life through his good actions. So Jesus asks the lawyer what he thinks the law says. The man answers with part of the Shema, saying, "'You must love the Lord your God with all your heart, all your soul, all your strength, and all your mind.' And, 'Love your neighbor as yourself'" (10:27).

When Jesus tells the man that he's right, the man pushes further, probably trying to get out of the second part of the command. He asks who his "neighbor" is. Then Jesus answers with a parable about a severely wounded man and the Samaritan (someone Jews viewed negatively at that time) who helps him. A "neighbor" is anyone you meet, even if they're your enemy.

TODAY'S GOD SHOT

Jesus is the ultimate Good Samaritan. The Samaritan and Jesus are both rejected and despised, but they concern themselves with the hurting. They both pay the price for healing and rest. And they both promise to return. In the parable Jesus tells, the Good Samaritan does something good and true and beautiful, and it points to Jesus! Everything we do on earth is temporary; everything Jesus has done or will do is eternal. He's where the joy is!

LUKE 12–13

ZOOM IN

So don't be afraid, little flock. For it gives your Father great happiness to give you the Kingdom.

Luke 12:32

While Jesus is preaching, a man interrupts and asks Him to settle an argument about money. Jesus cautions the man that life isn't measured by money; then He tells a parable about a foolish man who plans to build new barns to hold all his wealth, but God tells him he'll die that night. We don't know how long we will live and Jesus could come back at any moment, so we need to prepare for eternity. And preparing for eternity means answering this question: *Do we know Jesus or not?* A relationship with Jesus is the only preparation we can have, and it's the only preparation we need!

Jesus tells another parable about a man who plants a tree that's fruitless for three years. Most Bible teachers say this parable shows God as the planter, Jesus as the gardener, and Israel as the tree. Jesus has ministered to Israel for three years, but Israel isn't repenting. The man is patient with the tree, and God is patient with Israel.

TODAY'S GOD SHOT

God delights in giving His kids good gifts! He doesn't want us to be afraid, because He is with us. He pays attention to us, He delights in us, and He gives us good gifts. And the best gift of all? He gives us Himself! He's where the joy is!

ZOOM IN

His father said to him, "Look, dear son, you have always stayed by me, and everything I have is yours. We had to celebrate this happy day. For your brother was dead and has come back to life! He was lost, but now he is found!"

Luke 15:31–32

Jesus has dinner at a Pharisee's house, where He meets a man with a dangerous medical condition. The condition makes his body swell up. Since it's the Sabbath, Jesus asks the Pharisees if it's legal for Him to heal the man. (Of course, Jesus knows the answer!) The Pharisees don't answer, so Jesus heals the man and sends him home. Jesus tells the Pharisees to humble themselves now or else they'll be humbled later.

Then Jesus tells three parables about lost things: a sheep, a coin, and a son. In each parable, the lost item is found and celebrated!

~TODAY'S GOD SHOT~

God celebrates us! It seems almost too good to be true, doesn't it? In the parables of the lost sheep, the lost coin, and the lost son, there is rejoicing when what was lost is found. Jesus says that in the same way, God rejoices when a sinner repents. He celebrates us, and He's where the joy is!

LUKE 16–17

ZOOM IN

The Kingdom of God can't be detected by visible signs. You won't be able to say, "Here it is!" or "It's over there!" For the Kingdom of God is already among you.

Luke 17:20–21

We read a few stories Jesus tells today, and some of them are confusing. Just like in the Old Testament, when you come to a passage of Scripture that you don't understand, have patience. Pray that God will teach you something about Himself.

Jesus tells the disciples that they can't spend all their time and energy worrying about their money. They need to spend their time and energy learning about God and how to live His way. In another story, Jesus encourages His disciples to be humble, living as servants of God.

The Pharisees want to know when God's kingdom will come. They think God will send a political or military leader to wipe out their enemies and bring peace, but Jesus tells them it won't happen that way. Jesus says He *is* the kingdom of God.

TODAY'S GOD SHOT

Jesus tells His disciples about the coming of His kingdom, and His speech is full of heavy and confusing information, such as "The time is coming when you will long to see the day when the Son of Man returns, but you won't see it" (17:22), and "That night two people will be asleep in one bed; one will be taken, the other left" (17:34). But He also tells them the best promise: *He's coming back!* And on that day, those who know Him will be united with Him. Even when we don't understand everything else, that's the comfort we can cling to. He's where the joy is!

SEVEN-DAY ROUNDUP

ZOOM OUT

We read some of Jesus's most famous parables in the last seven days: the man who owed a great debt, the Good Samaritan, and the lost son. In each story, He taught the disciples more about Himself and His kingdom. The Pharisees are getting angrier by the day, trying to trap Him into breaking the law. But of course, they can't. Jesus is the only person who's ever kept God's law perfectly.

APPLICATION

The Good Samaritan shows his neighbor love like Jesus's love. He sees a need and meets it. He makes sure the man gets the care that he needs. Do you have a neighbor who needs to see Jesus's love? Pray that God will show you someone who is hurting and in need. Then talk with a grown-up who loves Jesus about ways you can show your neighbor love like Jesus's kind of love.

JOHN 11

Mary and Martha—who we've met before—send a message to Jesus to let Him know their brother Lazarus is very sick. But instead of going to their house right away, Jesus says Lazarus's sickness will be used to glorify God. By the time Jesus and His disciples arrive, Lazarus has been dead for four days. When Jesus sees His friend Mary, He breaks down and cries.

Jesus says to roll the stone of Lazarus's tomb away, prays and thanks the Father, then calls Lazarus out of the tomb—and he comes out, fully alive! *Whoa!* Some people in the crowd believe in Jesus, but others run straight to the Pharisees to report what happened. Caiaphas the high priest becomes a prophet—accidentally for him, but on purpose by God—when he says, "You don't realize that it's better for you that one man should die for the people than for the whole nation to be destroyed" (11:50). So the religious leaders start to plot Jesus's death.

TODAY'S GOD SHOT

Jesus waits for Lazarus to die before He goes to the family's house. This miracle of bringing a dead man back to life sets into motion the plan to kill Jesus. When Jesus cries, we don't know for sure what He's thinking about. The heartbreak of His friends who are mourning over their brother? The brokenness of the world He came to save? His own death, which will happen soon? Whatever His reasons, we get to see that Jesus is both fully human—weeping over death—and fully God—*defeating* death. Even in weeping, He's where the joy is!

ZOOM IN

"Yes," Jesus replied, "and I assure you that everyone who has given up house or wife or brothers or parents or children, for the sake of the Kingdom of God, will be repaid many times over in this life, and will have eternal life in the world to come."

Luke 18:29–30

Jesus encourages His disciples to pray about what's really on their hearts and to not give up. He tells them a parable about a wicked judge who gives in after a widow won't stop bugging him. This *isn't* a direct picture of God hearing our prayers; God is *better* than this. So if even a wicked judge gives in to a widow's desperation, imagine how much *more* a loving, caring, generous Father will do for His kids! When we pray for something and God gives it to us, we're reminded of how generous He is.

Jesus meets a rich man who wants to know how to get into heaven. He claims he has obeyed the law, but Jesus pushes him to think deeper—to examine his *heart*. The man realizes he isn't willing to give up the security of his wealth in order to follow Jesus, and he leaves sad.

Jesus tells His disciples again that He'll die soon, and this time He gives them more heartbreaking details, but they don't understand Him yet.

TODAY'S GOD SHOT

Jesus promises that whatever we lose for the sake of His kingdom won't compare at all to what we gain. He takes what doesn't serve us or His plan for us, and He gives us so much more in return! He's always giving life, hope, peace, healing, freedom, justice, and joy, because He's where the joy is!

MATTHEW 19; MARK 10

ZOOM IN

Whoever wants to be first among you must be the slave of everyone else. For even the Son of Man came not to be served but to serve others and to give his life as a ransom for many.

Mark 10:44–45

The Pharisees ask Jesus a question about divorce, and Jesus answers them. It's a hard teaching because it's so strict, and His disciples tell Him it sounds like it's easier not to get married at all. Jesus tells them that for some people, this is true. When you're an adult, being married can be hard, and being single can be hard too. God's plans for His kids are different, and whatever plan He has for your life, it won't be easy, but He'll be with you!

James and John ask Jesus if they can sit at His side in the kingdom of heaven, and He tells them no. James and John might not understand what He means yet, but in the kingdom, Jesus will be seated at the right hand of the Father. They'll understand then!

TODAY'S GOD SHOT

Jesus came as a servant. When He died, He took Himself away from them physically, but left them something that will last forever. By sacrificing His life, He offers us eternal life. He gave up everything to give us everything, and He's where the joy is!

ZOOM IN

He noticed a fig tree beside the road. He went over to see if there were any figs, but there were only leaves. Then he said to it, "May you never bear fruit again!" And immediately the fig tree withered up.

Matthew 21:19

Jesus tells a parable about a vineyard and its workers. The vineyard owner pays everyone the same amount of money, even though some of them work longer hours. The parable teaches us that everything God gives us is a gift of His grace.

Jesus continues His journey to Jerusalem. It's time to celebrate the Passover, but He's also going to be crucified. On the way, He sees a fig tree that doesn't have any fruit on it. It's not fig season yet, so why is Jesus angry? The fig tree probably represents Israel. God has waited and waited for Israel to bear fruit, but it hasn't. And Jesus knows what is going to happen soon.

Jesus teaches in the temple and tells two more parables. In both parables, judgment is coming for those who reject Jesus as the Christ.

TODAY'S GOD SHOT

Jesus has power over life and death. He speaks life and healing so many times, but to the fig tree, He speaks death. He could have spoken death at any time to the people who would kill Him, but He didn't. He came to fulfill the Father's plan to bring God's kids into His kingdom forever. He's where the joy is!

DAY 306

LUKE 19

ZOOM IN

For the Son of Man came to seek and save those who are lost.

Luke 19:10

In Luke's telling of the story, Jesus hasn't yet gotten to Jerusalem. He's on His way there when He meets Zacchaeus, a tax collector. Zacchaeus is healthy and rich, so he isn't looking for a blessing, but he has heard about Jesus and he's curious. He climbs a tree so he can see Jesus, and Jesus sees him, calls him by name, and invites Himself over to dinner. Zacchaeus is changed by Jesus and has a heart of repentance.

Jesus sends two of His disciples for a colt, a young donkey. Fulfilling the prophecy from Zechariah 9:9, the King of the universe enters Jerusalem on a donkey, a sign of someone bringing peace. As He looks over Jerusalem, He weeps. He loves the city and the people in it, but they don't see Him for who He is, and they don't understand the reason He came.

~TODAY'S GOD SHOT~

Jesus tells a story with you in it. When He says that He came "to seek and save those who are lost" (19:10), that's you! In fact, it's all of us. Jesus does all the work here: He comes, He seeks, and He saves. We could never save ourselves, so thank God that Jesus does it for us. He's where the joy is!

ZOOM IN

Now my soul is deeply troubled. Should I pray, "Father, save me from this hour"? But this is the very reason I came! Father, bring glory to your name.

John 12:27–28

Jesus goes to Mary, Martha, and Lazarus's house for dinner. Mary takes a jar of expensive perfume and pours it on His feet. Then she wipes His feet with her hair. Judas—the disciple who will soon betray Jesus—says the perfume should've been sold and the money given to the poor. But really, he just wants to sell the perfume and steal the money. Jesus defends Mary and points again to His coming death.

Jesus wants to be rescued from what's about to happen. He's fully God, so He knows what He's about to endure, and He's fully man, so He's distraught about the suffering that's coming. He knows that there is no other way to accomplish His mission: He must be the perfect sacrifice to pay the debt for our sins.

TODAY'S GOD SHOT

Jesus can bring the dead back to life, stop a powerful storm, multiply food, and so much more. But when it comes to His death, He submits to the plan. Jesus is God the Son; He's not just a miracle worker or a good teacher. Yet He still obeys God the Father. He knows that even though His death will be the most horrific pain anyone could experience, God's plan is the best plan. He's where the joy is!

MATTHEW 22; MARK 12

ZOOM IN

Jesus called his disciples to him and said, "I tell you the truth, this poor widow has given more than all the others who are making contributions."

Mark 12:43

The Pharisees ask Jesus questions about taxes, trying to trap Him into breaking the law. Jesus tells them to keep the government's laws, even if the government is oppressing them. Then the Sadducees try to trap Him with a made-up situation about the afterlife. Jesus answers their question with truth, then points out that the Sadducees don't even believe in the afterlife. And then, He corrects their wrong belief about the afterlife by pointing out the Scriptures they've been ignoring.

Then, a Pharisee scribe asks Jesus which commandment—there are over six hundred in the Old Testament—is the most important. Jesus answers with the Shema, summarizing all six hundred of the laws into two: Love God with your entire being, and love your neighbor like you love yourself.

TODAY'S GOD SHOT

God's heart is for the poor. He sees and cares for the people who have nothing, and Jesus wants His disciples to do the same. He points out to them the widow who gives pennies and says she's given more than even the rich gave. He sees and cares, and He's where the joy is!

SEVEN-DAY ROUNDUP

ZOOM OUT

Over the last seven days, we followed Jesus back to Jerusalem as He prepares for His coming death. His warnings about His death have been coming more frequently, as He's preparing His disciples for life afterward. Meanwhile, even though Jesus is troubled about what will happen to Him, He knows God's plan is perfect.

APPLICATION

In Matthew 22:37–40, Jesus says that the entire Old Testament law can be summarized into two laws: love God and love people. Make a list of some of the ways you can love God. Then, make a list of some of the ways you can love people. Pray and ask God to help you love Him and others. We can't love anyone without His help!

MATTHEW 23; LUKE 20-21

ZOOM IN

When you hear of wars and insurrections, don't panic. Yes, these things must take place first, but the end won't follow immediately.

Luke 21:9

In Matthew's gospel, Jesus's seven warnings to the Pharisees are all in one place, and they're serious. Like Isaiah warned Israel about their six woes, Jesus warns the Pharisees about the troubles ahead for them. The Pharisees try to make themselves look righteous, but they're actually greedy and selfish. Jesus tells the crowds to do what the Pharisees say but *not* what they do.

Jesus says His followers will be able to endure even the darkest times on earth because He'll make them able. He warns that we shouldn't get caught up in the things of this world, but we should focus on what's eternal.

TODAY'S GOD SHOT

Jesus says we shouldn't panic when we hear about wars and fighting. He knows how it all ends, so He can tell us with truth and authority that we don't need to worry. He never says that things in life won't be scary or hard, but He promises that we won't be alone. Whatever scary thing happens in the world, it's no match for God! He's where the joy is!

---ZOOM IN---

You, too, must keep watch! For you don't know when the master of the household will return—in the evening, at midnight, before dawn, or at daybreak.

Mark 13:35

As Jesus and His disciples leave the temple, one of them remarks on how beautiful and impressive it is. Jesus tells them that soon it'll be destroyed. (And about forty years later, it happens.)

They go up to the Mount of Olives, and Jesus's closest disciples ask Him questions about the end of the earth. They want to know two things: *how* they'll know it's happening and *when* it'll happen. He explains how they'll know it's happening but doesn't tell them *when*. He knows it won't help their faith. However, He does instruct them what not to do: worry. And He tells them what to do now: stay awake, keep watch, stand firm, endure, and pray.

～TODAY'S GOD SHOT～

Jesus promises that God's kids will have hard times, and He also promises that He'll protect us from eternal harm. He's honest that trials will come. And He's also encouraging when He says that because of His salvation we'll endure. He's building an unstoppable kingdom, and His kids are a part of it! He's where the joy is!

MATTHEW 24

ZOOM IN

So you, too, must keep watch! For you don't know what day your Lord is coming.

Matthew 24:42

It's the final week of Jesus's life, and He tells His closest followers that the temple will be destroyed, Jerusalem will fall to Rome, and they will endure many trials. These aren't easy messages for His disciples to hear, but He tells them not to worry.

Jesus encourages His followers with reminders that His kingdom will keep going and growing. What they're building is eternal. The gospel won't die out and it can't be killed off. It will keep reaching people of all nations until the day that He returns!

TODAY'S GOD SHOT

Jesus tells His followers how to prepare. He doesn't tell them to spend all their time trying to figure out the exact moment that He's coming back. Instead He tells them to stay awake (be aware) and keep watch (look forward to it). When we know Him, it's easier to trust Him. And whenever He comes back, it'll be the perfect moment. We can wait for His return while we trust that His timing is perfect. No matter what happens or when, He's where the joy is!

ZOOM IN

Then the King will say to those on his right, "Come, you who are blessed by my Father, inherit the Kingdom prepared for you from the creation of the world."

Matthew 25:34

Jesus teaches His followers how to wait well. He will die soon, and they'll have to spend the rest of their lives waiting for Him to return. We might spend the rest of our lives waiting for Him to return too, so it's important that we wait well.

Jesus uses more parables to explain how to wait: We must spend our time wisely, and we must use our gifts wisely. The more we know and trust God, the easier it will be for us to use our time and our gifts in generous ways that please Him and bless us.

Jesus explains that everyone will have eternal life. Everyone will be brought before God, and like a Shepherd, He'll separate the sheep from the goats. The goats will have eternal punishment. But the sheep—God's kids—will have eternal life with Him.

TODAY'S GOD SHOT

God has been preparing His kingdom for us since He created the world, and He's eager to share His blessings with His kids. What a beautiful day that will be! He's where the joy is!

MATTHEW 26; MARK 14

ZOOM IN

He replied, "It is one of you twelve who is eating from this bowl with me."

Mark 14:20

Jesus tells the disciples that He has only a few days to live. Judas realizes he can make money by turning Jesus in, and he makes a deal with the chief priests.

Jesus celebrates the Passover meal with His disciples, telling them the bread is His body and the wine is His blood. As followers of Jesus today, we observe this meal too; it's called the Lord's Supper, and it reminds our forgetful hearts that Jesus's body was broken and His blood was poured out for our sins. It's the best meal we can have because every time we eat it, we remember how much God loves us.

Even though there was always lamb to eat at the Passover meal, the Bible doesn't mention the disciples eating lamb. At the first Passover, the Angel of the LORD passed over every home marked by the blood of a lamb, leaving the children inside safe. Because of His death, Jesus's blood will keep His kids safe and give them eternal life. *Jesus* is the Passover Lamb.

TODAY'S GOD SHOT

Jesus feeds Judas, the one who will betray Him. Jesus knows what Judas will do, and He shows him this act of grace and mercy anyway. Through His death, Jesus offers life. Jesus offers life to everyone who believes in Him, and He's where the joy is!

ZOOM IN

So he got up from the table, took off his robe, wrapped a towel around his waist, and poured water into a basin. Then he began to wash the disciples' feet, drying them with the towel he had around him.

John 13:4–5

John says that Satan put the idea in Judas's heart to betray Jesus. Jesus still trusts the Father's plan. What Satan intends to use for evil, God uses for good. So at the Last Supper, Jesus serves even Judas, who He knows will betray Him. Jesus tells His disciples to love each other as He has loved them. Jesus tells Peter that he'll deny Him three times before the morning comes.

Jesus goes to the garden of Gethsemane to pray. It's a place where olives are crushed for their oil, and it's a place where Jesus is crushed with the weight of what's going to happen to Him. Since He is fully man, He is deeply troubled by the thought of going to the cross. He even sweats what might be blood. And since He is fully God, He knows that this is the will of His Father, and the only way for salvation.

Soldiers come to the garden to arrest Jesus and take Him to the high priest's house. Peter follows. Three different people ask him if he knows Jesus, and three times, he says no. Jesus looks at Peter, and Peter weeps—he knows what Jesus predicted about Peter's denial has come true.

The officials blindfold Jesus and beat Him and mock Him.

TODAY'S GOD SHOT

Jesus washes His disciples' feet. Without paved roads, at the end of a day of walking in sandals, the disciples' feet would've been filthy. Washing feet was a servant's job. Peter tries to refuse Jesus's act of humility, but Jesus does it anyway. The King and Savior of the universe humbles Himself like a servant. He's where the joy is!

JOHN 14–17

ZOOM IN

So you have sorrow now, but I will see you again; then you will rejoice, and no one can rob you of that joy.

John 16:22

John gives us more details about what Jesus says to His disciples before His death. Jesus is going away, and He tells the disciples that though they can't follow Him right now, they'll follow Him one day. And then they'll be with Him forever. Jesus says He'll prepare a room for them in His Father's house, which means they're family!

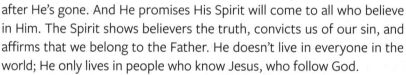

He explains that they'll continue to do the works of God after He's gone. And He promises His Spirit will come to all who believe in Him. The Spirit shows believers the truth, convicts us of our sin, and affirms that we belong to the Father. He doesn't live in everyone in the world; He only lives in people who know Jesus, who follow God.

Jesus prays for His disciples, and He prays for all believers. (If you follow Jesus, that's you too—Jesus prayed for you!) He prays for unity among us and that God will be glorified through us.

TODAY'S GOD SHOT

Jesus is with us, so we have everything we need. He gives us moments of peace and joy now, even in the middle of sorrow. And one day, He'll give us perfect peace and full joy for all of eternity. We won't be able to think of a single thing to ask Him for because we'll have everything we need. Our joy will last forever because we'll be with Him, and He's where the joy is!

SEVEN-DAY ROUNDUP

ZOOM OUT

Jesus taught His disciples, served them, and prayed for them. He prayed for us too. And then, He was arrested, blindfolded, beaten, and mocked. He went through six trials in eight hours, preparing to be killed. He knows this is the only way to save the world.

APPLICATION

Jesus is coming back one day, and until He does, His kids have work to do! In Matthew 25, Jesus told His disciples two parables about how to wait well. In one, the lesson is how to use time wisely, and in the other, the lesson is how to use gifts wisely.

Make a list of some of the ways you can serve God with your time. Then, make a list of some of the ways you can serve God with your gifts. Pray that God will show you how to use both your time and your gifts wisely until the day He returns.

MATTHEW 27; MARK 15

ZOOM IN

When they were finally tired of mocking him, they took off the purple robe and put his own clothes on him again. Then they led him away to be crucified.

Mark 15:20

Judas is overcome by the weight of his betrayal. He takes his own life.

Jesus has been declared guilty in three different religious trials. Now He is taken to the Roman governor, Pontius Pilate. The people accuse Jesus of claiming to be a king. Pilate apparently tries to avoid making a decision by sending Jesus to King Herod, but Jesus is sent back to Pilate.

Pilate says Jesus is innocent, but he gives the people a choice: He can release Jesus or Barabbas. Barabbas has been convicted of robbery and murder. The people choose to set Barabbas free. We are just like Barabbas—our sin means we deserve death, but Jesus takes our place and His blood atones for our sin.

Fulfilling God's plan, Jesus dies a terrible death on the cross. A follower of his named Joseph prepares His body for burial. He wraps His body in linen and places it in a tomb, then he rolls a giant stone in front of the tomb's entrance.

TODAY'S GOD SHOT

Jesus took the punishment we earned so we can be with Him forever. He was betrayed and mocked and beaten and denied by the people He came to serve, and that includes us. Judas's sin, Pilate's sin, and our sin sent Him to the cross. He covers us with the blood of His sacrifice, bringing us all peace, hope, and—of course—joy. Even in His death, He's where the joy is!

ZOOM IN

The light from the sun was gone. And suddenly, the curtain in the sanctuary of the Temple was torn down the middle. Then Jesus shouted, "Father, I entrust my spirit into your hands!" And with those words he breathed his last.

Luke 23:45–46

On His way to the cross, Jesus is beaten even more. The prophet Isaiah said the Messiah would be beaten beyond human recognition, and here, Jesus is. His body is so broken and weak that a man named Simon has to carry His cross. He's crucified at Golgotha, which means "The Place of the Skull."

Jesus asks God to forgive the soldiers, and He invites the criminals on either side of Him to join Him in the kingdom. One of them believes.

Right before Jesus dies, He cries out, "It is finished." The work of salvation is done because of Him. It's midday, but the sky goes dark. Joseph, Nicodemus, and a few women wrap and anoint His body. They roll the stone over the entrance of His cave tomb.

TODAY'S GOD SHOT

God does so many miraculous things. In Matthew's account of Jesus's death, dead people rise from their graves and walk through the city. *Wow!* In John's account, Pilate becomes an accidental prophet, writing that Jesus is the King of the Jews. And Luke mentions what two other writers do too: that the sky goes dark at noon, and in the temple, the curtain is torn from the top to the bottom—God opens up His presence to His people in a new way. Praise God, our miracle worker! He's where the joy is!

MATTHEW 28; MARK 16

ZOOM IN

Jesus said to them, "Don't be afraid! Go tell my brothers to leave for Galilee, and they will see me there."

Matthew 28:10

It's been three days since Jesus died, and now it's early Sunday morning, before the sun rises. Mary Magdalene and some other women disciples go to visit Jesus's tomb. An angel tells them not to be afraid and that Jesus has been raised from the dead! He invites them to see the empty tomb, and then tells them to spread the word.

As we know from Luke's and John's gospels, when Peter and John hear the women's story, they run to the tomb to see for themselves. The stone has been rolled away, and the linen cloths that wrapped Jesus's body are folded up and set aside. Thieves would've stolen the expensive fabric—and they certainly wouldn't have wasted time folding it up—so the disciples know the grave hadn't been robbed, but they're not sure what happened.

Jesus's eleven remaining apostles go back home to Galilee. Jesus meets them there, and they worship Him. He tells them to go and make more disciples. And He promises to be with them.

TODAY'S GOD SHOT

Jesus tells Mary to let His brothers—the disciples—know that He's alive! The last time they were all together, He told them that they'd turn their backs on Him and deny Him. They did. But despite their betrayals, He still calls them His brothers, and He can't wait to see them. What great love and forgiveness God has for the sinners in His family! He's where the joy is!

ZOOM IN

They said to each other, "Didn't our hearts burn within us as he talked with us on the road and explained the Scriptures to us?"

Luke 24:32

Back at the tomb on Sunday morning, Mary is weeping; it's all too much. She sees the outline of a man, but in the early morning light she doesn't recognize the person. But when Jesus says her name, she *knows*. It's Him!

Later that day, Jesus joins two men on the road to Emmaus. They're talking about Jesus and everything that's happened over the last three days. Jesus explains the writings of the prophets to them, and just when they recognize Him, He disappears.

Jesus appears again to His disciples as they fish, telling them from the shore to put their nets on the other side of the boat. He did this on the day He first called them, and this is just like what happened then—their nets overflow with fish! Then Jesus cooks them breakfast. After Jesus asks Peter if he loves Him three times, He tells Peter to feed His sheep.

A few weeks later—forty days after His resurrection—Jesus ascends to heaven from the Mount of Olives.

TODAY'S GOD SHOT

God makes our hearts burn for Him! The men on the road to Emmaus say that when Jesus talked to them (that's prayer) and explained the Scriptures to them (that's Bible study), their hearts burned (they were awakened). God is the one who makes His Word come to life. He makes our relationship with Him beautiful. He's where the joy is!

ACTS 1–3

Suddenly, there was a sound from heaven like the roaring of a mighty windstorm, and it filled the house where they were sitting. Then, what looked like flames or tongues of fire appeared and settled on each of them. And everyone present was filled with the Holy Spirit and began speaking in other languages, as the Holy Spirit gave them this ability.

Acts 2:2–4

Jesus tells the apostles to stay in Jerusalem until the Holy Spirit comes to them. After Jesus ascends to heaven, His followers go to the upper room, where they'd eaten the Last Supper, to pray. The eleven remaining apostles are there, along with Jesus's female disciples, Jesus's mom, and His brothers (their hearts changed, and they believe in their brother now!). The apostles replace Judas with Matthias, so there are twelve of them again.

A week later, during a holiday called Pentecost, the disciples gather. A strong wind blows inside, and something appears over their heads that is similar to fire. They're filled with the Holy Spirit and can communicate in other languages so that people from other nations can finally understand them. These people can hear the gospel for the first time! When Peter preaches, three thousand people repent and are baptized! God brings unity through sending His Spirit.

TODAY'S GOD SHOT

God doesn't usually do things the way we imagine. He promised to send the Holy Spirit, but probably no one imagined He'd do it like this! There's an indoor tornado, fire holograms, and people speaking languages they've never learned. God's ways are always so much better and bigger than ours. He's where the joy is!

──ZOOM IN─────────────────────────

For Jesus is the one referred to in the Scriptures, where it says, "The stone that you builders rejected has now become the corner-stone." There is salvation in no one else! God has given no other name under heaven by which we must be saved.

Acts 4:11–12

Jesus's death and resurrection have made tensions in Jerusalem worse than ever, but the apostles keep doing what Jesus told them to. As we saw in our previous reading, Peter and John healed a man who couldn't walk and then preached the gospel. They get thrown in prison, but Peter and John keep talking about Jesus there too!

A faithful believer named Barnabas sells some land so the apostles can take care of the poor believers. Ananias and Sapphira pretend to be generous like Barnabas, but the Holy Spirit tells Peter that they're lying.

As the church grows, the government feels jealous and threatened. They put Peter and John in jail again. The church has to figure out how to live and work together, and they put more men in charge to take care of decision-making, like how to take care of widows. One of those men is named Stephen.

~~TODAY'S GOD SHOT~~~~~~~~~~~~~~~~~

Jesus Christ, the Messiah, is the only way to heaven. Some people say that God leaves people out, but He actually shows everyone the way *in*. He's kind and loving, and He tells us exactly how to get into the kingdom of heaven: by believing in Jesus. He's our invitation, our salvation, and our only hope. And He's where the joy is!

ACTS 7–8

ZOOM IN

But the believers who were scattered preached the Good News about Jesus wherever they went.

Acts 8:4

Stephen is falsely accused by unbelieving Jews and is put on trial. When he is allowed to present his defense, he doesn't talk about himself at all. He tells everyone listening about Jesus: His life, His death, and His resurrection. God gives Stephen a vision of heaven, and he seems to be at peace. The rulers kill Stephen by throwing stones at him; he becomes the first **martyr** of the church.

Saul—who is also called Paul (we'll get to that soon)—is there at Stephen's murder. After Stephen dies, the persecution of the church gets even worse. Saul goes from house to house, dragging believers from their homes and throwing them into prison. Many believers leave Jerusalem, and wherever they go, they take the good news of Jesus with them.

An angel sends Philip to an Ethiopian official who is confused reading Isaiah. Philip shares the good news of Jesus, and the man believes! After baptizing the man, Philip disappears and then reappears on the coast.

TODAY'S GOD SHOT

God uses for good even what the enemy intends for evil. When Stephen was murdered, the leaders were trying to stop the gospel from spreading. But the opposite happens! The believers who leave Jerusalem take the gospel with them, and they tell everyone. They know they might be persecuted, but that doesn't stop them. They know that He's where the joy is!

SEVEN-DAY ROUNDUP

ZOOM OUT

We've now read the first four books of the New Testament (the Gospels), and we've read forty-three books total! This week, we read about how God's power was shown at the resurrection and Pentecost. After Jesus's death and resurrection, His apostles and disciples spread the good news, and His church starts to grow!

BIG PICTURE: MATTHEW

In Matthew's gospel, one of Jesus's apostles and a former tax collector writes about Jesus as King. Jesus—a descendant of David and the Son of God—brings the kingdom of heaven to earth.

BIG PICTURE: MARK

In the gospel of Mark, Paul's assistant—John Mark—shows Jesus as the Servant who came to serve and give His life as a payment for our sin.

BIG PICTURE: LUKE

In Luke's gospel, the early missionary shows Jesus as a man who came to turn the world upside down, bringing good news not only to Jews, but to Gentiles, women, the poor, and the oppressed. He's the Savior of all who believe in Him!

BIG PICTURE: JOHN

In the gospel of John, one of Jesus's first apostles writes about Jesus as God, the long-expected Messiah who came to restore man's broken relationship with God.

WORD TO REMEMBER

- Martyr—someone who is killed because of their faith

APPLICATION

Jesus's followers couldn't stop sharing the good news about Him! What is the good news about Jesus? Practice what you would say if a friend asks you. Then pray for an opportunity to share that good news with someone!

ACTS 9–10

ZOOM IN

Instantly something like scales fell from Saul's eyes, and he regained his sight. Then he got up and was baptized.

Acts 9:18

Saul continues his hunt for Jesus's followers, tracking them down in different cities and bringing them back to Jerusalem for punishment. But God has a different plan for Saul. On the road to Damascus, a great flash of light knocks him to the ground. He hears a voice from heaven that asks, "Saul! Saul! Why are you persecuting me?" (9:4).

This event leaves Saul blind, and God sends a believer, Ananias, to him. Ananias has heard about what Saul does to believers, so he's scared, but he does what God tells Him to do. Ananias prays over Saul. Saul regains his sight, is filled with the Spirit, is baptized, and preaches that Jesus is the Son of God!

God uses a Roman centurion and a vision to show Peter that God's family is beautifully diverse, filled with people of different races and backgrounds. The church is facing persecution and death threats, but the Holy Spirit gives them peace and comfort.

~TODAY'S GOD SHOT~

God is sovereign over the salvation of His people. Saul was determined to destroy the spread of the gospel, but God had other plans for him. When God has chosen someone for His family, they're His. If you're praying for a friend or family member who has rejected the gospel, be encouraged because God gets the final word! God will save anyone He chooses. He's where the joy is!

ZOOM IN
We can see that God has also given the Gentiles the privilege of repenting of their sins and receiving eternal life.

Acts 11:18

Peter returns to Jerusalem and helps the believers there understand that God's family includes Jews *and* Gentiles. The Jewish people are confused about this, since throughout history, God had told them *not* to mix with foreigners. But Peter explains that Jesus told them this would happen. The believers understand and rejoice: God is growing His family!

Barnabas goes to a new church in Antioch to make sure things are going well there. He brings Saul with him, and they stay for a year, encouraging the church there as it grows. Here, we see the word **Christian**—a believer of Jesus Christ—used for the first time in the Bible. The Christians at Antioch send money to Jerusalem to care for the Christians there during a famine.

A new King Herod is on Rome's throne, and he is brutal. He persecutes Christians and murders James, one of the apostles. Herod has Peter arrested, but the church prays hard for him. During the night, an angel punches him awake. *Whoa!* He gets up and his chains fall off; he's free! Peter tells his fellow believers about the miracle, and the church continues to grow.

TODAY'S GOD SHOT

God gives repentance. It's easy to think of repentance as a gift we give to God, but the Bible says repenting is a privilege *He* gives to *us*. What a beautiful gift: We are given eyes to see, ears to hear, a mind to understand, and a heart to surrender to the truth! He's where the joy is!

ACTS 13–14

ZOOM IN

In the past he permitted all the nations to go their own ways, but he never left them without evidence of himself and his goodness. For instance, he sends you rain and good crops and gives you food and joyful hearts.

Acts 14:16–17

In Antioch, the believers are worshipping God and fasting when the Holy Spirit tells them that Barnabas and Saul are going to be missionaries. The Christians pray for them, and they start their journey. Their first stop is Cyprus, where Saul starts going by the Gentile version of his name, Paul. This makes sense since he's now a missionary to the Gentiles—he's adapting to other cultures to remove what might get in the way of the gospel message.

Paul and Barnabas go to another city that's *also* named Antioch. The leaders of the synagogue ask Paul for encouragement, and he tells them what Jesus has done for them. The Jews who aren't Christians think they're better than the Gentiles, but Paul isn't surprised. He tells them that this is God's way of opening up the gospel to the Gentiles. Many of them believe!

In Iconium, the Jews who don't believe in Jesus work against Paul and Barnabas. In Lystra, the enemies of the gospel stone Paul. He's hurt so badly that people think he's dead, but he isn't! The missionaries go back to the places where people have tried to kill them, to strengthen and encourage the Christians there.

TODAY'S GOD SHOT

God makes Himself known to everyone, even when people reject Him. Because of God's goodness, everyone on earth receives His *common grace*, like sun, rain, bountiful crops, food, and happiness. He's so generous, making Himself and His kindness known to everyone. He's where the joy is!

ZOOM IN

If you need wisdom, ask our generous God, and he will give it to you. He will not rebuke you for asking.

James 1:5

James, Jesus's half brother, used to mock Him. But like we saw after Jesus's resurrection, his heart changed. James calls himself "a slave of God and of the Lord Jesus Christ" (1:1). He writes to Christians living outside of Israel. (By the way, his name is actually Jacob, but it was written as *James* when the Bible was translated to English. Since your Bible says James, that's what we'll stick with here.)

The church is running into trials, but James says they're growing stronger because of them! He tells them to ask God for wisdom because God will always answer yes. James writes a lot about perfection, which can be confusing for Christians to read, because we know we're not perfect. But it points us to the wholeness that only God can give. *Jesus* is our perfection!

James tells believers the kinds of things that show others God has changed them: purity, peacemaking, gentleness, mercy, and sincerity. When they've really been changed by God, James says others will take notice.

TODAY'S GOD SHOT

Jesus lived a perfect life; the rest of us are all sinners. James is a book that can feel like a checklist of how to live a perfect life. But it's really a book that points us to our perfect God. Right at the beginning of the book, James says that if you need wisdom—and we all do—you can ask God and He'll give it! He's so generous to sinners, and He's where the joy is!

ACTS 15–16

ZOOM IN

He made no distinction between us and them, for he cleansed their hearts through faith.

Acts 15:9

Paul and Barnabas travel to Jerusalem to correct the Jewish Christians' teaching. Some of the Pharisees are wrongly teaching that Gentile Christians have to follow Jewish ceremonial law like circumcision. Peter insists that—because of Jesus—God makes no distinction between Jews and Gentiles.

Barnabas and John Mark team up on a missionary journey, while Paul teams up with Silas. Paul and Silas travel to Lystra, where they meet Timothy and prepare him for his missionary journey. In Philippi, they meet Lydia. God opens her heart to the gospel, and her whole family decides that day to follow Jesus!

Paul and Silas are thrown in jail because they free a girl from a demon. An earthquake shakes open the prison gates, but they stay put because they see a chance to share the gospel. They tell the good news to their prison guard, and he and his whole family become believers!

TODAY'S GOD SHOT

God cleanses our hearts by faith. He uses faith like a silversmith uses a fire: to purify and refine our hearts. Having true faith in our hearts gets rid of everything that doesn't belong there. He gives us faith, and He's where the joy is!

ZOOM IN

There is no longer Jew or Gentile, slave or free, male and female. For you are all one in Christ Jesus. And now that you belong to Christ, you are the true children of Abraham. You are his heirs, and God's promise to Abraham belongs to you.

Galatians 3:28–29

Paul writes letters to churches in different places, and this letter is written to a church in Galatia that he started on his first missionary journey. Your Bible may call this book The Epistle to the Galatians; **epistle** is the Greek word for "letter."

Paul explains again that Gentiles don't need to follow Jewish ceremonial law to become Christians. Paul says that changing the gospel in any way makes it a false gospel, and he says God will judge anyone who preaches it.

Even though God has a special relationship with Jews, Gentile Christians are counted as Abraham's descendants too. God promised Abraham that all nations of the earth would be blessed through him, and because of Jesus, we are! Salvation is a gift from God, given by grace alone, through faith alone, and in Jesus alone.

TODAY'S GOD SHOT

God's salvation belongs to all who believe in His Son. No matter your background, Paul makes it incredibly clear that the only requirement for eternal life in God's kingdom is belief in Jesus. Because of Christ, the door is open to everyone. And because of the Holy Spirit, we are united in spite of our differences. He's where the joy is!

GALATIANS 4–6

ZOOM IN

But the Holy Spirit produces this kind of fruit in our lives: love, joy, peace, patience, kindness, goodness, faithfulness, gentleness, and self-control. There is no law against these things!

Galatians 5:22–23

Since we are children of God, we are also His heirs along with Jesus! And as coheirs, we inherit everything. But there's even more good news. We also inherit the Holy Spirit. Because of the Spirit at work in us, we can call God our Father.

If we depend on our good works to save us, we may as well go back to being slaves. Paul begs the Galatians not to go back to their old ways. It would be absurd for children of the King to want to be slaves.

Our salvation comes through faith in Jesus alone. We can't earn it, but we don't get a pass to sin as much as we want either. Instead, we have an opportunity to show others who God is and how much He loves us!

TODAY'S GOD SHOT

God planted us like trees in His garden, and the Spirit started working in us, producing fruit. The word *fruit* in 5:22 is singular; this means there is *one* fruit with *nine* characteristics. When that fruit shows up in our lives, that's the Holy Spirit at work. Do you see love, joy, peace, patience, kindness, goodness, faithfulness, gentleness, or self-control in your life? If you do, thank God! He does the work. He gets the glory and you get the joy, because He's where the joy is!

SEVEN-DAY ROUNDUP

ZOOM OUT

We've finished reading forty-five books together so far! Now we're digging into the spread of the church throughout the world. As missionaries of the gospel continued to travel, both Jews and Gentiles became Christians. The apostles encourage believers and correct false teachings; God is patient with them as they figure out how to be the church. As the gospel is preached to all nations, more churches are started, and God's family grows!

BIG PICTURE: JAMES

James writes a letter to Christians scattered outside of Israel, teaching them that if God has truly changed them, their faith will result in good works. True Christians won't just hear God's Word; they'll do what it says.

BIG PICTURE: GALATIANS

Paul writes a letter to the church in Galatia, rebuking false teachers and reminding the believers that salvation is a gift from God, given by grace alone, through faith alone, and in Jesus alone.

WORDS TO REMEMBER

- Christian—someone who believes in Jesus Christ as their Savior
- Epistle—the Greek word for a letter

APPLICATION

A Christian is someone who believes in Jesus Christ as their Savior. If someone asks you how they can become a Christian, what would you say? You could use the ABCs to help you: Christians 1) **A**dmit that they are sinners in need of a Savior; 2) **B**elieve that Jesus's death and resurrection paid the price for their sins and made a way to be with Him forever; and 3) **C**ommit to living life God's way. Practice your answer so that you'll be ready any time someone asks you how they can become a Christian!

ACTS 17

"For in him we live and move and have our being." As some of your own poets have said, "We are his offspring."

Acts 17:28 NIV

Paul and Silas spend three days in Thessalonica. Paul teaches in the synagogue there and uses the Scriptures to show people how Jesus is the Messiah. Like we've seen before, some believe and some don't. The Jews who don't believe start a riot, and Paul and Silas leave in the middle of the night.

After another synagogue stop in a different town, where many of the people *do* believe in Jesus, Paul moves on to Athens. In Athens, the people want to learn as much as they can—but only about science, art, philosophy, and religion. They don't want to find the truth about Jesus, enjoying questions more than answers. Paul changes the delivery of his message to better reach the Athenians. There is an altar in Athens dedicated to "an unknown god." Paul tells the people that he knows who this God is, and He's the one who made them! Some of the people mock Paul, but others believe.

TODAY'S GOD SHOT

God is the source of everything good, true, and beautiful. Paul used popular Greek poems to reach the people he preached to: "For in him we live and move and have our being" (17:28 NIV). God gives us life; God shows us the way; and God makes us who we are. The Gentile Greek poets were pointing to God! He's everything good, true, and beautiful, and He's where the joy is!

ZOOM IN

We always thank God for all of you and pray for you constantly. As we pray to our God and Father about you, we think of your faithful work, your loving deeds, and the enduring hope you have because of our Lord Jesus Christ.

1 Thessalonians 1:2–3

Paul writes two epistles, or letters, to the church at Thessalonica. He knows God has chosen them to be a part of His family because they have received, are living out, and are sharing the gospel. Paul's first letter is full of encouragement, reminding them to keep living lives of honor and purity, even when they face persecution.

Before Paul writes his second letter to the church at Thessalonica, things get worse for them. They face more persecution, and they're confused when letters that are written by someone *pretending* to be Paul tell them to live the opposite of God's way. Paul tells them that God will give them relief and that He can be trusted to handle justice.

～TODAY'S GOD SHOT～

God gives faith, love, and hope. We can't make ourselves more faithful, loving, or hopeful, and neither could the Thessalonians. But we can pray and ask God to do it for us. Paul gives God all the credit for how they are growing in their faith because he knows God is the one doing the work! Do you want more faith, love, and hope? Ask God. And thank Him when it starts to grow in your heart. He's where the joy is!

ACTS 18–19

ZOOM IN

One night the Lord spoke to Paul in a vision and told him, "Don't be afraid! Speak out! Don't be silent!"

Acts 18:9

Paul continues his missionary journey, going to Corinth, where he meets Aquila and Priscilla (we'll call them A&P), a married couple who were forced out of Rome. They're tentmakers, which is Paul's job too. They all stay together for a while, and Paul keeps preaching the gospel. Then Paul takes A&P to Ephesus, where they meet Apollos. A&P help Apollos understand the parts of the gospel that he was missing, then he becomes a teacher and missionary too.

In Ephesus, Paul decides to teach in a gathering space meant for non-religious teachings. Many people travel through Ephesus to do business, so they hear Paul's teachings. They take the gospel home with them, and the good news about Jesus spreads through Asia!

TODAY'S GOD SHOT

God makes every little detail of our lives work together for His plans! Because A&P were kicked out of Rome, they met Paul. And because they were all three tentmakers, they became friends. And because they became friends, A&P went with Paul to Ephesus. And because they went to Ephesus, they met Apollos, who helped build the early church. And because the people in Ephesus were stubborn, Paul moved on to a new location, which is how the gospel spread to Asia. From jobs to rejection to timing, God works in and through all the details. He's where the joy is!

1 CORINTHIANS 1–4

Paul writes to the church in Corinth. He discusses some of their problems and answers some of their questions. He reminds them that God is the one who called them into His family, and God is the one who will keep them there!

After reminding them how much God loves them, Paul has some strong words for the church at Corinth. The people are worshipping their leaders, so Paul tells them they've got it all wrong and that their arguing makes them look like children. They need to remember what *Jesus* did for them. Paul also reminds the Corinthians that they should boast only in God, not in themselves. He asks whether he should visit them with rebuke or with love. He doesn't want to have to rebuke them.

TODAY'S GOD SHOT

God gives righteousness, sanctification, and redemption. Being declared righteous points to the moment in the past when you became a Christian: when you repent from your sins, believe in Jesus, and commit to living His way. The rest of the time we live—including right now—is our sanctification, the ongoing process of becoming more like Jesus. And the redemption of our bodies will happen in the future, when Jesus comes back! Your past, present, and future are all gifts from God. He's in every part of it, and He's where the joy is!

1 CORINTHIANS 5–8

ZOOM IN

But for us, There is one God, the Father, by whom all things were created, and for whom we live. And there is one Lord, Jesus Christ, through whom all things were created, and through whom we live.

1 Corinthians 8:6

The Corinthians say that because God set them free, they're free to sin as much as they want. Paul tells them this is wrong! Being free in Christ means we're free *from* sin, not free *to* sin. Paul says that Christians must honor God with our bodies, since they're gifts from God and the place where the Holy Spirit lives. God cares about our bodies, and He cares about what we do with them.

Paul gives his opinions on marriage. These aren't God's laws, but Paul believes the Holy Spirit has led him to these opinions. He says marriage is good, but it's better to be single to focus on the work of the church. From a lot of other places in the Bible, we know that both marriage and singleness are gifts from God, and the one who gives the gift is the one who chooses what gift to give. There is joy in whatever gifts God gives us. So when you're older, if God gives you the gift of marriage, you can rejoice and serve Him. And if He gives you the gift of singleness, you can rejoice and serve Him. Both marriage and singleness are great places to serve God!

TODAY'S GOD SHOT

God is the source, supply, and goal. He starts it all, sustains it all, completes it all, and it all points back to Him. All things are from Him, through Him, and for Him, and He's where the joy is!

ZOOM IN

The temptations in your life are no different from what others experience. And God is faithful. He will not allow the temptation to be more than you can stand. When you are tempted, he will show you a way out so that you can endure.

1 Corinthians 10:13

Even though God has always been with them, protecting and providing for them, God's people have always struggled with idolatry. And now, Paul warns the church at Corinth against making idols out of themselves. We all can fall into this: putting ourselves and our desires in charge and ignoring God. Paul says we'll all be tempted to sin, but God gives us power to resist it!

Paul says that in a marriage, God is the head of Christ, Christ is the head of the man, and the man is the head of the woman. Paul isn't putting down women; he writes many times in his letters about the value of women. Women are made in the image of God, and they have the same value as men. But some of their roles are different.

Paul reminds the church that **Communion**—or the Lord's Supper—is done in remembrance of Jesus, and they should remember His command to love one another.

~TODAY'S GOD SHOT~

God will never give us more than *He* can handle. It's easy to misunderstand 10:13 and think it's about our own strength in the face of temptation. But that belief ignores the last sentence: "When you are tempted, he will show you a way out so that you can endure." *He* is the one who shows us a way out of sin. Trust Him to provide you with everything you need to obey Him. He is faithful, and He's where the joy is!

1 CORINTHIANS 12–14

ZOOM IN

There are different kinds of spiritual gifts, but the same Spirit is the source of them all. There are different kinds of service, but we serve the same Lord.

1 Corinthians 12:4–5

Paul teaches the Corinthian Christians about the gifts of the Holy Spirit. It seems like they're confusing personality traits with spiritual gifts. Personality traits can be connected to spiritual gifts, but they aren't always. Someone could be shy, but the Holy Spirit could give them the gift of preaching. Someone else could struggle with reading, but the Spirit might give them the gift of great wisdom. God gives His people unique gifts that make His church better!

Paul explains what love is, and he reminds the Corinthians of the greatest love story of all time: God's love for His kids. Paul says that out of faith, hope, and love, the greatest is love. Why? Because when Jesus comes again, our faith and our hope will be fulfilled and made complete. But love will go on forever and ever, through all eternity.

The end of chapter 14 may have been confusing to read. It's important to remember that Paul was writing to a specific church at a specific time. Many Bible scholars believe these verses prohibit women from *interrupting* church meetings, not from participating in them. Paul wants these women to help create peace and unity and prevent distraction and confusion.

TODAY'S GOD SHOT

God is creative and loves diversity. He made each one of us different, with unique gifts. Together, we glorify God and build each other up. He builds a kingdom full of all different types of people. He's where the joy is!

SEVEN-DAY ROUNDUP

ZOOM OUT

We have finished reading forty-seven books of the Bible! This week we followed Paul during another of his missionary journeys, where he continued to preach the gospel. He also wrote letters to new churches as he got word of how they were doing. He wrote words of encouragement as well as words of correction.

BIG PICTURE: 1 & 2 THESSALONIANS

Paul writes these two letters to the persecuted church at Thessalonica. In the first letter, he writes to encourage and restore their hope. In the second letter, he writes to correct their false beliefs about the day of the LORD. And in both letters, Paul reminds the church that Jesus will come again, which will be a glorious day for believers!

WORD TO REMEMBER

- Communion—a small meal of bread and wine taken by Christians to remember Christ's body and blood given for our salvation, also called the Lord's Supper or the Eucharist

APPLICATION

Paul wrote letters to Christians to encourage them and to correct them. Imagine if Paul wrote a letter to you. What would he say? In what ways do you show faith, hope, and love? Are there sins Paul would correct? What would he remind you about being a Christian? Write yourself a letter, and put it somewhere that you'll find it again in a few months.

1 CORINTHIANS 15–16

ZOOM IN

But whatever I am now, it is all because God poured out his special favor on me—and not without results. For I have worked harder than any of the other apostles; yet it was not I but God who was working through me by his grace.

1 Corinthians 15:10

Some of the Corinthians don't believe that Jesus was resurrected from the dead. Paul reminds them that there are over five hundred eyewitnesses, and he says many of them are still alive. The most important thing about our faith is Christ's resurrection. Because He had victory over death, everything changed! We are free from our sin, free from death, and free to hope for the day He comes again.

The Corinthians who don't believe in the resurrection are falling into sin; they think their actions don't really matter. Paul reminds them that this life isn't the end.

Paul asks the Corinthians to collect money to give as an offering to the oppressed church in Jerusalem. He tells them to collect the money on the first day of the week, which suggests that the church now meets on Sundays (to remember and celebrate Jesus's resurrection) instead of Saturdays (the traditional Jewish Sabbath day). The resurrection changes everything!

TODAY'S GOD SHOT

God works through us by His grace. Paul knows this and explains that he doesn't deserve to serve God as an apostle, but by God's grace, he gets to be a part of God building His church. Paul's sinful past doesn't determine his future; God determines his future. God gives us everything we need to serve Him; He's where the joy is!

2 CORINTHIANS 1–4

ZOOM IN

For God, who said, "Let there be light in the darkness," has made this light shine in our hearts so we could know the glory of God that is seen in the face of Jesus Christ.

2 Corinthians 4:6

After Paul's last letter to the church at Corinth, some of the people repented of the sins Paul addressed, but some rebelled even more. God used Paul's next visit to turn their hearts back toward Him.

Paul and his fellow missionaries endured many trials in Asia, and it led to despair. But God carried them through. Paul asks the people to pray for them, telling them prayer helps. Through prayer, we connect with God and encourage other believers.

People who carry Christ with them carry a light that God shines into and through their hearts. Even though Paul and his traveling companions are being beaten and hurt, the light God put in their hearts is shining all around—to other prisoners, jail guards, and officials. Paul and his friends can't stop speaking the truth, and if they are killed because of it, it will be so that others might live.

TODAY'S GOD SHOT

God shines light in our dark hearts so we can know Him more! When we "know the glory of God" (4:6), we see God for who He is, what He's doing, and how much He loves His kids. Are you growing in how much you know God? He's doing that work in you and for you. He shines in the dark, and He's where the joy is!

2 CORINTHIANS 5–9

Our hearts ache, but we always have joy. We are poor, but we give spiritual riches to others. We own nothing, and yet we have everything.

2 Corinthians 6:10

Paul is suffering, but he doesn't fear death. He knows he'll either be alive here on earth, or alive with Christ. Because of Jesus, Christians don't have to fear death, because we have the promise of eternal life!

Paul says to love Christ most of all, which makes it easier to obey Him. He says not to be unequally yoked with unbelievers. Remember how a yoke connects two animals so that they can work together? It's important for Christians to partner with people who are also following Jesus with their lives. Then you can work together as a connected team for Him!

Paul reminds the Corinthians to be generous in their offerings for the struggling Christians in Jerusalem. God has been generous with them, so they should be generous too. God gives us blessings so that we can bless others and so that He will be praised!

TODAY'S GOD SHOT

God gives joy. Even though Paul and the other missionaries were going through extreme oppression and persecution, Paul can't stop talking about their joy! Trials have a way of showing what really matters to us and *through* us. No matter what happens to Christians, we can have joy because He's where the joy is!

2 CORINTHIANS 10–13

ZOOM IN

Each time he said, "My grace is all you need. My power works best in weakness." So now I am glad to boast about my weaknesses, so that the power of Christ can work through me.

2 Corinthians 12:9

Paul wants the Corinthians to repent of their sins before he comes to visit them again. Through the power of the Holy Spirit, he'll shine a light on the truth, punish disobedience, and tear down the enemy's lies about him.

God has helped Paul endure many trials, such as imprisonment, shipwrecks, beatings, hunger, thirst, freezing, and being stoned. But most of all, Paul says his biggest burden has been the one he has for the church. He loves them and wants them to live God's way.

Paul tells the story of when God gave him a vision of the "third heaven," the spiritual realm—above where the birds fly and past where the stars shine. It was an incredible gift that came with a "thorn in his flesh." This "thorn" could be a vision problem or another physical trial, but whatever it is, when Paul asks God to take it away, God says no. But God promises to show His strength through Paul's weakness.

TODAY'S GOD SHOT

God is strong when we are weak. And when we speak about His power working in spite of our own weaknesses, we get more of His power! Praising God for who He is and what He's doing gives us strength. He's where the strength is, and He's where the joy is!

ROMANS 1–3

ZOOM IN

For everyone has sinned; we all fall short of God's glorious standard. Yet God, in his grace, freely makes us right in his sight. He did this through Christ Jesus when he freed us from the penalty for our sins.

Romans 3:23–24

Paul writes a letter to the church in Rome. He writes it to Jewish and Gentile Christians: all the people "who are loved by God and are called to be his own holy people" (1:7). Paul says God has made it obvious that there is a Creator in charge of everything, but many people choose to ignore the truth and live life their way.

But Paul also reminds Christians to be humble. It's easy to look down on people who are caught up in their sin, but it's only by the grace of God that He called us out of our sin. His grace is what makes us turn from our sin.

Paul says that all of us—Jews and Gentiles—are under the curse of sin and we all need God's rescue. Jesus is the only Savior, and He can save anyone! His gift of salvation changes us and makes us want to obey God and honor His laws.

TODAY'S GOD SHOT

God gives us all the gifts that make us right with Him: grace, faith, justification, and redemption. He gives us everything we need and everything we didn't know we needed. He gives it all, and He's where the joy is!

ZOOM IN

He was handed over to die because of our sins, and he was raised to life to make us right with God.

Romans 4:25

Paul wants Jewish Christians to embrace Gentile Christians as brothers and sisters in the same family. None of us can earn our salvation; we accept it as the free gift that it is! When we are justified—declared righteous—because of Jesus, we are made right with God the Father.

Paul says the law teaches us what sin is, which is important. We need to know that we are sinners to understand why we need a Savior. The law is a helpful tool for us, but because of Jesus, it's not how we measure our righteousness.

Paul lives in the struggle between who he was and who he is. He examines his heart to make sure he wants what God says is right.

TODAY'S GOD SHOT

Jesus "was handed over to die because of our sins, and he was raised to life to make us right with God" (4:25). Christ's death saves us and makes us right with God. We get mercy and we get grace. We get forgiveness and we get adoption. He saves us from punishment and gives us blessing. What an amazing Savior! He's where the joy is!

ROMANS 8–10

Believers must set our minds on the things of the Spirit. We choose wisely what we think about, because what we think becomes what we say and do. It's hard to control what we think about, but the Holy Spirit helps us!

The Spirit prays for us while we wait for the day when Jesus returns. And when God the Spirit prays for us, those prayers always line up with God the Father's plans. God the Son prays for us too!

Because of our sin, we all deserve punishment, death, and separation from God. But in His mercy and kindness, He gave us Jesus and adopts us into His family. Paul wishes everyone knew this kind of freedom and love.

TODAY'S GOD SHOT

God is going to adopt more people into His family, so we must share the gospel with them! Paul teaches us how to do this: He goes from place to place, enduring persecution and writing letters, spreading the knowledge of God and the hope of the gospel. We can do that today too! Spread the good news that He's where the joy is!

SEVEN-DAY ROUNDUP

ZOOM OUT

We've finished forty-nine books of the Bible, including Paul's letters to the Corinthians. This week, we started reading his letter to the church in Rome. We've seen Paul encourage believers who are being persecuted and give God the glory for the gift of salvation.

BIG PICTURE: 1 & 2 CORINTHIANS

Paul writes a few letters to the church he started in Corinth; two of his letters have survived. In the first surviving letter, Paul reminds the believers to repent from their divisions and to build each other up, working together for the gospel. In the second surviving letter, Paul teaches that God uses our weakness and suffering to reveal His strength and grace.

APPLICATION

Romans 10:9 (ESV) says, "If you confess with your mouth that Jesus is Lord and believe in your heart that God raised him from the dead, you will be saved."

Draw a picture of yourself. Next to your mouth, write what Paul says you must confess. Next to your heart, write what Paul says you must believe. If both of these are true for you, then praise God that He has saved you!

ROMANS 11–13

ZOOM IN

Oh, how great are God's riches and wisdom and knowledge! How impossible it is for us to understand his decisions and his ways!

Romans 11:33

Paul addresses a question that many of his readers have: Has God written off the Jews as His people? No! God has preserved a remnant from Israel, just like He did during the exile. Those who know God will be preserved, and that includes both Jews and Gentiles.

God is the Gardener who makes wild branches part of His vine because God wants His kingdom to be beautifully diverse!

God is sovereign over all earthly authorities, even the evil ones. He's always working on His plan and preserving His people. No matter who's in charge, God can be trusted. And as people who trust God, we must show respect to people in authority, even the ones we disagree with.

TODAY'S GOD SHOT

God is impossible to fully understand; His decisions and His ways are so far beyond what our human brains can possibly comprehend. But in His great kindness, He makes Himself *knowable*. Even though we can never fully understand Him, we can *know* Him. What a beautiful mystery! He's where the joy is!

ZOOM IN

The God of peace will soon crush Satan under your feet. May the grace of our Lord Jesus be with you.

Romans 16:20

Paul reminds the Romans that there is room in the body of Christ for different people with different opinions and preferences. When we fight with each other, someone is usually left feeling like they're "less" than others; this shouldn't happen! We should let the Spirit guide our convictions about how God wants us to live, while also trusting Him to guide others too. Paul says it's better to disagree than to argue to prove your point.

Paul challenges the church in Rome to hold firmly to their faith, living out their convictions and letting their faith show up in every part of their lives. Being a Christian means our faith should always be personal, but never private.

Paul reminds them to live in peace with each other, building each other up with what God is teaching them. We learn not only from God but also from each other, so it's important to surround ourselves with people who love Jesus.

TODAY'S GOD SHOT

God brings peace with His power. God doesn't ignore the chaos and destruction that Satan causes; He defeats it. "The God of peace will soon crush Satan under your feet" (16:20). God has already won the battle, and in doing so, He brings us peace! He's where the joy is!

ACTS 20–23

ZOOM IN

That night the Lord appeared to Paul and said, "Be encouraged, Paul. Just as you have been a witness to me here in Jerusalem, you must preach the Good News in Rome as well."

Acts 23:11

Paul is on his way to Jerusalem to deliver the financial support from other churches. He preaches in Troas until midnight, and a man named Eutychus falls asleep and falls out of a window and dies! Paul raises him from the dead—*wow!*—then keeps preaching until sunrise.

The Holy Spirit has warned Paul that imprisonment and affliction are waiting for him. But Paul presses on because he knows all of the suffering—and even his own death—is in God's plan. He will keep sharing the message of God's love as long as he lives.

Some people spread lies about Paul bringing a Gentile into a Jewish temple; this is a crime punishable by death. So the people beat Paul until a local leader, who thinks Paul is someone else, arrests him. God tells Paul that he won't die in prison. He'll go to Rome to tell people about Him first.

TODAY'S GOD SHOT

God lined up every single detail about Paul's life before he was even born so that the gospel would spread. Paul survived his arrest because he was a citizen of Rome, was educated, spoke Hebrew and Greek, was a Pharisee, and might have even looked like an Egyptian. And even though he was in prison, Paul still spread the gospel! God isn't just in charge of the big picture; He's in charge of every tiny detail that makes up the big picture! He's where the joy is!

ZOOM IN

But God has protected me right up to this present time so I can testify to everyone, from the least to the greatest.

Acts 26:22

Paul defends himself by telling the truth. He lives with integrity and tries to honor God in everything he does. Governor Felix wants to learn more about Christianity—which was called "the Way" at that time—so he tells the soldiers to treat Paul well in prison. Felix keeps visiting with Paul to hear more about the Way, and Paul tells him. He shares the gospel and obeys the rules of being a prisoner. After Felix leaves his job, a man named Festus replaces him. Governor Festus decides to take Paul back to Jerusalem for a trial. Because Paul is a Roman citizen, he says he'd like to make his case to Caesar instead.

A few days later, King Herod Agrippa II comes to town, and he asks Paul to tell his side of his story. Paul shares the gospel beautifully, but Festus says Paul has lost his mind. Paul insists that he's not crazy and says King Agrippa agrees with him. Agrippa says he's not ready to make a decision to follow the Way yet, and Paul says he wants everyone to become a Christian, no matter how long it takes.

TODAY'S GOD SHOT

God protects His kids, even during the worst of trials. Paul has faced false accusations, beatings, shipwrecks, and prison, but he still says God has protected him. Paul has his mind and his heart set on God, and he knows that God's protection is for eternity. He gives up temporary comfort for eternal glory. Paul knows that He's where the joy is!

ACTS 27–28

ZOOM IN

For the next two years, Paul lived in Rome at his own expense. He welcomed all who visited him, boldly proclaiming the Kingdom of God and teaching about the Lord Jesus Christ. And no one tried to stop him.

Acts 28:30–31

It's time for Paul to be taken to Rome for his trial in front of Caesar. He's allowed to take some friends with him, and they set sail on a ship. Paul warns the sailors that they're going to lose supplies and shipmates, but they don't listen to him. When the storm comes, the sailors throw supplies overboard, and Paul gives them another message, this time from an angel: They'll lose the boat, but they'll all live. Two weeks later, they shipwreck on the island of Malta.

The sailors plan to kill the prisoners so that they don't escape, but a centurion named Julius stops them. While Paul is building a fire, a snake bites and holds on to his hand. Paul shakes off the snake and lives, so the people in Malta think he must be a god. While they stay in Malta, Paul heals many people.

When they finally get to Rome, Paul is given more freedom and rights than other prisoners. Paul shares the gospel with everyone who visits him.

TODAY'S GOD SHOT

God provided for Paul by appointing Julius as his centurion; Julius eventually spared Paul's life. Julius saw God speak to and through Paul, and he watched Paul humbly encourage his enemies, survive a snakebite, and heal people in Malta. Julius probably couldn't deny the truth about God after seeing all of that! Maybe God assigned Julius to Paul not just for Paul's sake, but for Julius's too. God can save anyone, and He's where the joy is!

COLOSSIANS 1–4; PHILEMON 1

ZOOM IN

Christ is the visible image of the invisible God.

Colossians 1:15

Paul wrote the two letters we read today while he was in prison, probably in Rome. The first letter is to the church at Colossae; Paul doesn't know them personally, but he's friends with one of their church leaders. The Christians there are having some problems, and he reminds them that God forgave their sins and made them alive! Their new life in Christ calls them to compassion, kindness, humility, patience, love, peace, and thankfulness. This will show up in the way they live in the world and in their homes.

Paul writes another letter to Philemon, a wealthy Christian, on behalf of Onesimus. Onesimus was Philemon's servant, but he stole from Philemon and ran away. Onesimus later became a Christian and met Paul. Paul asks Philemon to forgive Onesimus and welcome him back, not as a slave but as an equal.

TODAY'S GOD SHOT

Jesus shows us what God is like. Colossians 1:15–20 tells us that He reveals God, He's always existed, He made everything and everything serves His purposes, He rules over everything, and He is God. Jesus brought His full self—both God and man—to the cross, and because of Him, everything will be restored. He's where the joy is!

EPHESIANS 1–6

ZOOM IN

Put on all of God's armor so that you will be able to stand firm against all strategies of the devil.

Ephesians 6:11

Many Bible teachers think Paul wrote this letter to a number of churches in and around Ephesus, which could explain why it doesn't address any specific problems. Instead, it offers general encouragement. Paul reminds the Christians that they were chosen by God before He made the world. Every believer was dead in sin until God intervened and made us alive in Christ. And we'll get to enjoy Him forever!

Being grateful for everything God has given us helps us view ourselves and God rightly. When we view God rightly, we love Him more, and when we love Him more, our hearts are drawn toward Him and away from sin.

TODAY'S GOD SHOT

God gives us everything we need for battle. If you put on all of God's armor listed in Ephesians 6, there's an uncovered part: your back. In ancient battles, archers stood back-to-back so they could protect each other. God doesn't intend for us to fight alone, or even walk alone. We need each other. For every battle we face, He gives us each other and He gives us Himself. He's where the joy is!

SEVEN-DAY ROUNDUP

ZOOM OUT

We finished *five* more New Testament books, which means we've read fifty-four books of the Bible! We saw how God protected Paul even during the worst of trials and how Paul couldn't stop sharing the good news of Jesus.

BIG PICTURE: ROMANS

Paul writes to the Roman church to bring unity to the Jewish and Gentile Christians. He wants them to remember that the good news of Jesus binds them together as they live a new life marked by holiness.

BIG PICTURE: ACTS

In Acts, we get an account of the church's early days after Jesus's resurrection. We see Jesus's apostles take the gospel to the ends of the earth, inviting all people to follow Christ. Though they're persecuted and some are even murdered, they don't give up, and the church grows.

BIG PICTURE: COLOSSIANS

The church in Colossae has started to believe a lie about Jesus. Paul writes to remind them that Jesus is God, Lord over all creation, and has defeated the powers of sin and death. Because of Him, Christians are redeemed!

BIG PICTURE: PHILEMON

Paul writes a personal letter to Philemon on behalf of a former servant. By sharing Onesimus's story, Paul shows how the power of the gospel changes lives.

BIG PICTURE: EPHESIANS

In Ephesians, Paul writes that Christ has united all kinds of people to Himself and to each other. Because of Him, Christians reject their old sinful selves and live as new creations.

APPLICATION

In Acts 26:29, we read that Paul wanted everyone to become a Christian. Is there someone in your life who you want to become a Christian? Write their name down and commit to praying for their salvation. Ask God to give you the strength to keep praying, no matter how long it takes.

PHILIPPIANS 1–4

ZOOM IN

Fix your thoughts on what is true, and honorable, and right, and pure, and lovely, and admirable. Think about things that are excellent and worthy of praise.

Philippians 4:8

Paul writes an encouraging letter to the church at Philippi, a church he watched grow. He reminds them that God will finish what He started. Paul tells them to "work hard to show the results of your salvation, obeying God with deep reverence and fear" (2:12), which is sanctification. When we're sanctified, God does the work of making us more like Him, and we are faithful in living His way.

Paul encourages them to be faithful even through persecution and suffering. He's the perfect person to deliver that message because he's writing to them from jail! God can use anything for His purposes. Paul says that through Christ, he can endure anything that comes his way. He thanks them for providing generously for him while he's been in prison and reminds them that just as they've provided for him, God has provided for them.

TODAY'S GOD SHOT

Jesus is all of the beautiful things Paul lists in 4:8: true, honorable, right, pure, lovely, admirable, excellent, and worthy of praise. So when we fix our thoughts on Jesus and who He is, our minds are filled with beauty. He's where the beauty is, and He's where the joy is!

ZOOM IN

Yet true godliness with contentment is itself great wealth. After all, we brought nothing with us when we came into the world, and we can't take anything with us when we leave it.

1 Timothy 6:6–7

Paul writes this letter to his friend Timothy, who is a young leader at the church in Ephesus. Timothy has to fight hard against their patterns of pagan worship, even among people who want to be leaders. Paul tells Timothy that the people need to learn humility. He wants them to be the kind of people who draw outsiders *to* the church, not the kind who push them away.

Paul outlines the requirements for church leaders, like elders and deacons; the list is long because leaders have a lot of responsibility.

Paul reminds the people that they're free to enjoy the gifts God has given them, but the Giver is the one to be worshipped. He says money is a blessing that should be used to honor God. Money itself isn't the problem; *the love of money* is. Generosity is the right perspective.

~**TODAY'S GOD SHOT**~

God's Word says that knowing Him and becoming like Him makes us rich: "True godliness with contentment is itself great wealth" (6:6). Someone could be the richest person in the world, but if they don't know God and aren't **content** with what He's given them, they'll feel like they have nothing. May our hearts truly believe that knowing Christ is enough. He's where the joy is!

TITUS 1–3

ZOOM IN

I have been sent to proclaim faith to those God has chosen and to teach them to know the truth that shows them how to live godly lives. This truth gives them confidence that they have eternal life, which God—who does not lie—promised them before the world began.

Titus 1:1–2

Paul writes to his friend Titus, who is a minister on an island named Crete. The people there are used to all kinds of sin, so they have a hard time understanding what living God's way looks like. Paul tells Titus that if the church there shows people how beautiful their faith is—that God's gift of grace and eternal life changes *everything*—then others will be drawn to it.

Like he told Timothy, Paul tells Titus the qualifications for church elders. And like he told Timothy, he reminds Titus that the church leaders should be humble. Our humility can show up the most when we disagree with someone. In that case, Christians should be gentle, show kindness, and avoid arguing.

TODAY'S GOD SHOT

God promised us eternal life "before the world began" (1:2). The good news of our salvation has been God's plan since before any of us were born. He created the world, carried us through the fall of sin, and sent His Son to live and die for the sins of the world so that we could be rescued. We're not just His creation, but His children and His heirs. Praise God! He's where the joy is!

ZOOM IN

In his kindness God called you to share in his eternal glory by means of Christ Jesus. So after you have suffered a little while, he will restore, support, and strengthen you, and he will place you on a firm foundation.

1 Peter 5:10

The apostle Peter writes to encourage the Gentile believers who are being persecuted. He reminds them that God hasn't forgotten or betrayed them, but that He chose them. Their trials won't destroy them, but rather make them stronger.

Peter teaches the Gentile Christians that they have a high calling to be royal priests. But how can that be, since they're not royalty or Levites or even Jewish? Because of Jesus, every believer can approach God directly like priests used to do. *Wow!* Jesus is the only **mediator** we need. This is called *the priesthood of the believer*.

Peter says God wants people to notice how Christians have beautiful souls. What matters is what you look like on the inside.

TODAY'S GOD SHOT

God will give you all you need, even when you're suffering. Peter reminds the Christians who are suffering that nothing they're experiencing now is eternal. It'll all pass, and God hasn't forgotten them. He's called them to eternal glory and He's coming to their rescue! So when you suffer, be on the lookout for God to restore, support, and strengthen you. Whether it happens on earth or in eternity, He'll do it! He's where the joy is!

HEBREWS 1–6

ZOOM IN

God also bound himself with an oath, so that those who received the promise could be perfectly sure that he would never change his mind.

Hebrews 6:17

The author of Hebrews is a mystery. It seems to be written to early Jewish Christians and focuses right from the start on how Jesus has no comparison: He created the world, He sustains the world, He is God, He purified us from our sins, He's seated at the Father's right hand, and He will never change.

Christians shouldn't ever forget these things, remembering that we've been set free from the fear of death! We should stand firm in our faith, which is evidence that He lives in us. If someone truly knows God, they'll continue to believe in Him, even if they wander away from His ways for a time. If someone stops following Jesus forever, it's because their heart wasn't truly changed to begin with. True believers in Jesus can be confident of the hope that is in Christ Jesus: His sacrifice was final!

TODAY'S GOD SHOT

God deals gently with all of us who wander away from Him. We've all wandered, either on purpose or by accident. But God is always gentle with us, drawing us back to Him, teaching us, and loving us. It's such a relief to know we can never go too far for Him to find us! He's where the joy is!

ZOOM IN

And so, dear brothers and sisters, we can boldly enter heaven's Most Holy Place because of the blood of Jesus. By his death, Jesus opened a new and life-giving way through the curtain into the Most Holy Place.

Hebrews 10:19–20

In the Old Testament, priests followed the old covenant, making sacrifices on behalf of the people to atone for their sins. Because Jesus is the new and eternal high priest, there is a new covenant that's infinitely better. There is no need for daily sacrifices anymore because Jesus was the ultimate sacrifice; He finished it—once and forever!

The old covenant and the system of sacrifices provided a temporary solution to a permanent problem, but Christ's death solved the problem once and forever. Because of the new covenant, our sins have been paid for, and God doesn't accept any other payment. There is no other solution but Jesus.

The author of Hebrews calls Christians to endure, as it shows what our hearts believe. Jesus will come back again, but not to be sacrificed. Instead, when He returns, He'll be *celebrated*!

TODAY'S GOD SHOT

Jesus made the way for us to be united to the Father. When Jesus died, the curtain in the temple that sectioned off the Most Holy Place was torn from top to bottom. God's place of dwelling was no longer in the temple; it's in the hearts of all believers! Jesus made the way for God the Spirit to dwell in us. He's where the joy is!

HEBREWS 11–13

"Faith shows the reality of what we hope for; it is the evidence of things we cannot see" (11:1). Faith isn't just positive thoughts and good vibes. Faith has an object: Christ. The people in the Old Testament were saved by faith too. They had faith in Christ, even though they didn't know His name, because they had faith in YHWH—the one true God—and Jesus is God.

Faith doesn't mean that God will bless us with the things we want or an easy life. Faith empowers us to endure through trials. And because we're God's kids, we'll also have to go through His discipline sometimes. Every good parent disciplines their kids.

The author encourages Christians to walk in unity and holiness. Christians should love each other well, be kind to strangers, care for those in need, honor the purity of marriage, and be content.

TODAY'S GOD SHOT

God rewards those who truly seek Him. And the best reward He can give? More of Himself. Nothing is better, and nothing lasts longer, and there's nothing else that can't be taken away. He is the Rewarder, He's the Reward, and He's where the joy is!

SEVEN-DAY ROUNDUP

ZOOM OUT

You spent seven days reading more letters to the early church, learning what a healthy Christian life should look like. You have eight days and seven books left in your journey through the entire Bible, because we've already read fifty-nine books together! God has shown you so much about Himself!

BIG PICTURE: PHILIPPIANS

Paul writes to the church at Philippi to thank them for their generosity and encourage them. He reminds them about the process of sanctification and the importance of setting their minds on the things of God. He teaches all Christians that even though suffering will come, we can have joy.

BIG PICTURE: 1 TIMOTHY

Paul writes to Timothy, teaching him how to lead the church. In this first letter, Paul teaches that true Christians live lives that demonstrate their faith to others.

BIG PICTURE: TITUS

Paul gives Titus a picture of a healthy church: It's made up of people whose faith has changed every part of their lives. The work of the gospel produces godly living in Christians, and true godliness will draw others to Christ too.

BIG PICTURE: 1 PETER

Peter writes to churches around Asia. In this first letter, he encourages Christians to endure persecution with hope and remember that God keeps His promises.

BIG PICTURE: HEBREWS

In Hebrews, Christians are encouraged to keep Christ as the object of their faith and to endure whatever trials come. Jesus is our once and forever sacrifice, and the only way to eternal life!

WORDS TO REMEMBER

- Content—believing that what you have is enough
- Mediator—someone who goes between God and people. In the Old Testament, priests did this for the Jewish people. After Jesus's life, death, and resurrection, He has done it forever for all Christians!

APPLICATION

In many of the letters in the New Testament, we see that contentment is one of the characteristics that marks a Christian. One way to build contentment is through gratitude. Paul models gratitude when he thanks the churches for their support. Build contentment in your own life by making a mental gratitude list before you fall asleep. Thank God every night for three gifts He's given you, and watch how contentment grows in your heart!

ZOOM IN

All Scripture is inspired by God and is useful to teach us what is true and to make us realize what is wrong in our lives. It corrects us when we are wrong and teaches us to do what is right.

2 Timothy 3:16

From a Roman prison, Paul writes the second letter to Timothy; he's awaiting his trial and expects that he will be killed. He wants to give Timothy some final instructions, and he's probably also feeling lonely. After all, many people have abandoned him because he keeps going to prison. He reminds Timothy that if we aren't actively growing in our faith, we'll fall into fear.

God is at work in us and through us, and He'll accomplish everything He has promised to us and for us. So Paul encourages Timothy to keep doing the hard work of spreading the gospel. He also tells him not to be surprised when it's hard, and urges him to be willing to endure whatever it takes for the gospel to reach all who will believe it.

Paul knows God will rescue him, even if rescue comes in the form of earthly death, because that means eternal life. And God did rescue him. Church history tells us that Paul was a martyr, killed for his faith shortly after he finished writing this letter.

TODAY'S GOD SHOT

God gave us His Word for many reasons: to rebuke us in our hardheaded sin, to correct us in our foolish choices, and to train us in righteousness. His Word is a gift to us, and it's how we get to know Him better. His Word is one way we find out that He's where the joy is!

2 PETER 1–3; JUDE 1

ZOOM IN

So I want to remind you, though you already know these things, that Jesus first rescued the nation of Israel from Egypt, but later he destroyed those who did not remain faithful.

Jude 1:5

Both of today's letters deal with church leaders who are trying to stop false teachers' lies. Peter wants his letter to be passed from church to church, reminding Christians to hold tightly to the truth. Even in persecution—which he is experiencing too—Peter says that God has given them everything they need.

The false teachers say that the church leaders are lying, but Peter stands firm in the gospel. The good news of Jesus is the truth. And God's Word is written by the Spirit's guidance. Peter says that when a teacher says something that goes against the Word of God, it's a lie. The Bible can always be trusted.

Jude was most likely written by one of Jesus's brothers; like James, he went from mocking Jesus to worshipping Him! He retells stories of God punishing the wicked while sparing the righteous; the wicked false teachers think they won't see God's judgment, but Jude says they will. He tells the church not to be afraid, because God is keeping them in His love.

TODAY'S GOD SHOT

Jesus hadn't yet been born as a human when the Israelites were rescued out of Egypt, but Jude says that Jesus Himself rescued them! Jesus has always existed. He's in the Old Testament, doing miraculous things to save His people. Then, now, and always, He's where the joy is!

ZOOM IN

We love each other because he loved us first.

1 John 4:19

Most Bible scholars agree that 1, 2, and 3 John were written by one of Jesus's first apostles, John. But the author of these three letters is less concerned with people knowing who he is and more concerned with people knowing who *Jesus* is. False teachers are caus-ing church division and spreading lies about Jesus. John gets right to his point: Jesus has always existed because He's truly God, and John and many others saw Him and touched Him and talked to Him because He's also truly man.

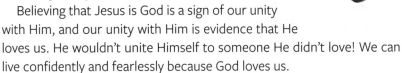

John says that Jesus hasn't re-turned yet, but He will one day. And when He does, we'll be trans-formed. We'll get to live in the new heaven and the new earth in our new bodies. But until that beautiful day, we can't forget to grow in righteousness.

Believing that Jesus is God is a sign of our unity with Him, and our unity with Him is evidence that He loves us. He wouldn't unite Himself to someone He didn't love! We can live confidently and fearlessly because God loves us.

TODAY'S GOD SHOT

God loved us first, and He makes us able to love Him and others. We wouldn't be able to love anyone without His help. Love was His idea! He's where the love is, and He's where the joy is!

2 JOHN 1; 3 JOHN 1

I say this because many deceivers have gone out into the world. They deny that Jesus Christ came in a real body. Such a person is a deceiver and an antichrist.

2 John 1:7

John starts his second letter by saying that he loves the church and its people, and that everyone who loves truth should *also* love the church and its people. This can be hard because the church is made up of people like us: sinners. But God has poured out so much grace to help us!

If we really believe that what Jesus says is true, then love is living it out. Love without truth is foolish, and truth without love is boastful. Love and truth go together, like Jesus demonstrated.

John encourages the church to stay strong and to display God's goodness to everyone around them.

TODAY'S GOD SHOT

Jesus came into the world fully God and fully man, and John says that anyone who teaches otherwise is an anti-Christ (someone who is against Christ). This is a hard teaching, but remember that the good news and the hope of the gospel is that God loves to rescue those who are against Him and make them part of His family forever! There is hope for everyone who doesn't know God yet. Pray that all will come to know and believe that Jesus is the way, the truth, and the life, and that He's where the joy is!

ZOOM IN

When I saw him, I fell at his feet as if I were dead. But he laid his right hand on me and said, "Don't be afraid! I am the First and the Last. I am the living one. I died, but look—I am alive forever and ever! And I hold the keys of death and the grave."

Revelation 1:17–18

Jesus's apostle John was sent to a tiny prison island because Rome couldn't figure out how to kill him! While John is on that island, Jesus gives him a **revelation** about Himself to write down and share with people. While the book does tell us about the end of the world, it's not a puzzle we have to solve or a riddle we have to figure out. The purpose of the book is that Jesus *reveals* something important to people, making it known, so His message isn't hidden away.

Jesus tells John to write a letter to seven churches. Some of the people in those churches have fallen into sin, some are being persecuted, and some are growing in Christ. He speaks warning, encouragement, and hope to the churches accordingly. And Jesus reminds all of them to listen, obey, and persevere.

John gets to peek inside God's throne room. God holds a scroll that is sealed closed. When Jesus shows up and takes the scroll, everyone falls down to worship Him.

TODAY'S GOD SHOT

Jesus says not to be afraid! Revelation is a book that can feel scary, but because we know Jesus, we don't have to be afraid. Who He is helps us see everything rightly. We can read this book without fear because the King of Glory is by our side. He's where the joy is!

REVELATION 6–11

ZOOM IN

Then the seventh angel blew his trumpet, and there were loud voices shouting in heaven: "The world has now become the Kingdom of our Lord and of his Christ, and he will reign forever and ever."

Revelation 11:15

Today, Jesus opens the seven seals on the Father's scroll, one by one. The first four seals give us four horses and four horsemen; these are enemies of God that bring death, disease, and destruction. But they're still under God's control. The final three seals have to do with God's people: martyrs, the great day of the Lord, and the multitude of believers.

Seven angels blow seven trumpets. The first four trumpets bring disaster on earth and in the skies. At the fifth trumpet, a star falls from heaven, and there is an attack of locusts (possibly armies). The sixth trumpet brings a plague. But the seventh trumpet will mark the beginning of God's kingdom.

Lampstands and olive branches may represent the faithful witness of the church in the end times. God gives His people power in the midst of tragedy. When the enemy appears to be winning, God proves that He can't be defeated.

TODAY'S GOD SHOT

Jesus has already won the battle, and He will reign over His kingdom forever and ever. Many people who talk about Jesus's return wind up being scared, but Christians who remember His words can look forward to it instead! For believers, the end times are really just the beginning. It's when we can fully experience the kingdom of God. We can be excited for Jesus's return, knowing that He's where the joy is!

ZOOM IN

Together they will go to war against the Lamb, but the Lamb will defeat them because he is Lord of all lords and King of all kings. And his called and chosen and faithful ones will be with him.

Revelation 17:14

John's vision is filled with signs and symbols, including one of a woman who gives birth to a child who would rule the nation, and a beast who doesn't like this and tries to put a stop to it. The woman lives in the wilderness, where God takes care of her. Most Bible scholars agree that the woman represents Israel; the dragon represents Lucifer; and the stars swept by the dragon's tail are the angels who joined the side of the enemy. War breaks out in heaven, and when Lucifer and his angels lose, they wage war on earth. God protects Israel, so Satan's angels go off to attack God's other kids, the Gentiles.

Seven angels appear carrying seven bowls of God's wrath. And when the world's armies meet in Armageddon, the last angel pours out his bowl and Babylon drinks the wrath. After a woman on a beast hurts God's people, an angel declares that Babylon's rule has ended. God's people rejoice at His victory!

TODAY'S GOD SHOT

Jesus will defeat His enemies; in fact, He already has the victory! As His "called and chosen and faithful ones" (17:14), we get to be with Him, but He's the one who does all the defeating. His victory over death and darkness was His victory over His enemies. He's our conqueror, and He's where the joy is!

REVELATION 19–22

ZOOM IN

He who is the faithful witness to all these things says, "Yes, I am coming soon!" Amen! Come, Lord Jesus!

Revelation 22:20

Heaven is having a party over God's victory! The multitudes praise God, and then it's time for a wedding: the marriage of Christ and the church. Jesus appears on a white horse, wearing a robe dipped in blood. He's followed by the armies of heaven, likely the people of God. His Word is His weapon; He brings justice and is victorious over His enemies.

Satan will eventually suffer total defeat in eternal torment. Everyone will be judged by their works, but those whose names are in the Lamb's Book of Life will be pardoned because their sins are covered by Christ, the Lamb.

After this, heaven and earth will pass away, and the new heaven will come down and merge with the new earth. We will live in that magnificent place in our new bodies, forever! The angel says to spread the word; people need to know that Jesus is really coming back, that judgment is really going to happen, and that the blessing of living with God for eternity really waits for us!

TODAY'S GOD SHOT

Jesus says three times that He's coming back soon. Knowing that an incredible, glorious future awaits us, John says God's kids will join with the Spirit and beg Christ to return. So when Jesus says, "Yes, I am coming soon" (22:20), John leads our answer by saying "**Amen**!" or "Let it be so!" We trust in Jesus's promise and join in John's prayer, saying, "Amen! Come, Lord Jesus!" *You are* where the joy is!

EIGHT-DAY ROUNDUP

ZOOM OUT

You finished the entire Bible: thirty-nine books of the Old Testament and twenty-seven books of the New Testament, for a total of sixty-six books! Congratulations! As you finished the final letters of the New Testament and the Revelation of Jesus Christ, I hope you were reminded of who God is, what He's doing, and how much He loves His kids.

BIG PICTURE: 2 TIMOTHY

Paul writes a second letter to Timothy, teaching him how to lead the church. He calls on Timothy to continue boldly sharing the gospel, no matter what suffering comes.

BIG PICTURE: 2 PETER

Peter writes to churches around Asia. In this second letter, he reminds his readers to live godly lives and trust that God will rescue them.

BIG PICTURE: JUDE

Jude writes a letter urging the church to fight against false teachers and for the one true faith. He wants them to look at the big picture of how God has preserved the righteous, and to be faithful for their whole lives.

BIG PICTURE: 1, 2, & 3 JOHN

John writes three letters to remind Christians to obey God and be faithful to Him. By walking in truth and love, believers live out their faith.

BIG PICTURE: REVELATION

John is given a revelation of Jesus Christ, showing events that are to come at the end of the world. Jesus has already won the battle, and He promises that He's coming back! Then His believers will live with Him forever in the new heaven and the new earth.

WORDS TO REMEMBER

- Amen—the end of a prayer, meaning "let it be so, Lord"
- Revelation—when something important is revealed, or made known

APPLICATION

Is Jesus in the Old Testament? Yes! Not only is He prophesied about as the Messiah, but He's actually there, rescuing His people. Reread these passages and find Him in each one.

Judges 6:12

Isaiah 37:36

Daniel 3:25

Praise Him that He's been there since the beginning. He'll be back soon, and then we'll get to be with Him forever!

WORDS TO REMEMBER

Definitions for each word can be found on the page number beside it.

Abundance—47

Afterlife—143

Amen—436

Ancestor—47

Angel—39

Apostle—345

Ascent—143

Atone—71

Attribute—191

Bible—12

Christ—353

Christian—393

Chronicle—151

Chronological—23

Church—353

Communion—401

Compassion—71

Consecrate—63

Content—426

Conviction—175

Covenant—23

Defile—231

Demon—337

Descendant—47

Disciple—337

Epistle—393

Eternal—143

Exile—143

Fast—263

Fear—63

Flattery—207

Genealogy—151

Gentiles—319

Glory—63

Gospel—337

Grace—23

Heir—223

Holy—63

Humble—183

Idolatry—103

Inherit—39

Intercede—87

Jews—319

Justification—71

Knowledge—199

Lament—135

Martyr—385

Mediator—426

Mercy—23

Messiah—159

Missionary—337

Monarchy—143

New Testament—12

Offering—31

Old Testament—12

Oppress—119

Pagan—127

Parable—345

Passover—55

Pentateuch—111

Persecute—353

Pharisees—337

Prophecy—31

Prophet—31

Providence—31

Rebuke—119

Redeemer—31

Redemption—95

Refuge—119

Remnant—271

Repent—39

Restore—39

Resurrection—103

Revelation—436

Sabbath—55

Sacrifice—39

Sadducees—353

Sanctification—71

Sanctuary—295

Scholar—311

Scripture—12

Shema—103

Sin—23

Sovereign—23

Sustain—303

Tabernacle—63

Tithe—79

Transfiguration—353

Trinity—23

Torah—111

Understanding—199

Unity—159

Vengeance—223

Vulnerable—63

Wisdom—199

Woe—247

Wrath—239

Yoke—345

Zion—263

BIG PICTURE

Summaries for each book of the Bible can be found on the page number beside it.

ACKNOWLEDGMENTS

This project would not have been possible with the passion and dedicated work of Emily Pickell. Your talents, wisdom, and friendship have been a blessing to me for more than a decade, and it's a true joy to watch God use you to bless so many others as well!

Tara-Leigh Cobble is a *Wall Street Journal* bestselling author, the creator of *The Bible Recap* line of books, and the creator and host of the daily podcast *The Bible Recap*, which has garnered over 300 million downloads. She also hosts a popular daily radio feature called *The God Shot*, on which she teaches through passages of Scripture verse by verse.

Tara-Leigh's zeal for biblical literacy led her to create and develop an international network of Bible studies called D-Group (Discipleship Group). Every week, hundreds of men's and women's D-Groups meet online and in homes and churches around the world to study Scripture.

Tara-Leigh speaks to a wide variety of audiences, and she regularly leads teaching trips to Israel because she loves to watch others be awed by the story of Scripture through firsthand experience.

Her favorite things include sparkling water and days that are 72 degrees with 55 percent humidity, and she thinks every meal tastes better when eaten outside. She lives in a concrete box in the skies of Dallas, Texas.

For more information about Tara-Leigh and her ministry, you can visit her online:

WEBSITES: taraleighcobble.com | thebiblerecap.com | mydgroup.org

SOCIAL MEDIA: @taraleighcobble | @thebiblerecap | @mydgroup